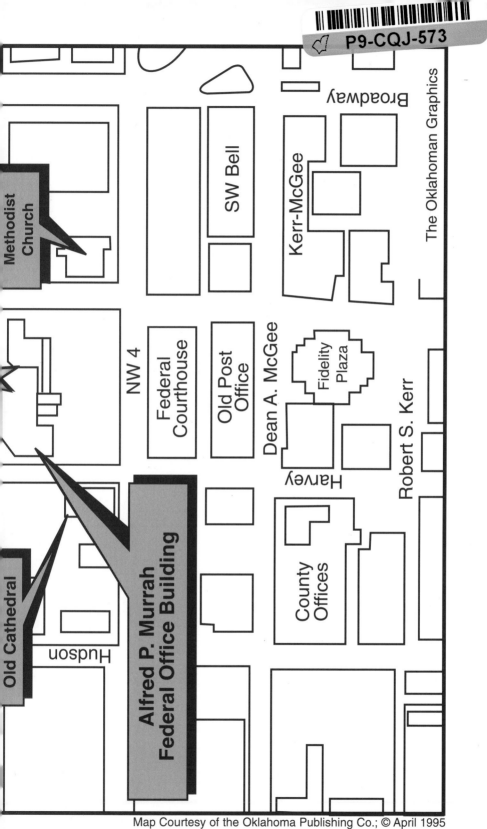

P9-CQJ-573

Broadway

The Oklahoman Graphics

Methodist Church

SW Bell

Kerr-McGee

NW 4

Federal Courthouse

Old Post Office

Dean A. McGee

Fidelity Plaza

Robert S. Kerr

Harvey

Old Cathedral

Alfred P. Murrah Federal Office Building

Hudson

County Offices

"Much of the power of *Forever Changed* comes from the sheer number of those who have contributed their personal accounts. The eighty-one stories of loss and survival are a painful reminder of the enormous gap left in the lives of those left behind."

—Andrew Phillips, *Maclean's*

"A moving account of the aftermath of the Oklahoma City bombing from the all-too-often forgotten perspective of the victims. The compelling accounts from victims and survivors force reflection on the terrible impact of crime and the need for society to respond to it."

—Paul G. Cassell, Professor of Law
University of Utah College of Law

"The farewells and remembrances collected in this powerfully written book carry the messages that should linger with us always. This book, written straight from the heart, travels straight to the heart of the reader."

—Julie DelCour, *Tulsa World*

"The strength and courage of the survivors will not let us forget the human costs of American homegrown terrorism. Through the tears, the victims come back to life, exhorting us to lead graceful, peaceful lives and to stand firm against the reactionary fanaticism that has left us forever changed."

—Marc Levin and Daphne Pinkerson, Producers
Oklahoma City: One Year Later

"In the media, the bombing investigation and subsequent trials unfortunately obscured the heart-wrenching tales of loss and survival that stemmed from the tragedy. *Forever Changed* is a gripping and powerful meditation on the magnitude of what was unleashed that horrible morning."

—Phil Bacharach, *Oklahoma Gazette*

"The human cost of the Oklahoma bombing is something that can never be measured, only felt. The stories of families and survivors in Kight's book are a legacy that shows the human spirit triumphs after all."

—Ben Fenwick, Reuters

"Each story in *Forever Changed* will help you understand the enormous devastation and pain caused by violence. Perhaps through that understanding, you will be motivated to demand of your legislators, that which we deserve—a safer nation. We can and must honor the memories of our victims by guaranteeing future generations an end to violent crime."

—Fred Goldman (Ronald Goldman's father)

"Just when I thought I'd heard it all in my three years of covering this tragedy comes another poignant recollection, another stretch for understanding, another layer of loss. This book has them all, as told by anyone's neighbor, colleague, sibling, grocer, or pal. Their voices are as varied as their injuries, their outlooks as diverse as their faces and names. We all know one of them. We all want to know more."

—Penny Owen, *Daily Oklahoman*

"*Forever Changed* profoundly confronts universal themes of loss, fear, courage, spirituality, redemption, the fragility of life, and the realization that everything can change in a split second. Ultimately, *Forever Changed* is about triumph over evil. Even in the face of profound loss, the vivid and poignant first-person accounts of the tragic events of April 19, 1995, give rise to hope and the indomitable ability of the human spirit to rise above adversity."

—Marc Klaas, KlaasKids Foundation

"From the gripping prologue to the very last word, the resolve to commemorate the lives of special people intertwines with the pain of separation from them to create a mosaic to be treasured forever."

—Norman S. Early Jr., Former Denver District Attorney, NOVA Board Member

"*Forever Changed* paints a very personal picture of the 1995 Oklahoma City bombing. Each person's firsthand account lets you see that day through their eyes.... *Forever Changed* simply and eloquently tells their stories of pain and loss...of love and courage."

—Tony Clark, CNN America

Forever
CHANGED

Remembering Oklahoma City,
APRIL 19, 1995

CHANGED *Forever*

COMPILED BY MARSHA KIGHT
DIRECTOR, FAMILIES AND SURVIVORS UNITED

 **Prometheus Books**
59 John Glenn Drive
Amherst, New York 14228-2197

Photo credits

Page 31, Ann Shirley Banks, © 1996 Glamour Shots
Page 49, Mark A. Bolte, © 1995 Woodland Photograph
Page 60, Brett Brooks, © 1995 Glamour Shots
Page 67, Shirley E. Brotherton, © 1997–98 Motophoto & Portrait Studio
Page 78, Joseph E. Chicoraske, © 1997–98 Motophoto & Portrait Studio
Page 82, Richard Clough, © Professional Images
Page 179, Marla Hornberger, © 1995 Moto
Page 205, Frankie Ann Merrell, © 1992 Whitaker Portrait
Page 255, Mark, Laura, and Carly Oak, © 1995 Olan Mills
Page 304, John Karl Van Ess III, © Professional Images
Page 323, Julie Marie Welch, © 1989 Karen Moore

Published 1998 by Prometheus Books

02 01 00 99 98   5 4 3 2 1

Library of Congress Cataloging-in-Publication Data

Forever changed : remembering Oklahoma City, April 19, 1995 / compiled by Marsha Kight.
    p.   cm.
    ISBN 1–57392–238–2
    1. Oklahoma City Federal Building Bombing, Oklahoma City, Okla., 1995.
2. Victims of terrorism—Oklahoma—Oklahoma City. I. Kight, Marsha.
HV6432.F65   1998
362.88′09766′38—dc21   98–8519
                                                                          CIP

Printed in the United States of America on acid-free paper

Contents

Acknowledgments

*F*irst, I'd like to mention Brandon Stickney, author of *All-American Monster*, who befriended me during the trial of Timothy McVeigh. Brandon cared about this book and submitted it to the acquisitions committee of Prometheus Books. I also extend my thanks to editor-in-chief Steven L. Mitchell, marketing director Jonathan Kurtz, and associate editor Mary A. Read for their support and guidance.

To Lori Doggett, who poured her heart and soul into this book. She interviewed many of the family members and survivors for this book and assisted with the editing. Lori said, "The price of my part of this project has been the breaking of my heart and the wounding of my spirit, but the rewards are beyond measure. April 19, 1995 has left my life 'forever changed,' and I am grateful for the opportunity to have a part in giving a voice to our silenced angels and for telling the courageous stories of those who survived. Thank you for allowing me to share your hearts."

To Suzette Hatfield, who also assisted in gathering stories. While interviewing the survivors and victims' families, Hatfield observed,

"It was clear that those recovering were turning outward to God and others. Others retreated from society and disintegrated emotionally." Hatfield calls on citizens to take a renewed role in their government and communities. "It's time to pull away from the TV and become activist, compassionate citizens to redeem our country."

To Dorian Leigh Quillen. When Dorian began interviewing survivors and family members, she did not know what to expect. What she found were people in various stages of grief, anger, and recovery struggling with the great questions of life with a variety of views on fate, God, capital punishment, and crime. Dorian said, "I am indebted to those who allowed me into their homes and entrusted me, a stranger, with their stories. They have reminded me of everything I love about being from Oklahoma City—their friendliness, faith, strength, practical resolve, and that genuine, familiar goodness that the world has come to know as the 'Oklahoma Standard.'"

To Tom Huber, the photographer responsible for the front cover, thank you. The picture was taken on the east side of the Athenian restaurant across the street from the Murrah building. Tom said, "Even though I did not know anyone personally affected in the bombing, my heart and mind have been changed forever by this national tragedy."

A special thanks to each individual who participated and shared a special story. We have been each other's strength and support, when we could not stand alone. We have been each other's teachers. You are an inspiration, because of your extraordinary resiliency, to emerge from something so devastating. Your stories show the world how often we underestimate the sheer tenacity of the human spirit. I hope this book is a way we can reclaim some of our power, while giving something back, sharing our hearts and experiences and our hopes for a better tomorrow.

Last, but not least, to all my family and friends who have stood by me and supported me. Thank you, for your love and for understanding the importance of this book.

Marsha Kight
Director, Families and Survivors United

Prologue

*O*n April 19, 1995, at 9:02 A.M. a bomb exploded in Oklahoma City and the echoes of that day still reverberate in the countless souls that were shattered by its impact. In a split second the Alfred P. Murrah Federal Building was reduced to rubble and thousands of lives were just as surely splintered and crushed. One hundred and sixty eight lives were violently destroyed. Those who survived the "War Zone" carry their scars for life. As a nation, we all carry the emotional scars. The veil of innocence was ripped from our eyes and our lives forever changed. The blood of the innocent was the price of hatred and its toll of grief and anguish will be exacted for a lifetime.

There has been much written about the bombing itself and how its victims died. This book is a testimony to how they lived, by telling the stories of those who died and the magnitude of goodness that was stolen that tragic spring day.... Legacy after legacy of loved ones who were robbed of their futures and whose lives were ended far too soon.... Families struggling to cope with the tremendous void left in their hearts, images of their loved one's death haunting their minds and tormenting them in the night.... Daily living with the strife of trying to make sense of the senseless.... Families that were once close now torn apart by the emotional wake of the bomb.

Those who survived the blast also share their stories of physical and emotional wounding. All of them carrying deep scars, some that can be seen and some that cannot. They saw unspeakable horrors that day and will live for the rest of their lives struggling with the sights, smells, and sounds forever burnt into their very souls. Each of the one hundred and sixty eight people who were lost was also a co-worker and a friend to many of the survivors. Survivors lost more friends in one moment than most people could in several lifetimes. They often had to attend four to five funerals per day. Grief that enormous is difficult to comprehend and even more difficult to carry in one's heart. The survivors were truly the heroes of April 19, 1995. They were the ones who disregarded their own injuries and their own safety to rescue co-workers from the rubble. Many of them going back into the building instead of away from it in order to help the injured. Many of them lovingly tending to the wounds of others with no thought to their own. These are our real heroes.

We hope that in reading these stories, America will feel our loss and will realize that when innocent people are murdered and maimed, it affects us all. For when goodness is taken from this world, then all of society suffers.

The bomb not only ripped through the concrete and steel of a building, it tore through the hearts and minds of many lives as well. The shockwaves of the explosion produced fallout that is still extending outward. Within these pages, those who were most affected by unfathomable loss and trauma share their experiences as they travel this difficult path. We hope that our experiences will transcend the bombing and will be a beacon of hope to all who are forced to walk this bitter path of grief. There are no scales by which to measure pain or grief, and though circumstances may vary, the thread of anguish weaves itself through any loss.

We also hope that this book will be a wake-up call for the nation. Retaliating against the government with violence only kills innocent people. The government did not suffer loss. Those who suffered grievously were mothers, fathers, children, husbands, wives, brothers, sisters, and friends. One hundred and sixty eight is a huge number, so in putting names, faces, and lives to this number, as well as to the hundreds upon hundreds of survivors, it is our hope that America will cease to grow indifferent to terrorism within our borders. Terrorism, if left unchecked, will be our own demise. Let us do all we can as a nation to end violence and make this world a safer place for all our children. In doing so we will honor the memory of the one hundred and sixty eight lives that were so tragically taken.

Families of victims and survivors of the blast have drawn much strength as we have united together. We are many people from many walks of life, woven together by the intertwining of suffering and compassion to form a tapestry—a tapestry made stronger by the threads of shared grief, pain, love, and understanding. We have tasted each other's tears and have formed bonds that will last a lifetime.

Lori Doggett
Marsha Kight

No man is an island entire of itself; every man is part of the main. …Any man's death diminishes me because I am involved in mankind, and therefore never send to know for whom the bell tolls; it tolls for thee.

—John Donne

Give sorrow words; the grief that does not speak whispers the o'er-fraught heart and bids it break.

—William Shakespeare, *Macbeth*

God employs several translators; some pieces are translated by age, some by sickness, some by war, some by justice.

—John Donne

Let Victims' Rights Ring Across America

Marsha Kight

*A*pril 19, 1995, was the worst attack of terrorism in the history of this country. Its target was the U.S. government, but instead it shattered innocent lives. I lost my daughter, Frankie Merrell, and my five-year-old granddaughter, Morgan, lost her mother. In the months that followed I found myself in a downward spiral. There was no question—my life had to change if I was to continue to live.

I knew that, for myself, I must find a voice to survive this tragic loss. I became an advocate for victims of the Oklahoma City bombing, and through that experience, I exposed myself to the plight and pain of so many others. For all of us who joined together in this way, the veil of innocence was removed. Among other things, we determined that the silence of the victims had to end.

This book has been our effort to act on that belief, to put our memories into words. I am proud of our collaborative efforts to give voice to our pain. But in the years following the bombing, as that crime has been prosecuted in the courts, I have learned that it is not sufficient for the victims to speak to anyone willing to listen, they must also have the right to be heard in the justice system.

There have been millions of victims before the Oklahoma bombing and, sadly, many are yet to follow. My hope is that the good which comes from this tragedy will shine as a beacon of hope for all victims of crime everywhere, and that it will act as the catalyst for positive change in American laws on victimization. That hope has yet to be realized.

Every time innocent people are murdered, it should and does affect us all. Every time an act of violence happens, every American loses some sense of security and freedom.

How many more of our sons and daughters, brothers and sisters, friends, spouses, mothers, and fathers have to be slaughtered before we unite in an effort to stop violence in our country, and the disrespectful ways in which our government treats victims afterward?

The constitutional protections, so important in criminal proceedings, were put in place by our founding fathers to "provide for the common defense and ensure domestic tranquillity." Civil liberties were recognized as fundamental for everyone in establishing this nation.

On a June 1996 morning, Judge Richard P. Matsch informed family members and survivors who were seated in his courtroom that they had the lunch-hour recess to decide whether or not they would remain as observers of the trial, either in the Denver courtroom or in Oklahoma City on the closed-circuit television, or be impact witnesses during the penalty phase of the trial, if McVeigh was found guilty. For the victims, who had lost their loved ones, and the survivors, this was a shocking, painful event and yet another victimization—this time by the judicial process.

Although a grueling decision like this normally requires very careful thought, we were given no time. Every family member and survivor present tearfully made his or her choice that noon hour. Many, who had just arrived for the hearings, left in dismay, excluded from the most important judicial process in their lives and in the history of this nation.

I opted to remain in the courtroom as an observer, but upon my return to Oklahoma City I began seeking a way to reverse Judge Matsch's decision on behalf of families and survivors, as well as all victims of crime.

Paul Cassell, a Utah attorney and professor of law, and Bob Hoyt and his associates at the Washington, D.C., law firm of Wilmer, Cutler and Pickering took up our cause. They filed an emergency permit with the Tenth Circuit Court of Appeals in Denver, Colorado, asking that the court rescind Judge Matsch's order. Professor Cassell specifically cited an act of Congress that permitted victims to observe court proceedings without prejudicing their right to also speak at sentencing. Without a hearing, the Appeals Court's there-judge panel ruled that victims did not have the right to be heard on this violation of their rights, that we had no "standing" to even have our challenge to this cruel exclusion from judicial proceedings considered, much less vindicated.

We then filed an En Banc petition, asking that all judges in the Tenth Circuit Court of Appeals review this decision. Supporting our request for review were all the attorneys general in the Tenth Circuit, forty-nine members of Congress, and the Department of Justice. The court refused to hear the case. Once again we were turned away.

Knowing the time constraints before the trial, the decision was made by all concerned to take our case to the United States Congress. In a nonpartisan act, the president and the Congress took a giant step toward the fair treatment of victims by enacting the Victim Allocution Clarification Act of 1997.

The victim's right to be heard must be made as sacred as the defendant's right to counsel, and must be protected as zealously as the accused's right to remain silent.

Indeed, we cherish the constitutional protections for the accused, to ensure that all participants in the criminal justice system perform their duties honorably, ethically, and in accordance with the highest standards. We also support the ideal that no one should be convicted of a crime unless that conviction is backed up with proper evidence, obtained in full compliance with the rules of criminal procedure.

But we have learned from experience that these protections for defendants must be balanced with constitutional considerations for the rights of victims, their families and representatives, to fully participate in each and every stage of the justice process: through the investigation, indictment, bail, motions, trial, sentencing, appeals, and parole.

Society itself is harmed by violent crime, through assaults on the peace, dignity, and good order of its people. Only the direct victims of a criminal act can testify to both the physical and emotional pain caused by such an act. Just as defendants have the right to introduce mitigating circumstances at sentencing and parole hearings, victims, too, must have the right to share the impact of the crime on their lives with presiding officials.

The right of victims to present impact statements at all appropriate stages of the judicial process must be absolute. Never before in the history of our country have so many been so negatively impacted as victims of ever-increasing violent crime. And even if the annual roster of new victims is declining, it is wise to remember that they join a huge number of other victims whose wounds have not healed.

Crime victims are liberals and conservatives; rich and poor; for and against the death penalty; vengeful and forgiving; weak and strong; black, white, and every color in between—none of us should be barred from speaking as a result of our views or social status.

I do not take lightly the idea of advocating an amendment to the U.S. Constitution. I am aware of the fact that this country has seen fit to add only twenty-seven such amendments since its inception a little over two hundred years ago. But never before in the history of our country has violent crime been so pervasive, and never before have so many victims been impacted by such horrific crimes.

I have been saddened, confused, and hurt by my experiences with the criminal-justice system, which seems to defend itself by sending conflicting messages to victims.

Now is the time for all of us to make certain that the voices, the experiences, and the presence of the victims are given legitimate standing in every court, on every level, throughout America. The only way to guarantee that is by enforceable and meaningful rights enshrined in the U.S. Constitution. I call upon each person who reads this book to contact their members of Congress and ask them to support this amendment. If not the Oklahoma City bombing, what will it take? The death of your loved one?

Marsha Kight
Director, Families and Survivors United
6488 Avondale Drive, Suite 301
Oklahoma City, OK 73116
Web Site: FamiliesandSurvivors.com

War Is Hell

Berta Altizer

*O*n April 19, 1995, downtown Oklahoma City resembled a war zone on that never-to-be-forgotten day, and war is hell. My husband worked in the Murrah Federal Building, the target of the manmade explosion, and was at his desk on the eighth floor when the world turned upside-down. He had worked in the Murrah building for seventeen years. One of his duties included that of emergency preparedness officer for the eighth floor. As such he was, for example, the last one to leave his floor during a fire drill, making sure all persons had safely left the building before him. That is easy in a drill, but what about the real thing? What happens when the drill turns into reality? How would you react in a moment of crisis? You can never prepare for a bomb, "an unknown quantity."

My husband was virtually untouched by the bomb blast itself. He was tossed around quite a bit and was trapped in the remains of his office by a tremendous amount of debris. What had happened? Moments before, people were talking and laughing just outside his office. When the noise of the blast and falling debris stopped, there was an eerie silence. His next words were, "Hello,

Ken and Berta Altizer

is anyone there? Can anyone hear me?"

He began digging his way through the debris, yelling all the while. After ten or fifteen minutes of digging and yelling, finally came a response. The voice did not come from the direction my husband needed to go to escape the collapsing building. He altered his path, struggled over more rubble, and found an injured co-worker, Ruth Heald. Her face was covered with blood and she had lost sight in one eye. My husband and another co-worker carried Ruth over the remains of walls, ceilings, file cabinets, and down eight flights of stairs.

When these survivors emerged from the building, my husband's shirt was soaked with blood. It was not his blood, but that of Ruth. My husband could have thought only of himself and escaped the building as soon as possible. He says he would have felt guilty the rest of his life if he had just looked out for himself and fled down the stairs. He had to make sure that he had done everything he could to help rescue anyone else.

Minutes before the explosion he had gone down to the seventh floor and spoken with Gene Hodges, and then come back to the eighth. There was a fax for the legal department. He strolled over there and talked with all of the legal staff, and at 9 A.M. he walked by Tony Reyes's office to say hi. As soon as he did, Tony's phone rang and Ken walked to his own office. He sat down in his chair at 9:01 A.M. He was the last one to see these dear friends alive. It was so sad. Families were calling him that night wanting to know if he had seen them that morning. They were hoping that their loved ones had not made it to work yet.

I talked to my husband at 8:50 that morning. My brother, Cliff

Culp, is a fireman, and he called me at 9:15 A.M. and told me what had happened. I was in denial. I had just talked to Ken. I immediately picked up the phone to call him and had no answer. I went into shock. I went to find a television and looked at that building where I had worked and a lot of my friends still worked. (I had worked at HUD for seven years and knew thirty-two of the thirty-five people killed.) The big piece of concrete that hung dangling from the eighth floor fell in front of my husband's office. In my mind I said, "There's no way he made it out of there." After a couple of hours, my brother called and said someone had seen Ken walking around, so I knew he was alive. At this point I did not realize how bad things really were.

When I finally made it to Ken, we hugged and he said, "Berta, they can't find Trish." She had been my supervisor at HUD and he knew we were really close. She had sent me a birthday card on April 13 with the sweetest note. Then one friend after another…Diana Day, who used to carpool with me; Colleen Guiles, who was a wonderful friend; Kim Clark, who was getting married in a couple of weeks and whose wedding shower was going to be that Friday night. And there were so many, many more friends. I had a story for each one of them. We tried to go to most of the funerals. Some were at the same time and we had to choose; some were out of state. There were days when we went to several. No one should have to go to that many funerals in a lifetime, much less in two weeks.

I could go on. Even to this day, I find myself crying about all of it, just remembering. Our lives are forever changed.

A Story of Extremes

Caye Allen

*H*ow can I begin to tell a story of extremes? Extreme love, extreme happiness, and extreme tragedy. Ted and I met when we both worked at the Department of Housing and Urban Development. As we both lived in Norman, we, along with a woman named CiCi, rode together in a car pool for about three years. During our eighty-minute round-trip daily treks, we shared a lot of thoughts and had lot of disagreements. We went through CiCi's boyfriends, an accident, the birth of Ted's daughter, Meghan, and the birth of my daughter, Rachel. Eventually, CiCi moved, I changed jobs, and Ted went to work as the Director of Planning for the City of Moore, Oklahoma. I would see Ted occasionally around Norman, but, basically, we lost contact until December 31, 1987, when, now both divorced, we attended a New Year's Eve party of a mutual friend. Shortly thereafter, we were a couple, and Lord, what a couple we made. We were totally in love. I felt as though I was on a fast-moving train that I just could not stop. Neither of us was the type of person to move so quickly, but we were both positive we had found our soul mate—to have and to hold forever. On June 3, 1989, we

Ted Allen with family. From left to right: Jill, Spencer, Meghan, Ted, Rachel, Caye, Gretchen, and Austin (Front)

were married in an intimate wedding in our backyard. Because our children were so important to us, we had a special service particularly for "blended families." I had never been so happy. I had a husband I adored and who felt likewise about me. Ted had joint custody of his four children: Jill, Gretchen, Spencer, and Meghan, and I had Rachel. Suddenly, I had *five* wonderful children! What more could a person ask for? On June 19, 1990, our extreme love grew, and a beautiful baby boy, whom we named Austin, entered our perfect life. You have never seen a family so excited over the birth of a child.

Life continued to be perfect. In a time when, in my opinion, families don't spend enough time together, we quickly became a very close-knit group. Ted and I attended every basketball game, soccer game, pompom performance, cheerleading performance, dance recital, and school program of every child and loved every minute of it. Ted coached basketball and soccer teams every chance he got. We took family weekend camping trips and vacations to Florida, Tennessee, and South Padre Island, Texas, in our travel trailer. Everyone teased us about being the Brady Bunch, and, I must admit, we were just as corny as the Brady Bunch.

Ted and I loved being together. We cleaned house together, worked outside together, cooked together, and even went to the grocery store together. So, when Ted came back to work for the federal government in June 1991, and we could again ride to work together, we were ecstatic. We ate lunch together every day, and people at our offices used to needle us about always being together.

Our youngest child, Austin, was enrolled in the day-care center in the Murrah building in September 1990. When he was two, we had a difficult decision to make. Austin's name had come up on a waiting list at another day-care center. All of our other children had attended this day care, and we wanted him to go there, too. But having him with us on the trip to the city each day and being able to go see him at the day care was very nice also. We considered the pros and cons for a few days and ultimately made what later turned out to be the best decision we ever made. Thank God, we moved Austin from the day-care center in the Murrah building in August 1993.

Twenty-one months later, the most extreme event of all occurred. April 19, 1995...who will ever forget that date? For our family, it started as any other day. Spencer, Meghan, and Rachel were shuffling around getting ready for school. I took my van to the car dealer to have some routine maintenance, and Ted and Austin picked me up for the ride to work. When we dropped Austin off at his day care, Ted, as usual played with the children. Ted was six feet six inches and weighed 275 pounds and the four-year-olds in Austin's class delighted in running and hiding under the tables, screaming, "The giant is here!" Ted would grab them and hug them, and I believe Ted and the kids got a lot of joy out of this little daily routine.

Because we were thirty minutes later than usual, traffic was light, and we made the twenty-two-mile trip without any difficulty. We arrived at the Murrah Building and pulled into the underground parking garage to drop Ted off. We had driven to work that day in Ted's

1991 Chevrolet pickup. Because of his love for that truck, the family jokingly called it "The Shrine." Ted kissed me goodbye as he did every day of our married life, looked me in the eye, said "I love you," and then, true to form, added, "Don't hit any curbs with my tires!" I sighed and replied, "Ted, you love this truck more than you love me!" He chuckled, shook his head, smiled his wonderful smile, and said, "Jeez, Caye!" It was 8:55 A.M. I would never see my husband again!

Three blocks south of the Murrah building, at First Oklahoma Tower, I put my bagel in the microwave oven. As I shut the door, I heard and felt the sound that would change my life forever. It was 9:02 A.M. I ran into my office, looked out the window, and yelled to Gina Penny, a co-worker, "What in the heck was that?" No sooner had I said that, then another co-worker, Nick Lillard, came down the hall and said the words that stopped my heart: "I've been in Vietnam, and I'm telling you, that was a bomb." I feared he was right.

Linda Mitchell, another co-worker, and I arrived at the site about 9:07. It didn't look like anything in the United States. Glass and debris were everywhere. People were walking down the street, in shock, with blood on their faces, arms, and hands. The strangest thing I remember is the silence. There were people everywhere, but there were no cries of pain or fear. It was eerily quiet and then I noticed the sirens. Rescue vehicles were coming from every direction and the noise was deafening. I couldn't think straight. I was already in shock. I just couldn't believe this was happening in Oklahoma City.

By noon, after three hours of constant walking, I knew Ted was badly injured. I knew that if he were able, he would have found me by now. He would never have let me live this nightmare alone. I convinced myself that he was stuck somewhere in the building, just waiting to be rescued. But that evening when I got home at 10:30 P.M. and saw the north side of the Murrah building on television for the first time, I knew the love of my life was dead. The largest hole was exactly where Ted would have been sitting on the eighth floor. If he was at his desk, he did not have a chance. But, I didn't tell anyone. I wanted others, especially the kids, to be able to hang on to that glimmer of hope for as long as possible. The older ones figured out

the inevitable, but, finally, on Sunday, April 23, 1996 (we were notified of positive identification on April 26), I had to tell Austin what
had happened. He was only four years old and absolutely worshiped
his daddy. Because Ted traveled often in his job, Austin was not too
concerned that he had not come home. He knew something was up
though because of the constant flow of people through our house;
but he was having so much fun being entertained, I think he was
afraid to ask, afraid his entertainment would end. I took Austin into
my bedroom and told him what had happened. Of course, he began
to cry, and said, "Do you mean Daddy is an angel now?" I was so
thankful that Austin, at four years old, had found a positive way to
view this death. We later went outside because, like in *The Lion King*,
Austin wanted to find his Dad's star. He picked the North Star and
when I asked why, he said, "Because Dad was so fat!" Oh, from the
mouths of babes.

The next day, our family made the decision that we were going to
view this death in a positive light. We were truly blessed by having
the most wonderful husband and father. We had so much that many
families never get to share. We decided to focus on what we *had* and
not on what we lost because we had so very, very much. In order to
share what we had, Spencer made a heartfelt video about his dad that
was shown at the services, and Jill did the eulogy. It was a very
touching dedication to Ted with many wonderful memories. By the
end of the service, I believe that every one of the more than one
thousand people there had been touched in one way or another. The
funeral was a beautiful celebration of Ted's wonderful life.

They say time heals all wounds. We are all much better now, but
we will never, ever be healed. The kids have all picked themselves
up, brushed themselves off, and carried on in a manner that would
make Ted proud. Ted was not one for self-pity, and he would be
extremely disappointed if any of us wallowed in it. I have worked
very hard with the kids to keep this in the proper perspective
because I know I will see Ted again and when I do, I want him to
open his arms to me and be able to say, "Job well done."

Whoever did this took a wonderful man from our family. However, we will not let them take away our life. We will not let them win

again. They have damaged us badly, but we are not broken. Since the bombing, Jill, Gretchen, and Spencer are all in college and doing well. Meghan was in a car accident in August 1995 and had a blood clot on her brain, requiring surgery. She has recovered splendidly. She will graduate from Norman High School in May and will attend the University of Oklahoma. Rachel and Austin have also rebounded and adjusted very well. Pardon me for tooting my own horn, but these are outstanding kids! I told you this was a story of extremes. I had an extremely happy life. I had an extremely marvelous husband. The kids had an extremely remarkable father. We suffered an extreme tragedy, and we have made, what I consider, an extremely exceptional recovery. And, despite everything, I am one extremely lucky woman because of everything I have had!

The Force from Hell

Ann Banks

I take care of my nephew Carnell Newsom, and on our drive to school we were in deep prayer. Even after I dropped him off, I was still compelled to pray, for some reason. Once at work, I went to my desk and settled in. I made my way down to get water from the snack bar, then I took my place seated at my desk at the northwest corner on the eighth floor of the Alfred P. Murrah Federal Building.

I placed a call to the Choctaw Nation Housing Authority, and upon completing the call I heard a tremendous explosion. I felt the force of the vacuum, the building shake, the walls and the floors vibrate violently, as I was blown face downward on my desk. I was momentarily unconscious, and after coming to, I was able to raise my body back into my chair. At that point, I realized I was tangled in electrical wiring. Glass and debris were falling all over me. I was numb with fear.

I looked to the east and I saw the sky. I realized that most of the building was gone and right away I knew it was a bomb. I sat in shock and disbelief. File folders and papers were floating downward like snowflakes. At that same moment, I could hear telephones ringing throughout the building, which left me with an eerie feeling. I knew how close I had come to death and I then turned to Joe, a co-worker, who had the fear of death upon his face. We looked at each other but no words were spoken.

Finally, I climbed over the glass and debris on my desk to reach Joe. Calvin, my supervisor, came around the corner. We were all standing together in shock. I asked Calvin to stand on the desk and wave to

Ann Shirley Banks

the firemen. About that time, we were engulfed in bellowing black smoke. Panic and terror set in and I feared the building was getting ready to collapse.

Debris was piled at least five feet high and Joe decided to climb up on the pile of rubble to see what was left on the other side. There was flooring! Joe and Calvin took ceiling tiles to cover the glass, then the two of them pulled me up and guided me to our escape route, over the barrier of computers, file cabinets, wiring, and glass. The stairwell was on the west end. I could not get out fast enough. It was as though my legs carried me almost in flight. I recall a man telling me to slow down, that I was bleeding profusely, but all I could think about was getting out.

I felt my body shaking uncontrollably and I was bleeding heavily. I was sickened by the weight of fear, tears running down my cheeks, my back hurting. I can remember reaching the south plaza and seeing my co-workers. I tried to talk but I could not hear my voice. The paramedics called me one of the "walking wounded" and set me on a curb, putting pressure dressings on my wounds. While I was sitting there, I could see bodies being brought out in terrible shape. I felt dismay and disbelief. I no longer felt safe.

A female officer came by and I begged her to transport me to the hospital. She put me in the back of the police car. I was sitting between two women; a little girl was in the front seat.

The lady to my right said, "My baby was blown out of my arms." I grabbed her and we just sobbed uncontrollably.

Once we got to St. Anthony's Hospital, we were separated. The lacerations to my legs, hand, and back were cleaned and pressure dressings were applied. I remain under medical care and still receive psychological counseling.

Such an invasion into your normal life destroys the inner core of your being. It sets up a great magnitude of fear, of anxiety, and of panic. Nothing I have ever experienced has ever attacked my body with such a force. I call it "the blast and force from hell that has forever changed my life."

As a survivor, I must say I am privileged to have been acquainted with so many of the people who lost their lives in the Murrah building. I will never forget them, nor will I forget that day.

It Only Takes a Moment

Janet Beck

*S*hortly after 7 A.M. on April 19, 1995, I arrived at the Social Security office where I'd worked for almost thirty-one years. It was a beautiful day and I was looking forward to getting a lot of work done since this was my "down day"—a day without interviews. Before leaving the office the day before, I had organized my workload so I could start immediately.

On the way to my desk, located toward the back of the office on the first floor, I exchanged greetings with several co-workers. When I passed Richard Allen's desk, he told me the computer system was down and would be at least until noon. My spirits dropped—I would not achieve my goals for the day. Then I heard him laugh and knew he was teasing.

The atmosphere in the office was light. Several employees had been off work for the Easter weekend and had returned that morning. There was chatter and laughter coming from the break room as the monthly "birthday" donuts were brought in. Soon people were back at their desks getting ready for their day's appointments and trying to get as much work done as possible before the office opened to the public at 9 A.M.

Janet Beck

A few minutes before nine, some claims representatives went to the reception area and called their claimants back to their desks. Rex Irwin and I shared a common cubicle divider wall and I could hear him talking with his claimant whose wife had stayed in the lobby. I was busy working on my computer and chipped a fingernail. I grabbed my nail file to repair the damage and suddenly, everything became so dark I could not see my hand. The pressure was so heavy I couldn't catch my breath and thought I must be having a heart attack. I felt myself screaming and kept telling myself to stop—but I couldn't. I have learned since that even people who sat next to me did not hear me scream. The next thing I remember was my supervisor, LaQuita Cowan, who sat behind me, asking if I was okay. I could hear her and someone else calling names to see if everyone was all right. At that point I realized something had happened not just to me but to everyone.

Rex called my name and asked if I could get away from my desk. As I cleared away the ceiling tiles, lights, wiring, and whatever else had been blown or fallen on me and around my desk, I found I had blocked myself in. Rex said to stay where I was, he would come back to get me. He led some of our co-workers through what used to be the break room to the emergency exit at the east side of the building. The emergency door had been twisted but Rex was able to open it enough to get out. A beam of light came in through the partially opened door and I felt a calmness and peacefulness settle over me. I knew Rex would be back. Also, LaQuita and Richard Dean knew I was still there.

We continued calling out names to determine who was injured and what their condition was. One voice answered that she was drowning, and another person, who was trapped under her desk, just kept calling for help. I cannot remember any time in my life that I felt so helpless. All I could do was call out reassurances that someone would be back to get them. Rex fumbled his way back to his desk and found his flashlight. I had already climbed onto my desk because my feet were getting wet, and Rex held the light so I could see where to step. The file cabinets by our desks were gone and the other furniture was not where it had been. I crawled over the divider still standing between our desks, and we picked our way out the back door. He kept telling me to watch out for the electrical wiring hanging from the ceiling. That the electricity might still be live had not even crossed my mind since it was so dark. I was just relieved to be on my way out.

The first person I saw as I stepped up to the sidewalk was Laura Bode, a co-worker, lying at the top of the stairs. The man with her said she was in shock. Laura's sweater was full of fiberglass and she was having trouble breathing. She asked me to stay with her, and I assured her I would. Rescue workers kept coming around the corner in such a hurry that I was afraid someone would step on her. I finally got her moved to a safer place. People above us on the plaza yelled for ladders while more people ran up and down the street looking for others or trying to help. During my career with Social Security, we have had many threats, and as I looked around and saw windows blown out of many of the buildings south of the Murrah building, I felt a great relief that whatever happened was not directed at us. I still had no idea of what had happened.

While I sat with Laura, others were brought out of the building. One was so badly injured I did not recognize her. Richard Dean, one of my co-workers, who kept going back into the building to locate others, said he'd had to ask her name before he knew it was Sharon Littlejohn. I was beginning to realize something serious had happened. Reality hit when I learned that another supervisor, Carol Bowers, had been killed. Carol and I were in college together and had worked together for thirty years. Before long someone came to help Laura and me to an ambulance a block away. We were taken to the VA Hospital where the people there were helpful and concerned.

After I was examined for injuries, someone helped me to make a phone call to my friends Russ and Eula Simms. They had managed to get through to my daughters, Lynn and Teri, both of whom live in Texas, and then called my "adopted" son, Carl, who was living at home. Carl had been at the building by 9:20 looking for me.

I stayed at the hospital until Laura's mother got there, then the Simmses came and took me home. Carl was waiting and told me Teri and Lynn were both on their way. My brother and his wife from Tulsa were also coming. I really just wanted to be alone but later I was so thankful they all came. I was not able to do anything. They took phone calls for me and had to do all my thinking for me the next few days. I could not have made it without their help and support.

The few weeks after the bombing are still a blur. We were notified each time one of our co-workers was recovered. The survivors were constantly together: going to funerals, making hospital visits, or going to meetings. It seemed as if we were afraid to be apart; if we didn't have this continual contact, something would happen to another person.

A friend asked me if after surviving this, I was going to make some changes in the way I lived my life. At first I was offended. I thought I had been doing fine. Now I realize I have made many changes. My outlook is different and I don't put off doing things I really want to do. I still have many fears: being in the dark, being in crowded or unfamiliar places. It's hard to go to the grocery store or to places where I can't see around me. Situations which were part of my daily routine before are now very stressful. I've had to make many adjustments in my daily life.

Some good things have come from this horrendous event—the miracle of Sharon Littlejohn's continuing recovery, new friends I've made in different activities such as habeas corpus-antiterrorism reform* and the memorial committee. Of the few personal items I recovered from the building, the most meaningful is a magnet, one of several I had on my desk. It has a rainbow and a dove on it. I believe this is a sign to me of God's promise. I know He will take care of the survivors, the families, and all those affected. It does only take a moment for your life to be changed forever.

---

*A bill that was passed by Congress in April 1996 limits the number of appeals and time-processing of the appeals. *Ed.*

The Child of Light

Carol Beavis

---

*T*his poem was written by Carol Beavis, a co-worker and a friend of our family. It expresses our emotions, feelings, and the fond memories of our son, Derwin, who worked for Social Security. We will always love and cherish the time we had with our son.

THE CHILD OF LIGHT

In Memory of Derwin Wade Miller, May 4, 1967–April 19, 1995

> Into this world a special light was born,
> To soothe the night
> and bring joy to the morn.
> Into this life the light shone bright,
> growing and giving, never to slight,
> but each one of us receiving
> freely embraced by the light.
> This light was a child in the Springtime
> of life—

Derwin Wade Miller

Carefree and spirited with innocence
of strife.
The years came and the years went
Each full of experiences and promises
of undying friendships,
of a father's loyal respect,
and a mother whose face radiated
at the mere sound
of his name.
The seasons came and the seasons went
For Spring was almost spent.
Autumn was close at hand,
and this child was now a man.
His light shone forth for all to see
with a love of life for you and me.
God had a plan for this Child of Light.
Winter came early
As if in a hurry
For the world had to know and experience his plight.
He was to shine hope through the darkness
so the world could know
That through it all
Love will glow.

Carol Beavis

COLOR ME BLUE
IN MEMORY OF MY BROTHER
DERWIN MILLER

It seems as though
a long time ago
you left me in a daze

So when I am weak
I often think
of how much love you gave.

As years went past
good times did last
but often did I pray

To hear you laugh
my better half
I listened for that day

Precious as it went
Little time we spent
all gone but a memory

Nothing to replace
The empty space
that grows inside of me.

I look no more
like I did before
to heaven at God's feet

I have a prayer
That I will share
next time that we shall meet.

Tim Adams for La Sonja Heard

My Time to Speak

Arlene Blanchard

"Why am I still here?" This is the question that continually echoed through the confused and pain-riddled corridors of my mind, haunting and taunting me for weeks, even months, after the bombing on April 19, 1995.

Three weeks prior to the bombing, I had just celebrated my first wedding anniversary with my husband, Stan. Thoughts of the joy, peace, trials, and tribulations that we shared in our one year together made me reflect on the other husbands and wives who were lost and who had built a lifetime of memories with their spouses, children, loved ones, and friends.

I think about the young babies who hadn't even had their first birthday. The young toddlers just starting to comprehend small things in life. The unborn babies who had not experienced their mother's touch or their first cry as they entered this strange new world.

I had experienced so much and yet so little in my twenty-eight years of life. Why was I still here? I had traveled throughout the world while in the United States Army. I had lived in Italy, skied in Germany, dined in Greece, and saw the sights in Switzerland. Yet, I never had much love and compassion for others. I had never decorated my own Christmas tree, or held my own child for the first time.

As I reflected on the pluses and minuses of my life, I thought of the purpose this event had in my life. I had just nine days left before I was scheduled to depart the military and to embark on my new life as a civilian. I knew my life would change significantly, but I was excited about the change. I had no clue of how

Stan, Arlene, and Hunter Blanchard

dramatically my life was about to change in a split second. The Friday morning after the bombing, I had the opportunity to be on ABC's *Nightline* hosted by Ted Koppell. The interview with David Marash was on the same day they arrested Timothy McVeigh. Mr. Marash asked me what my thoughts were about the alleged bomber. I said, "It was even more painful to know that a citizen of the United States, an individual who shares the same heritage of this great nation, could do such a thing. I wish I could pull the plug on his life." I also mentioned that the second sketch of John Doe #2 looked very familiar to me. I could not say positively where or when I may have seen this individual.

The very next morning after the interview, at approximately 5:45 A.M., I received a call from the battalion's temporary headquarters and was told to report there as soon as possible.

I had to find someone to drive me there because I was not coherent enough to drive. I was made to wait two and a half hours before I was seen by anyone. Finally, I was led into a room, accompanied by my battalion sergeant major, to face one of the most hateful and noncaring individuals I have ever met. He was the head of Army Public Affairs for the United States Army Recruiting Command (USARC). He told me they were very displeased with my interview and my comments about possibly having seen alleged bomber number two, and that I was prohibited, by direct order, from doing any more interviews without their approval. Then I was told that I needed to wait again to speak with an FBI agent. This was another long wait that proved to be futile. Keep in mind that this was just three days after the bombing.

There was so much hatred and rage within me that I thought I would explode. I felt like Dorothy in the *Wizard of Oz*, with so many different emotions like a whirlwind around me, as though I was in the eye of a twister. There was no where to run, just like on April 19. I needed to vent. The loss of dear and close friends who could never be replaced. The thought that an American citizen who had served in the army as a fellow comrade, could be part of the most vile act against the people of this country. The fact that the very organization that I swore to serve and protect with my life would deny me one of the most basic rights as a citizen of this great nation—to speak out!

How dare they penalize me for being human and wanting to see justice done? My heart was bleeding from the savage, senseless wounds inflicted on me and countless others that day. What was I to say? How dare these people be so insensitive to what I had just experienced? They were not there! They were not held captive by this monster that would be with me for the rest of my life. They did not see all the blood. They did not hear the screams or the moans and groans for help. They did not experience the massive attack of confusion, or feel the sensation of going blind or of electricity coursing through their body. They did not have their whole life ripped to shreds in a matter of moments.

I had to deal with all these emotions even prior to attending any of the funerals of my lost friends. How could I cope? Who would help me diffuse? I had been to a group counseling session with some of the other survivors from the army, but this didn't help, it only made me more angry. I could truly feel their pain so it only compounded my own pain. Who has given me strength to handle this? Jesus! "Jesus," the name I called on immediately after I regained consciousness and calmed down from my hysteria. I called on Jesus as I squeezed my hands back and forth, as though He was holding my hand.

I remember that very instant when the bomb exploded and it felt like volts of electricity were penetrating my body. In total darkness, feeling completely isolated, I heard a small voice whisper in my ear, "If you were to go, you would be okay, because you know Him."

As I reflect back on the pluses and minuses of my life, I thought of the purpose this event had on my life. I no longer take simple everyday pleasures for granted. I now genuinely care about the needs of others. I have decorated my own Christmas tree. I am now a mom and held my child for the first time in January. I now have the opportunity to speak candidly and without being censored by the U.S. Army. "This is my time to speak."

What Would You Say?

Eva Bloomer

*T*he last conversation I had with my father was about getting my car fixed. Such a strange thing to think of but if only I had known at the time that it would be my last chat with Daddy, what would I have said?

Would I have been able to get away with a simple, "Don't go to work tomorrow, Daddy. Please come with me to get my car fixed?" Does fate work in such a way? Or would I have been denied the chance to give warning? If so, what, of all the things in my heart, would I have said?

Perhaps I would have brought up fond memories, like all those fishing trips to Bear Creek when I was a little girl. The two of us were quite a pair, once away from adult supervision (Mother, of course). She would pack us a few sandwiches, fix a big thermos of iced tea, and cheerily send us off, most likely happy to have the house to herself for an afternoon. Once on the road, we would sing silly songs, "Oh...froggy went a courtin' and he did ride...uh-huh," and miles would roll away. When we got close to the creek, we'd stop for bait and snack cakes. And when we were finally settled on the

44

bank, lines in the water—proud look on Dad's face that his little girl could bait her own hook with nary a girlish complaint—we would both be thinking of those snacks we just purchased. It was always my idea to break into them. Dad, counting on a child's need for sugar, never had to broach the subject himself, but instead waited patiently for me to ask if it was too soon for lunch. Though only

Glen Bloomer

ten in the morning, we would agree that if we just ate the cakes and saved the sandwiches for lunch, that it would be okay. On those trips, we were buddies. We would laugh and share jokes. He treated me as an equal, not as a child to be spoken down to. We were out in the wilds on an adventure and all we had was each other.

We never caught anything but perch at Bear Creek, but I had great times with a dear friend. I would thank my father for letting me be his friend and not just his daughter.

But maybe, instead of thanking him, for our last time to talk together I would say all those other things that rarely get said to anyone's satisfaction, once it is too late. Maybe I would have brought up all the rough times we went through while I was a teenager. I could explain to him how frustrating it was for me as a teen, that he and Mom were so often right in their warnings about the big, bad world, when I was just sure they were only interested in keeping me under their parental thumb. All those shouting matches, tears, and heartaches simply because he and I were so much alike (stubborn) and not about to admit it. All the terrible things I said to and about my daddy, convinced that he and Mom were just interfering in my life, which I had all figured out. Of course, as I got older, life showed itself to be not at all like I had figured, and Mom and Dad were proven to be the kind, loving parents that I had known as a child—and without a bit of smugness.

I would apologize to my father for all the pain, worry, torment, and anger that my thirteenth through eighteenth years caused him. Apologize for ever having doubted his love and wisdom. Apologize for there ever being a time in my life when I was not his friend.

No, I think, if granted one last talk with my father, it would be a talk about Mom. We would share all our wonderful memories of her. He could tell me the story again of how they met. How he fell in love with this beautiful woman, wearing a coral-colored outfit, when he first saw her. To his dying day, his favorite color remained coral. It may sound corny, but it is true. My father was a dyed-in-the-wool, bashful romantic, and he loved my mother more than I will ever know. I think he would like the idea of our last bit of time together being spent reminiscing about the delightful, smiling woman whom we both love and miss so much. I believe that it would be the most meaningful moments we could share—relishing the wonders of our life. We would come to glow with the understanding of how lucky we have been to have my mother in our lives, to have had the happy family that so few ever know. To have had each other to share this amazing, bittersweet adventure.

But our final chat was not about any of those things. It was about my stupid car because I didn't know that this was the last time I would ever see my father's beloved face again. In truth, it was not the last time I saw his face. For the sixteen days after the bombing that he was missing (he was pulled out of the building on the fifteenth day, but my family was not notified until the next day), I saw his face—his sweet face—in agony, alone, in the dark, and in pain. All my waking hours, for sixteen days, I willed my father to be alive and to hold on until they found him. But with that came visions of this handsome, dignified man with the twinkling eyes under a building, hurt, bleeding, scared, and alone. Horrible, heartbreaking visions that no one should have to endure. But what could I do? Hope for him to be dead and out of pain? No, I could not give up on my daddy; he would never have given up on me! So I would try to picture him in an air pocket, safe and sound, waiting to be rescued.

But the media does not like for us to have a hopeful picture of things when there is disaster afoot. The newscasters would go on and on, in an almost gleefully morbid tone, about how long "experts" say that a person can live without food or water. Then it would rain, and these touted "experts" would say that it was possible for rain to trickle down and give water to any who "might still be alive," and would seem to encourage hope again. Though I never gave up hope, not for a moment, as the days wore on, others gave up hope of finding anyone alive.

Let me tell you, no matter how hard you try to be optimistic, your mind will latch onto the "fear of the worst" and visions come, and there is no escape from the soul-wrenching atrocities that your mind can conjure. Throughout all these days, there was nothing to do *but* worry and agonize. Because there had been set up for the families a kind of headquarters at the First Christian Church in Oklahoma City, it was the only place we *could* be. All information went there first, and we were not allowed to be of any help to the rescue efforts. You couldn't go outside even for a smoke because of all the television cameras poised and ready to capture on film the tragic family members. There were even members of the media who tried to sneak into the church so they could harass the grieving families in our only refuge. While we waited for our twice-a-day report from the coroner—another body count—through all this madness my heart and mind focused on one thing, "Breathe, Daddy, keep breathing. Someone will get to you soon. Breathe, Daddy, keep breathing. Don't leave me, Daddy. Please hold on, they will get to you soon..."

All About Mark

Joyce Bolte

n October 21, 1966, Mark Allen Bolte was born in Bentonville, Arkansas. He was our first child and our pride and joy. He was chubby with a little bit of peach-colored fuzz for hair. He was happy and healthy and became the focus of our lives. As Mark grew into each new phase of his life we were constantly delighted with his antics and his developing personality. Mark was a good child. Oh, he had his share of spankings and he could be very stubborn, but he was also very loving. His favorite place to be was wherever his dad was. My husband worked out of town a good deal of the time and sometimes he would take Mark with him. Mark loved those outings and so did his dad. My husband loves football and so Mark developed a love for the game. By the time he was four years old, he knew all the National and American League helmets by heart. He was an avid Razorback fan and even had Razorback wallpaper in his room at home.

When Mark started to school he was not really into it, but he did okay. By the time he graduated from high school, he was an honor student with four years of perfect attendance. In high school he developed a love for basketball and we had a hoop in our driveway.

Every evening when Mark wasn't working, there would be a yard full of boys playing basketball in our driveway. Mark started working for Fred's Hickory Inn when he was sixteen. He would go to work after school and then come home to study. About this time he became interested in model airplanes. He would work constantly on them and every detail had to be perfect. Then he would carefully hang each one from the ceiling in his bedroom. They were still there when he died. As an adult, he continued that love of planes and loved to go to air shows.

Mark A. Bolte

When we walked into his apartment in Oklahoma City that first night, there was a card table set up with a model airplane partially completed and airplanes hanging from the ceiling.

When Mark was seven years old we were blessed with another son, Matt. He was a carbon copy of Mark and just as sweet. Mark was very good to Matt most of the time. Later Matt told us Mark had locked him out of the house one day and a few other brotherly love acts, but he was always there for Matt. One time Mark rode in a bike-a-thon. He placed third and there wasn't a prize he really wanted, but there was a small bike and he chose that prize for Matt.

We are of the Catholic faith and when Mark was in the third grade he became an altar boy. He continued to be one until he graduated from high school. He was Knight of the Year his senior year, and Don and I were so proud of him. Every year at Midnight Mass all of the past altar boys would serve. After Mark went to college, he would still serve. He was a religious young man and wherever he lived he always attended Mass. When we found his Bible at his apartment, I began to cry. It had been read much more than mine and I was ashamed of myself. I know that he is someone's guardian angel now.

Mark was also in the Boy Scouts. He and his friends stayed in Scouts even when they were in high school and it wasn't "cool" to be a Scout, because they loved the camping, activities, and their Scout leader. Guy J. Wilkerson played a major part in Mark's life. He loved those boys so much. One time he took Mark with him to the National Jamboree in Virginia. Mark enjoyed that trip even though they were caught in a hurricane and had to take all of the sleeping bags to town and dry them in dryers. He and his friends went on to become Eagle Scouts. Mark was very proud of that achievement.

When Matt became an Eagle Scout, Mark made a special trip home to be at the ceremony. Mark's interest in Scouts continued and when he moved to Oklahoma City he was an assistant scoutmaster for a troop there.

Mark's grandparents lived in northern Wisconsin When he was growing up we would go there every summer to visit. Mark loved going "up north" and visiting everyone. There were lots of relatives and we always had a good time. After Mark left home he would still go there as often as he could to see his grandma. He also had a favorite great-aunt in Tahlequah, Oklahoma, who he loved to visit. Every time he could, he would go to see her. We spent nearly every Easter with her and her family, so that was one of his favorite holidays.

Mark loved all holidays, but his very favorite was Christmas. It is also my favorite, so it is very hard to be happy at Christmas now. When he was little the Sears Christmas Catalog was his bible until after the holiday.

The first year that Mark was in college at Russellville, we bought him a tiny tree and he strung lights in his room and hung up ornaments that I had given him.

He took a picture and sent it home for us to see. He loved Christmas shopping and would spend hours picking out just the right present and card for people. He would send Christmas cards to everyone he knew because he loved doing it so much. Christmas was a tradition spent with his Aunt Helen, Uncle Larry, cousin Betty, and cousins from Louisiana. That was the most important time of the year for Mark. When he was home for Easter, just three days before the bombing, I told him, "Mark, you may not be able to be home for every holiday but I don't think I could stand it if you weren't home for Christmas." His reply was, "Mom, I will always be home for Christmas."

Mark grew up to be a big young man. He stood six foot five inches tall and weighed about 270 pounds. He was a very kind person even though he was stubborn. When he was ready to leave Vermont, he called his boss and asked if he could return their kindness to him. He bought all of the fixings for one of the few meals he knew how to cook and took them to their house, prepared dinner, and cleaned up the kitchen.

He had a temper but he never stayed angry for long. He loved jokes and loved to laugh. He had a laugh that could warm your very heart and make you laugh along with him.

When he was in Denver, he discovered snow skiing and loved it. He also discovered professional hockey. He became a great fan. He would buy hockey jerseys for Matt for Christmas and birthdays, and now Matt has all of Mark's. When he was in Montpelier, he discovered golf. That became the game of choice. He loved it and played every chance he got. He wasn't a very good golfer but one of his co-workers said he could hit a ball farther than anyone he had ever seen. It just didn't always go where he wanted it to.

When Mark graduated from Bentonville High, he went to Russellville, Arkansas, to Arkansas Tech. My husband and I followed him down to school with a load of his belongings. When we left him sitting in that dorm room alone with no one he knew on campus, I felt so bad. He came home as often as he could that first year. Then he joined Lambda Chi Alpha fraternity and was very involved in that. He made some very close friends there and they kept in touch after they parted. He then transferred to the University of Arkansas to complete his degree in Civil Engineering. The day he graduated was a beautiful day. He and all of his buddies were so excited to be out of school. Their futures were so full of promise. Mark was offered a job with the Federal Highway Administration and a job with the Missouri Department of Transportation. After much thought he decided he would take the federal government position because of all the traveling he would get to do and the benefits he would receive.

In January 1994 Mark left for his first assignment in Raleigh, North Carolina. From there he went to Wamic, Oregon; Denver, Colorado; Montpelier, Vermont; and then to Austin, Texas. We went to visit him everywhere but at Wamic. He was in Austin when he was offered the position of Environmental Specialist for the Federal Highway Administration for the State of Oklahoma. His desire was to go into the environmental field, and he would also be closer to home. I had worried every time he moved from one state to the other, and then when he settled where he wanted to be, we lost him in the April 19, 1995, bombing of the Alfred P. Murrah Federal Building. When Mark first left home we talked to him every Sunday night. Either he would call us or we would call him. That became a tradition that lasted until he was killed.

The night before Easter, during a visit home, Mark and Matt wanted to rent *The Lion King*. My husband and I had never seen it. We all sat and watched the movie, and the next morning Mark was going around the house singing "Hakuna Matata." He said, "Mom, do you know what that means? It means 'no worries.'" Some day I will watch that movie again but not for a very long time. The last time we talked to him was that Easter night when he called to tell us he had made it home okay.

The day we heard the news of the bombing we were glued to the TV. We looked constantly to see if we could see Mark. Friends started coming to the house to be with us. About 9:30 that night they called us to come to Oklahoma City. It was a very stormy night and we didn't arrive there until 3:30 A.M. We went to the church with the other families. Every day we watched the news and saw the ghastly destruction and knew that Mark was buried somewhere beneath it all. We waited for two horrible weeks before they found Mark. He was found the last day they looked for bodies. We were just so thankful that we had him to bring home.

Those were the most devastating days of our lives. Going to the church every day and returning to Mark's apartment every night to wait was dreadful. The numbness of what had happened kept us going, I suppose. Friends came from home every time they could. The telephone rang constantly. Finally it was over on Thursday, May 4, 1995. They came and told us they had found Mark. He was buried on May 9. The church was overflowing and there was an honor guard of altar servers lining the sidewalk into the church. It was a beautiful and moving service for a life that had ended all too soon.

I hope and pray that never again on American soil do people have to live through the horror that we and all of the other families and survivors had to live through. It has been a very difficult three years for us, but everyone loved Mark and there have been so many things done in his memory that he will never be forgotten. Our faith, the love of family and friends, and the realization that we have no choice but to go on has helped us this far. We still grieve every day for Mark, and life as we knew it has been destroyed forever. We will go on and do our best, but for all the healing time can do, it can never fill the hole that has been left in our hearts.

I would want Mark to be remembered as he truly was—a very kind and caring young man. He always thought of others and loved old people. He loved his family and loved God and I know that he is with Him now. As his boss in Austin told his new boss in Oklahoma City, "You are getting a great big teddy bear." That's what we told God and asked Him to please take care of Mark for us until we get to heaven.

To See
Another Day

Kathy Brady

My name is Kathy Brady. I work for General Services Administration (GSA) as an assistant building manager. On April 19, 1995, my life was changed forever.

At 9:02 A.M., I was at my desk on the first floor of the Alfred P. Murrah Federal Building in Oklahoma City, talking on the phone to an employee in Lawton. I never heard a "boom" but do remember my body feeling like it was expanding and then deflating, and then everything falling on my head and burying me.

I truly believe what saved me from much more serious injury was that my overhead systems furniture storage cabinet fell over on me, acting like a mini-bomb shelter. The blast never knocked me out of my chair, but buried me as I sat, and I remember just sitting there as everything fell and wondering what in the world had happened.

My first thought was that the construction contractor who had been working on the childcare center had brought the second floor down. After the initial debris stopped falling, I remember my exact thoughts: "You are alive, stay calm, and get the h—— out of here."

One of my most vivid memories was the total darkness and

feeling like my head was buried in a bucket of sand. My eyes, nose, and mouth were full of dust and debris. I slowly stood up and pushed the debris off of me and realized that at some time I had lost my shoes. I think the bomb literally blew my shoes off. This was later a standing joke with my co-workers, as I was known for running around the office with my shoes off. However, on this date I distinctly remember my shoes being on my feet.

Kathy Brady

After digging myself out, I was able to converse with several co-workers in my office. I continued to work my way to what had been the back door of our office, but my way was blocked by a file cabinet or bookcase. I now truly believe that when the adrenaline is flowing you can move things that under normal circumstances you probably could not budge. I moved the obstruction, and remember thinking, "We've been bombed. Nothing else could have done this kind of damage." I stood there for a short period of time wondering how I was going to get out of the building and yet needing to go back in and try and help my co-workers.

As I turned back toward the inside of our office, I felt a tug on my shirttail. I looked around and a gentleman, whom I recognized as someone who worked in the building, was asking me what I was planning to do and where I was planning to go. I told him I was trying to go back in and help my co-workers, and he told me to look closely. I did and saw there was a ceiling-high wall of debris blocking my way back in. This gentleman grabbed my arm and asked me if I knew the way out of the building.

I told him it looked like we might have a path toward the dock.

He slowly led me out of the building with my directions. At this time, we lost track of each other.

Several weeks later I was attending a group survivor meeting and saw this gentleman who possibly saved my life by not letting me go back into the building. I walked up to him and asked if he remembered me. He looked at me for a second and said, "Of course, you are the person who got me out of the building!"

He stated that he had been in the main elevator lobby at the time of the explosion, and that as long as he had worked in the building, he had never used any exit except the front door. He was standing there panicked and wondering how he was going to get out.

He said that the first sound he heard after the debris stopped falling had been someone yelling that they had made their way to the back door, and he simply headed to that voice, thinking they must know a way to get out. We were amazed at how each of us thought the other had probably rescued him.

Upon getting out of the building, a co-worker and I made our way south to see if we could possibly get up to the childcare center to try and help. This is probably one of the hardest things that I have had to deal with, in that without my shoes I was unable to get up on the plaza because of the glass, metal, and other debris.

I slowly worked my way to the corner of Fourth and Hudson where it has been described as a "war zone." I tried to help injured people down to the curb so they could sit, directed others to the cleared area, and asked everyone I saw what I could do to help.

Never in my life will I forget the look in the people's eyes—truly walking zombies—and also the injuries, the victims, the blood, and the total feeling of helplessness. I asked several people sitting on the curb if there was something I could do and was told to try and find some sort of bandage or cloth to help cover the wounds and possibly stop the blood from flowing. I saw an emergency medical kit on the sidewalk and grabbed packages of gauze, ripped them open, and gave them out as fast as I could.

Later, my co-worker Dot joined up with me and yelled that it looked like they were bringing out Melissa McCulley, a young college student who worked for us. We quickly made our way up to

Melissa and saw that they also had brought out Pamela Briggs, another co-worker, and laid them on the sidewalk next to each other.

I remember looking at Pam, who had a gash across her forehead, and seeing what I thought at the time was her brain, and thinking, "Oh, my God." I turned to Melissa, and I don't know why, but for me this seems to be one of the most striking memories of that day; I remember wondering why did something as horrible as this happen to such a little girl. Melissa is just slightly older than my son, and I guess motherhood just naturally kicked in.

Melissa was shaking, and Dot and I were trying to talk to her, afraid that she was going into shock. We could see that her knee was bent up and there was a tear in her pants and blood was coming through. She was begging us to please lay her leg down, and I remember a medical person opening the tear in her pants and being able to see all the way inside her knee.

Later that day, at a command center set up in a nearby hotel, John Cresswell, who was the maintenance personnel assigned to the operation of the Murrah building, arrived needing some medical attention for cuts on his arms sustained from trying to dig through rubble in the building. I remember him grabbing hold of me and starting to cry, "I've killed all those babies; I've killed all those babies!"

I kept telling him that a bomb had blown up the building and that it had nothing to do with something he had or hadn't done. All the time that he had been rescuing people, actually risking his own life, he had been feeling that he had in some way been responsible for the explosion. Nothing anyone said could penetrate his shocked mind that it was a bomb that had blown up the building.

Everyone who was able met at the command center the next morning. Some of these people came from all over the United States, many at their own expense. Never have I had more respect for what people can accomplish when there's a need, with no question on how many hours they have to work, or what they might be asked to do. That was when the "Oklahoma City Standard" was set—we don't shake hands, we hug. To this day, the people I work with and our co-workers in other parts of our region still do a lot of hugging.

I want to express my appreciation to the GSA for all they have done for us since the bombing to assist us in putting our lives back together.

And most importantly, I want to thank God for letting me live to see another day and to experience these days with my family and friends. I believe that God was not finished with me on this earth, and he had other things planned for me. I truly have a new outlook on life.

I think what has enabled me to make it through all of this is the desire to see my children to adulthood. I dedicate my story to my children, Michael and Andrea (Andi), the loves of my life. Michael —so I can see a young man become a fine grown man; Andi—who is severely mentally handicapped, knowing that God knew she needed me in more than the normal ways and would for a very long time.

The War Zone

Brett Brooks

*O*n April 19, 1995, I was at work. I work for the Oklahoma Guaranteed Student Loan Program, and at the time we were located in the *Journal Record* building at NW Sixth and Robinson, across from the Alfred P. Murrah Federal Building.

At 9:02 A.M. I was on the phone with a borrower, which was unusual, since normally I take my first break at 9:00, and head to the break room which is on the south side of the building.

While I was delayed in taking my break, the blast went off. It shook the building, unlike anything I've ever experienced in my life.

The blast blew me out of my chair and I landed on both ankles under my desk. When I got up, the ceiling tiles were falling down on my head and around the office. When I realized something had exploded, the first thought that came to mind was that a lot of employees were just standing in the aisles, shocked and scared. I was screaming at them to get out of there because a bomb had hit us. In fact, I thought the bomb was actually in our building, instead of across the street in the Murrah building.

Out of about 150 people in our office, most were out the door

Brett Brooks

within two minutes, with the exception of several of us who were searching for injured people. I heard screaming coming from the break room area, and when I got there, I saw that the blast had totally destroyed it.

Down in the executive office, the assistant director was walking around in a daze. His shirt was completely ripped apart. He had blood all around his neck, back, and face, as well as shrapnel and glass in his back. I helped pick glass out of his back.

The fifteen minutes I was in our building I inhaled enough smoke to cause lung damage.

The only way out of the building was the north stairwell and it was heavily damaged from rubble and glass. I slipped on the way down, either twisting or snapping an ankle bone.

When I went outside to see if anybody was out there, I turned around and looked at the Murrah building. What I saw was something I had never seen in a lifetime, not even on television. It was unbelievable!

The building was half destroyed. When I looked in the parking lot which separated the Murrah and *Journal Record* buildings there must have been twenty to thirty cars, and every single one was totaled and on fire.

I saw one person sitting in a car on fire. I saw a couple of body parts. What I saw was devastating. There was a huge crater in the street, like some kind of meteor had hit it. It was deep and wide. You could put two Greyhound buses in that hole.

Firemen were running up and down the street. Paramedics were everywhere. Glass was all over the streets. Just about everywhere on the sidewalks you could see blood. Lots of people were wrapped up with bandages covered with blood.

I was in a state of shock the whole time. They kept telling me that I needed to go be accounted for, because they were doing a count of every employee in the building. Then I heard a second bomb threat. All the doctors and nurses, and a wave of people were running toward us and they were telling us to get back.

I did not leave. A lot of our employees were on the ground and I stayed with them. A lot of other employees also stayed.

Finally, my ankle started swelling so that I couldn't walk anymore, so I decided to get in my car. The roof was caved in, and the sun roof had exploded. The cellular phone was dead because the phones were all jammed. I loaded some of my co-workers who had cuts and abrasions into the car and we went to St. Anthony's Hospital.

It looked like a war zone. There were people running everywhere with stretchers, wheelchairs, and chairs. They had every kind of employee from the flower girl, to the janitor, to security, grabbing people out of cars.

When I got to the emergency room I almost passed out from the stench of blood. It was on the walls and on the floor. People were lying down, throwing up, and passing out. I told them my left ankle was hurt and they said that only seriously injured people were going to be treated. I got back into the car and headed to my hospital.

I must have been one of the first people they treated because a lot of people were questioning me about what happened and asking if there were a lot of dead people. All I could tell them was, "Get ready, you guys are going to see more people than you've ever seen in your life."

The most vivid things that remain in my mind from the day of the bombing are my co-workers screaming for help, looking at the people in front of the Murrah building who were dead, seeing all the people in the emergency room crying and screaming, and the smell of blood. For about two days I could not get the smell of blood off me.

I am currently under a doctor's care. I've lost 50 percent lung capacity. I'm on an inhaler, and I take medication for water in my lungs and antibiotics to keep from getting respiratory infections. The injury to my foot and ankle required surgery. That's a permanent injury. I was told that in five years I will require a joint for my ankle.

For the rest of 1995 I missed a lot of work. I was hospitalized in June for a lung infection and an enlarged heart, and again in July for a phlebitis infection in my ankle and knee. I usually worked one to two weeks a month in 1995. I did not return to work on a regular basis until February 1996.

I have seen as many as six specialists. I currently receive counseling. I have not slept eight hours since the day before the bombing. I currently take all kinds of sleeping medication to try and help me sleep.

My life has been completely changed by this experience—physically, emotionally, and mentally. I have not seen anything good come out of this.

I see a lot of my fellow employees still suffering. I still see people jump at the slamming of doors or the breaking of glass. People cry from time to time. The employees I work with have permanent scarring on arms, faces, and legs that has totally changed their physical appearance. One employee's spouse left because he couldn't handle emotionally what his spouse had suffered.

The son of one of my employees was killed in the day-care center. That person has left the state, coming back only to handle business, but not to visit or live again. A couple of people who were injured are still completing skin-graft surgeries and bone replacements.

My employer has done everything humanly possible to take care of me and to make the work environment comfortable. I am still on light duty. However, I can personally say for me, things will never be the same.

The media so focused on the federal employees and did not have any sympathy toward anyone else, when there were many other people severely injured as well as some who were killed outside of the Murrah building.

If I had to do it all over again, I'm pretty sure I would have done what I did. The few lives I helped save made a contribution in the world. Had I not helped, they might not have been around to see their children grow up or spend the rest of their lives with family. I know the sacrifice I made and it has taken a great toll on me. I would not wish this on my worst enemy.

Oklahomans really pulled together. A lot of people who did not even know any of the injured came to the rescue with sympathy cards, money, donated blood, and donated time.

People came downtown to help out with whatever they could do. I guess it's unfair to say it was just Oklahomans, because we got a lot of help from all over the world, but basically the people of Oklahoma came to our aid.

Nobody was selfish, nobody was thinking of themselves. A lot of people risked their lives or serious injury to go back into the building. Just watching people lining up at blood banks and the hospital, as well as sending cards and letters to people they didn't even know, really was a big emotional lift.

As for the people who did this, there could not be enough justice in the world to make Oklahomans forget.

There's not enough money in the world to buy back the loved ones, to help you get through the stress you suffered or the injuries you have sustained. There's just not enough money in the world to buy all that back.

So I would say, try and live your life to the fullest, because tomorrow isn't guaranteed.

In Our Hearts

Minnie Mae Brooks

My sister Castine and I have always been extremely close. We have enjoyed a special relationship as sisters and as friends, for all of our lives together.

We all miss Castine so much. Castine was so much fun to be with, and she always greeted everyone with the biggest smile on her face. She was a stranger to no one, and everyone who knew her couldn't help but love her. She had such a love for life.

Her zest for life was something that Castine gave to her children. She was a wonderful mother and always took time to do many things with her children. She was constantly there for them, acting as chauffeur to various school activities, basketball games, judo lessons, and shopping. Castine was a person who worked hard to take care of her family. She taught her children to be good, and to always aim to achieve their best. She would be so proud of her three oldest sons Ronald, Timothy, and Cedric. They are doing such a wonderful job of caring for the three youngest children: Cathy, Hurtis, and Erick. Castine knows that I will always be there for her family. The children and I gather often and we talk about Castine, and all the good times that we shared with her when she was with us.

Castine's faith in God was something very important to her, a faith that she held from childhood throughout the rest of her life. She was a longtime member of St. John Missionary Baptist Church, and was an usher there, as well. All those who knew her, loved her dearly and she is deeply missed by all of them.

Castine was not only my sister, but also my friend. She would call me everyday from work, and we would talk about a little bit of everything. We would talk about her soaps on TV, and about what she was going to cook for dinner. How I miss those simple things.

Castine Deveroux

The tragic day of April 19, 1995, changed all of our lives forever. It is a day that I will never forget. I could not believe it when my son, Wendell, called me that morning and told me he thought there had been a bombing downtown. My heart dropped when I heard the news. I got on the phone to call Castine, but when I got no answer, I knew something was terribly wrong.

My family still cannot believe this awful thing has happened, even after so much time has passed since that tragic April day. This tragedy has taken a toll on all of us, but somehow, with God's help, we will make it.

Castine will be forever missed. We do not have her with us in body, but her presence is with us in spirit. We will always hold her in our hearts.

Time to Smell the Roses

Shirley Brotherton

*J*had prepared for work the morning of April 19 as usual, believing from that day on that the worst of the year was past. IRS Day was already over, I would surely get over my constant cold that had been bothering me since December 30, and it was my older son's birthday, a date signaling that the weather is usually very nice from that time on.

My husband drove me to work and we arrived at 6:35 A.M., our usual time. I stopped by Raymond's snack bar on the fourth floor as customary, and got a large snow cone that he created for me.

I reached my desk, performed all my routine tasks, then signed in. Some time later, I was reading something when I overheard Kim from the legal division talking to Betsy. Shortly after Kim left, at 8:47 by my watch (I keep my watch two minutes fast), because I knew the post office opened at 8:45, I took my purse and a package of books I was mailing to my cousin out of the drawer and told Betsy I was going on break.

Only because I wanted to mail those books to my cousin was I out of the office at that particular time. If I took a break in the mornings, it was usually later, and sometimes not at all.

I took the elevator down to the first floor and noticed Ron standing beside his door at the Social Security office, waved and said hello to him. He spoke and waved back, then I went out the door and walked across the street to the post office.

I got through quickly and made my way back to the Murrah building. I decided to stop at the first-floor women's restroom rather than waiting and going to the one on the seventh floor later, because I not only wanted to get some coffee, but also a small snow cone, and I didn't want to have to take my snow cone into the restroom.

Shirley E. Brotherton

I had just sat down in the booth with my coffee, then before I could zip my purse back up or take a sip of coffee—it happened! A loud BOOM! Then everything turned dark as black ink. I couldn't see anything. The table started shaking, with rubble piling up all around me, and my first thought was, We're having an earthquake and it feels just like the simulated one at Universal Studios. My grandson and I had been there just the month before during spring break. I held onto the table the way I had clung to the handle bar during the ride then.

I reasoned that the loud noise I'd heard was a natural gas line explosion because of the earthquake. The thought occurred to me to get under the table, but I couldn't because the rubble kept piling up and I was being buried in it, surrounded from the bottom and all sides. It was just a few inches from touching my head.

I felt something slam into me, and I was too stunned to even think. The next thing I was aware of was being concerned about breathing and thought, I'm going to have to claw my way out of here. Before I could panic, I saw a patch of beautiful, clear blue sky the shape of an oval. I was so grateful to see it because I knew that meant I would be able to breathe.

As soon as the shaking had stopped, I heard someone asking if anyone was in there. A man dressed in white pulled me out of the rubble. My vision was blurred and although I was aware that other people were around, the only face I clearly focused on immediately after the blast was Raymond's, from the snack bar, and I was relieved to see he was okay.

Later, Raymond stated that just as soon as he left the snack bar, the floor fell—that's how close I had come to being at the wrong place at the wrong time. If I had been just seconds later, or anywhere else except where I had been from 8:47 on by my watch that morning, I wouldn't be alive. I was sure that I was guided by some kind of divine intervention.

I firmly believe that those of us who survived did so because it was not our time to go, and that the ones who did not survive, their life's work on earth was finished.

The weeks and months following April 19 have not been easy for most of us, and some have not fared as well as others. For some, it is doubtful they will ever return to work. The rest of us are trying to carry on despite the memory lapses, short attention spans, and loss of co-workers and job place, not to mention having to start a complete new "normal level" on the job.

We all have to come to terms with the way we expect to carry on our lives. We can either choose to be miserable, blame God for what has happened, or, as difficult as it may seem, take the Scripture literally that says "All things work together for good to them that love God," and do our best to go on from there.

Faith is the one thing that cannot be taken from us. Since we have been exposed to what terrorism really is, we can never take safety and security for granted again, especially those of us who have experienced it firsthand.

I have definitely changed my priorities. Before the bombing, I was extremely obsessed with putting out and keeping up with a huge work-load to the point of, at times, being unfriendly and downright rude.

After the bombing, I realized there were people, even in my own work area in Housing and Urban Development, whose names I didn't know. I never took time to socialize because every minute was either dedicated to getting the work out or looking over documents in my computer. I had very little time to spare.

Besides, after speaking to workers for over eight years, it would be embarrassing to suddenly introduce myself and admit that I didn't know their names after all that time! So I just went along and pretended to know who they were.

The day after the bombing, I was wondering who had made it and who hadn't. The sad thing was, one of the people I was most concerned about—a lady I had met every morning and just about every break and lunch time—I didn't even know her name although I talked to her every day. I later found out that her name was Kathy Cregan, who worked for Social Security on the first floor—she hadn't made it. I didn't learn some of the HUD employees' names until weeks after the bombing.

From this day forward, I want to take the time to listen and talk to people when they feel the need to talk. I also want my co-workers to feel free to come to me and not feel the threat of having their head chewed off because I am under too much stress and strain. The work will get done, same way, anyway. Yes, my priorities have changed.

I want to be less critical of myself and others; to show respect and courtesy at all times; to dare to make mistakes and try to enjoy them, or at least later have a good laugh! I want to take the time to enjoy all facets of life, the beautiful scenery; to smell the roses; to appreciate the little things of life; to enjoy people, places, and things.

It is a relief to stop trying to be Superwoman, and to just be human and do my best, to try to live each day to the fullest because it may very well be my last.

The Story of...

Clifford R. Cagle

O n April 19, 1995, I was working at my desk at HUD on a solicitation that was to be mailed out the following week. When the bomb went off, I was knocked out of my chair by the force of the blast. Flying debris, concrete, and glass were imbedded in my face and neck. The next thing I knew, I was on the floor, choking on blood in my throat. I rolled over to let it roll out of my mouth. I know I heard people calling my name, but I couldn't answer them. I then heard someone call my name again, and I moved my hand so they knew I was alive. I passed out again and when I came to, I heard another co-worker calling my name. I moved my hand again to let them know I could hear them. I passed out again and came to when the rescuer put me on a stretcher. I woke up once while they were carrying me down from the seventh floor to the ground floor, then once again when I heard someone ask what hospital, and I told them the VA. Someone said no, so I told them Presbyterian. I realized they were taking X-rays and someone said I was all right and to relax. I didn't come to again until I was in ICU at about 9 P.M., after eight or nine hours of surgery.

The falling debris had crushed the left side of my skull and sliced my left eye into five pieces. My eye was hanging out of the socket by the nerve. I had lost 4.5 pints of blood by the time I reached the triage unit. While I was in the triage, the doctors and nurses thought they had lost me twice, as my heart stopped.

The nine hours of surgery were to remove glass and concrete from my face and neck. The concrete and glass had come within millimeters of my carotid artery. I also had a dime-sized hole in my skull, and the doctors thought I might have brain damage. Glass had penetrated the membrane between my skull and brain.

Clifford R. Cagle

My wife did not know about the bombing because she was running errands. When she arrived home, she turned the television on, not paying much attention to it, until they said the Murrah Federal Building had been bombed. She called me but could not get an answer.

My daughter told my wife that they needed to go to the hospital to try and find me. My wife said, "No, I think we should stay here so someone can get in touch if they have to."

Around 11 A.M., my youngest daughter called from school in a hysterical state, so my wife went to the high school and picked her up.

About noon, the hospital called my wife and told her I was in surgery and would be there for several hours and cautioned her not to hurry.

On the following Tuesday, I had another three hours of surgery to have my left eye removed and a prosthesis inserted, which was made of natural coral.

On April 25, 1995, I had another nine hours of surgery, this time to reconstruct the left side of my skull. The surgeon said my forehead was like putting a jigsaw puzzle together.

While I was in the hospital, some of the Dallas Cowboys players came to see me, including Michael Irving. I was joking around with him about being homeboys because I was from Florida also. After he left, the PR person for the hospital told me that Michael had invited me to a Cowboys game.

In May, I was fitted with a new prosthesis for my left eye. I also had to wear a mask to help reshape my eye and face. For a period of three months, and after all of my other surgeries, I had to go back every other day to have the mask reshaped.

In September, I had two more surgeries to tie the nerves back together on the left side of my face.

In December, I had eight teeth pulled to correct the jaw joint of the left side of my face because it had been damaged and the only way to correct it was to correct my overbite. So, I have to wear braces to straighten my teeth. Then my jaw will have to be broken to remove some of the jawbone.

In May 1996, I had another four hours of reconstructive surgery to fill in where the surgeons had cut some of my skull bone to use to reform my eye socket.

My eye doctor was to do some surgery on my eye also, but I believe he will do it all at once when I have my jaw surgery.

I went back to work in October 1995 and worked until November 1996. I can't stand the tension of going to work. I have a knot in my shoulder all day, my right arm is numb, and my neck is so tight it hurts. I was advised to take some leave to get away from the office. I am now applying for medical retirement because I cannot work with this much tension.

I Will Hurt Forever

John Henry Carlile

I met Catherine Mary Leinen in the winter of 1981. She was working for a bail-bond company and I was a police detective. We laughed and joked, and I knew right then and there that a long-lasting friendship had started. A year later, she went to work for the Federal Employees Credit Union which was located in the Murrah building.

Our friendship grew stronger as we discovered that we both enjoyed camping, craft projects, and just being together. As our friendship developed, we realized that it had grown into love. In 1991, we decided to spend the rest of our lives together.

Kathy was a very friendly and outgoing person with big brown, sparkling eyes. She made friends easily and was always willing to lend a hand to anyone in need. She enjoyed getting away from the daily routine by camping. She loved camping at the lake, visiting with camping buddies, and watching and feeding the different animals roaming about, especially the squirrels and the ducks. She also enjoyed strolling hand in hand on leisurely walks and watching the beautiful sunsets. I loved being with her and watching her love God's

Catherine Mary Leinen

creation. We were counting the days until she could retire so we could spend more time traveling and just simply enjoying life together.

Our plans, hopes, and dreams were torn apart at 9:02 A.M. on April 19, 1995, the day the world will remember—the day I wish I could forget. My life was forever changed.

On April 19, Kathy and I got up earlier than normal because I had to fly a training flight with the Air National Guard. As I left the house, I said, "Give me some lips" and I kissed Kathy goodbye, not knowing it would be the last time I would ever kiss her, hold her in my arms, or see her alive.

I drove to Will Rogers Airport and got ready for take-off. Around 8:50 A.M. I called Kathy at her office as I always did before take-off. I told her I loved her and would meet her at home at noon to take her to her doctor's office followed by her last therapy treatment. She had a broken shoulder from a fall in December. Those appointments would not be kept.

A few minutes later, I was standing on the north side of the operations building when I heard a loud boom. I literally felt the ground shake and a shock wave. I thought it was a sonic boom. However, when I went back inside, the TV was showing that the federal building had just been bombed. When I heard that, an eerie feeling came over me and I knew Kathy was gone. I didn't want to believe it, and I told myself she'll be fine and that she will call just as soon as she can get to a phone. I immediately drove home and tried to find out anything about her whereabouts. The minutes turned into hours and still no word. I stayed by the phone waiting for her to call to let me know she was fine. I called hospital after hospital trying to find out if there were any unidentified female patients who could possibly be Kathy. All my calls were met with negative responses.

The hours turned into days and still no word of Kathy. I prayed to God that she would be found alive. The restless days and sleepless nights that followed were as close to hell as I ever want to be. Every time the phone rang I knew it would be good news; instead it was very concerned family or friends wanting to know if I had heard anything. The answer was always the same—"no news."

The days had now become weeks and my hopes had changed: *Please find her body.* Let me bury my Kathy, let me see her one last time. On the evening of May 4, sixteen days after the bombing, the call I dreaded finally came. Kathy's body had been recovered.

I had to see her. I had to know for sure. I attempted to view her body that evening but was not allowed to until the next day at the funeral home. Having served on the police force for twenty-two years, I knew I could handle anything; I had seen it all. But this time it was my Kathy. Although it has been three years since the bombing, I can still see her battered and crushed body.

When people ask me how I'm doing, I usually say, "I'm fine," but if the truth be known, I will hurt forever for Kathy and for us.

After Kathy's funeral, my life was devastated. It seems families hurting so desperately look for outlets to appease their frustrations. Although Kathy and I did not have a marriage license, knowing we committed our lives to one another was all we needed, or so we thought.

Furthermore, the State of Oklahoma recognizes common-law marriages, or so we thought. But all of a sudden, my life with Kathy and what we had was being challenged by the very people who had acknowledged our marriage. The people who stood by me as we waited those never-ending sixteen days; the people who watched as I signed the death certificate "John Henry Carlile, surviving spouse." They were no longer *our* family, they were *Kathy's* family. The extra lot that they had purchased next to her would no longer be available for me. The headstone that was to mark her grave would not be set. Instead her grave would be unmarked until a replacement could be made without my name. Why was this happening?

After attending counseling at Project Heartland for nearly two years, I have found I am not the only one who had families turn against them. This is an untold story of many. Grandparents not speaking to their grandchildren, children at odds with their step-parents, in-laws against spouses; family pitted against family. Untold because of the hurt, the shame, and the greed. Families that should be holding onto each other and to the memories of the joy their loved one brought to this world.

I felt like I was losing every battle and I had no where to turn. And finally I did the only thing I could do, I turned to the Lord. I accepted Jesus Christ as my Lord and Savior and asked Him to forgive me of my sins and to come into my heart. On Easter Sunday 1996, I was baptized.

The battles have not gone away, and some days I wonder if I can cope with one more court date, knowing how much Kathy would hate this, but now there is peace in my heart. Now I know without a doubt that, although I cannot be buried beside her, I will see her sparkling brown eyes in heaven.

Black

Joseph E. Chicoraske

───────────────

*J*oy, my nine-year-old daughter, and I left home for school and work a little after 8 A.M. I gave her a hug and dropped her off at Villa Teresa School at about 8:30. I then went to the federal building, which was only six or seven blocks from the school. As I drove past the front of the building, I think I saw the Ryder truck parked at a meter in front of the eastern half of the building. I parked in my regular parking place on the C-level of the Murrah parking garage. I went to the eighth floor, signed in at 8:40, and then checked my desk for messages. My desk was the third one from the west wall, next to the north glass wall.

I got my coffee cup and went to the center of the building where the community coffeepot was located, behind the director's office. On the way back, the director asked me to find a particular file. I looked in the cabinet where I was sure it was and couldn't find it. I went back to see if it was on my desk—it wasn't. So I went back to the cabinet, very determined and muttering to myself. I dragged over a heavy wooden chair with a solid back and sat down, facing away from the windows, and started looking for the file one more

Joseph E. Chicoraske

time. The file cabinet was located four or five feet west of my desk and about fifteen feet from the north glass wall.

I had just started looking at the files when I heard what sounded like a tremendous clap of thunder, which almost immediately magnified in volume ten or twenty times. Then the floor began vibrating and shaking violently. I could not move from my chair. Debris from the direction of the windows was flying and hitting the back of my head and shoulders. I closed my eyes to protect them. During this, time slowed to a crawl. I thought it must be a gas-leak explosion since we have had gas leaks in the area. I began to realize that I might not survive and that I might never see my daughter again. I thought this can't be happening; being a single parent, I was all she had.

Then it all stopped and I felt very fortunate to be alive. There was an eerie silence, except for the barely audible building fire alarm. When I looked up, I thought I had been transported to a place full of distraction. The wall behind the file cabinets was gone. The cabinet I had been looking in was leaning toward me. There were bare concrete, sheet metal strips, electrical wires, and computer cables hanging where white fiberglass ceiling panels used to be. There were at least three or four feet of debris covering the floor. I looked over my right shoulder and could see my co-worker standing up. She looked like she was all right. I could also see that all the windows were blown out. Then I looked east and saw a black cloud coming up and moving rapidly toward us. I thought it was smoke, but once it enveloped me, I could tell by the taste that it was dust. It was unbelievably black—I couldn't see my hands in front of my face. I was having trouble breathing. Then a cool wind blew the dust away in an instant. As I was getting my breath, I heard what sounded like large caliber gunfire, and I could see black, rubber-smelling smoke. I was standing by the file cabinet and could not see down in front of the building—I could see out but not down. Later, I learned that the loud popping and smoke was from tires burning and exploding on burning cars in front of the building.

My supervisor, Calvin Moser, was at his desk in the northwest corner of the building, and my co-worker Ann Banks was at her desk, which was the next desk east of Calvin's. My desk was the next desk east of Ann's. My desk was just west of the last north wall support, which did not collapse. Ann and Calvin were all right.

I looked back to the east to try to see what had happened to the rest of the building. There was so much debris hanging down and on the floor that all I could see was that at least part of the north wall and floor were not there. I think my desk was still there, but it had collapsed because my computer, furniture, and other stuff had blown against it.

At this point, I realized that my shirt was wet, and I could tell I was bleeding. I could feel that the back of my head was very wet. I looked at my feet and did not see blood on the floor, so I hoped I wasn't seriously injured. Ann climbed over her desk to get to where I was, and then Calvin joined us.

We decided to try to get to the south side of the building where the elevators and stairwells were, rather than wait for help. I was greatly concerned about the stability of the building. We worked our way over and through the debris. There was still smoke and dust in the air, which gave things a dreamlike quality. As I got closer to the stairs, I saw a trail of blood drops going to the stairwell. This was the first sign that someone else had made it out.

My co-worker Ann went down the stairs first. I waited for Calvin. He was yelling to check for survivors. I didn't hear any response to his calls, so I went on down the stairs, thinking he was right behind me. By this time my shirt and pants were blood-soaked. I came out on the plaza and an emergency worker was already there, directing me to the southwest corner of the block. There was a large number of injured people on the plaza. I could not see well because I wear contact lenses and the dirt in my eyes and the bright sunlight made my eyes very sensitive. When I got to the southwest corner of the block, they bandaged my head. While waiting for transportation to the hospital, I saw other co-workers.

They helped me to a Marriott van and took two co-workers, a baby, two people on stretchers, and me to the Southwest Medical Center emergency department. When we got to the hospital, there were doctors and nurses waiting for us. They put some stitches and staples in my head and cleaned me up and released me. The hospital was able to notify my brother that I was all right as soon as I arrived, and they let him know he needed to pick me up. He was unable to contact the school because of problems with the phone lines.

My daughter's classroom had windows blown out, and it sounded like a loud sonic boom. It scared Joy because she knew I worked downtown. She said she really got worried when I did not come by to check on her like other parents did. Some friends picked her up and took her home with them until my sister picked her up. The telephone-line problems delayed us in notifying her that I was okay.

I did not realize how awful the disaster was until I got home and saw the destruction on television.

The Power
of Prayer
Richard Clough

---

*I*t was lonely in the office at 7:15 that morning. All the other
GAO staff was occupied except my assistant, Steve Pruitt,
who would be an hour late. I had hoped that Steve and I would have
our early business done by 8:00, ready to head over for our audit of
the Small Business Administration office. But, some mornings just
don't go as planned.

I looked at the clock. It was almost 9:00 when I patched the phone
lines to our Kansas City office for coverage in our absence. The next
thing I remember was hearing a muffled "puff" like I had heard many
times at fireworks displays—that little noise between the lighting of a
rocket and its explosion into a spectacular and beautiful display of
color. This one would bring horror, anguish, death, and destruction.

I was thrown to the floor. "What happened?" I asked myself. "Was
it a bomb?" There had been bomb threats in the past. I reasoned,
"No, it must not have been a bomb because we had no warning. It
must have been an earthquake." I dismissed that conclusion because
earthquakes are rare in Oklahoma, and when they do occur, they are
insignificant. As soon as my nose detected an odor like exploded

Richard Clough

gunpowder, I was convinced we had been bombed.

It seemed as though only a few seconds had passed when my thoughts turned to Steve. I called to him—no answer—again. Determined to find him, I started digging myself out of the rubble. A sharp pain ran through my left leg; it had been broken. My eyeglasses were nowhere to be found.

When I stood up on my right leg, I could see that the room had filled with dust and smoke. The area where Steve sat was buried in four feet of debris. I yelled desperately for him.

The north side of our office had been blown away. Beyond the dusty, smoky haze was blue sky. While I hoped that Steve had somehow survived, I feared he had not. I turned and saw an army officer and two or three ladies scaling a mountain of rubble to get to our office. The officer had blood streaming down both arms. I called to them to help me find Steve. They were too dazed to understand or respond.

One of the women crawled out an office window and onto the sloping outside wall of the building. I hurried over to help, pulled her back inside, and persuaded her to try to use the stairway near our office door.

I limped toward the stairwell; it wasn't where I thought it would be. The east wall and entry door had been destroyed. I reoriented myself and looked back south. There it was! One of the two doors leading to the stairwell from the hallway was gone, but the stairs were passable.

My heart rose to see others coming down the stairs.

Once on the street outside, I looked back. I was horrified to see that most of the windows on the south side of the Murrah building had been blown out and smoke shrouded the structure. Scores of people lay bleeding on the sidewalk, many screaming. My mind and body drifted into shock.

I struggled to the Oklahoma Natural Gas building about a block away to call my wife and the GAO office in Kansas City. I gazed at the broken windows surrounding me and was numbed even more. An ONG employee helped me make the calls and drove me several blocks to meet my wife.

After being treated and released by our family clinic, I called my mother.

Not until I saw the television coverage of the bombing several hours later did I realize the devastation caused by the blast and the miracle of Steve's and my survival. The next office, separated from ours by a narrow hallway, was the credit union. Twenty of thirty-three credit union employees died there when the north-side floors collapsed. Steve was only three feet from the precipice. He had been knocked unconscious by the explosion but was awake and calling for help when rescue workers arrived at about 9:40. I had been sitting only a few feet from the disintegration. The only passable stairway was the one just a few feet from our office entrance.

The entire nation has marveled at the response of Oklahomans to the Murrah building tragedy. Our strong religious heritage, our prayers, and the prayers of the faithful have sustained us across the country.

I Am Alive!

Sherri A. Coleman

*A*pril 19, 1995, started out like any other day. I got up and went to work, arriving there about 7 A.M. I went down and got a cup of ice at Raymond's snack bar on the fourth floor. I couldn't work at my computer since I was waiting for Sheila to fix it, which she finally did, leaving my desk around 9:00 to go to the ninth floor to teach a computer class. I had just turned on my computer to do some work when the bomb went off. I thought the computer classroom had blown up, but only over my desk. I didn't know that the whole building had exploded.

After debris stopped falling on and around me, I opened my eyes. I saw that there was no building on the north side. I heard a noise behind me and saw co-worker Carol Latimer coming from behind me, climbing over and under a lot of rubble. She looked like she was hurt very badly and had blood all over her face and clothes (later I found out she was bleeding from her ear, head, forehead, and arm). After we figured out that we were still alive, we started trying to get out. We heard another noise coming from behind us and saw another co-worker Wanda Webster coming from behind some debris. We helped her climb over stuff, and we started toward what we hoped would be a way out. We met yet another co-worker Cathy Coulter. Thank God she had not been at her desk. If she had, she would have died as her desk went down with the collapsing building. We went out together to the stairwell. We again had to climb over and under stuff to get out of the building, but we were alive!!!

Sherri A. Coleman

We saw destruction everywhere. I still didn't comprehend that it was our building that blew up. A few weeks earlier we had a scare when we had to evacuate the building because a gas line had burst. So I figured a gas line had burst again this time. I was standing on the south side of the Murrah building, and looking up at it I could see that the windows were blown out. The building was still standing so I didn't know that we had been hit. Then I turned and looked at the federal courthouse and decided that it had been hit. I know now that I was in shock. I was on automatic pilot. I was bleeding from my nose (which I thought was broken), head, back, and feet. I was a mess, but thank God, I was alive! The emergency workers asked me if I was hurt badly and if I had any broken bones. Though blood was dripping from my face, I told them I could wait until they got to those in ambulances who were hurt worse than I. They told me to have a seat on the curb and they would get to me as soon as possible.

People would come up and ask me if I had seen this or that person, and I would answer. I decided that I would get up and help look for some of my co-workers. Phoung Tran, someone I had worked with a long time ago, ran up to me, asking if I had seen her son, Christopher, who had been in the day-care center. I told her no, but that I would help look for him. I didn't know what he looked like, but I couldn't tell her to look for him by herself. Sonja Key, a co-worker, and I had to hold onto her because she was trying to go into the building. I don't blame her because I would have been doing the same thing had my child been in there. Finally, I looked up and saw a little boy in a rescue worker's arms and I asked Phoung if that was her son. She looked up and yelled yes! and ran to him. He was alive, but badly hurt.

I started around to the front of the building to look for some of my missing co-workers but I stopped halfway there. I could not have handled the destruction around the front of the building. I went to the back of the building and waited with some of the other people to be taken to the hospital.

Again an emergency worker asked me if I wanted to go to the hospital right then, and once again I told him I could wait if he needed to take someone more badly hurt than I. He told me he had a little girl who could not sit by herself and needed someone to hold her, so I went with her. When I got to the van I had to take a deep breath. I guess I didn't think she was hurt seriously until I looked at her. She had beautiful red hair and was cut all over her little face. She was groaning and I knew that she was hurting. Also at the van were two of my co-workers, Carol Latimer and Joseph Chicoraske. Patti Hall and Arlene Blanchard were lying on stretchers in the van.

They took us to Southwest Medical Center where the doctors and nurses gave us excellent care. They made sure I was taken care of, and that all cuts were cleaned and stitched or stapled. I finally got a line out to call my mother; her number was the only one I could think of at the time. She called my father and they both came to get me. I didn't know it at the time, but she didn't recognize my voice and thought it was someone else calling her to come to the hospital. They didn't know if I was dead or alive. Imagine how they felt when I walked through the waiting-room door! My mother took me home.

My son was home and was so glad to see me. I had to get word to my daughter that I was all right. She was still at school and didn't realize that the building I worked in was the one that blew up. I think that was a good thing. I sent my son and mother to get her. When she saw them, she knew something was wrong. That's when it came to her that it was the Murrah building, and she started to cry, but they told her I was all right and was at home waiting for her. After she saw that I was okay, I showered and then spent the rest of the day talking to concerned family and friends.

My husband, Kenneth, was in Liberal, Kansas, and had heard that a federal building had been blown up, but he didn't know which one. He was frantic with worry because he couldn't reach anyone in Oklahoma. All phone lines were down. He kept calling and finally got through to our house, and when I answered, he couldn't believe it. He made it home in record time and told me he was taking off work until he was sure that I was all right.

The next day I woke up (surprised that I could sleep) very sore everywhere. Today I have a long scar from my eyebrow to the end of my nose. I didn't have to have stitches on my face but I did get staples in my head and I have a deep scar on the back of my head. I had cuts and bruises on my back, arms, feet, and legs. I was a sight, but I was alive!!!

I was glued to the television trying to find out about my co-workers. I was happy that my husband was home. Jim Cook called a meeting at the Saddleback Inn for all the Office of Native American Division people. I was so very glad to see the people who survived, but also sad to not see everyone. I cried the whole time. Rescue workers were still looking for George Howard, Jules Valdez, Don Burns, Dave Burkett, and Lanny Scroggins of ONAP. Later we found out that they had perished in the bombing. We left the inn and went over to St. John's Baptist Church to meet with the HUD survivors. It was a very tearful reunion and I was so glad that Kenneth was here, I couldn't have done it without him.

They started finding bodies of friends who died in the bombing. I started going to funerals. There were sometimes four a day, but I felt like I had to go and say goodbye.

All this stress took its toll on Kenneth. His esophagus was troubling him. He went into the hospital as an outpatient and found out he has an esophageal reflux, hiatal hernia, and sores on his esophagus. I'm very worried about him and he is very worried about me.

I see Ryder trucks everywhere. I'm very afraid of them. I went to the store one day and a Ryder truck was parked right beside the building. I decided I would be brave and go in and I really tried but

I had to turn around and go home. Maybe one day Ryder will change the color of their vehicles and maybe one day I will get over my fear of them.

When the bomb went off at 9:02 A.M. on April 19, 1995, a different person walked out of the building. One day, maybe the person who went in the Murrah Federal Building at 7 A.M. will appear again.

Falling Through the Cracks

Robert "Russ" Compton

I ask myself, "Where are you? And where were you? Church
...friends...health organizations." April 19, 1995, was the
beginning of a significant and ongoing downturn in my life.

I lived in a building no one heard of, the Kirkpatrick Hotel,
across the street, one block north of ground zero. About sixty people
lived there above the beauty shop, restaurant, and loan companies. It
was lucky for me that the landlord was frugal (cheap, actually) with
regard to the central heat. I was still in bed at 9:02 A.M., blanket and
comforter pulled up over my head on that cool morning. Nights for
taxi drivers end very late.

A noise, like furniture dragging over a linoleum floor, interrupted my dreams. Mingled with it were the clamor of the hotel's
new fire alarm and a woman's scream. Only a moment later, it
seemed, I sat up in bed and what I thought was the tinkle of wind
chimes was glass shards falling from the bed linens. My room was
demolished; the east window was blown westward, the west door was
blown eastward! I still scratch my head wondering about it. Was I in
the middle of an implosion?

Robert "Russ" Compton

A line of people stood in the alley below me, staring and pointing. My first thought was that a gas line had exploded and that I'd better get out of there. I grabbed clothes and bolted into the bathroom. The back wall was gone!

Dashing out the front door, as I caught my first glimpse of the Murrah building, a cop was waving and shouting, "Go north!" Still I could only mutter, "Holy cow!" Later, I found out about the suspected second bomb.

For some reason, my mind latched onto renewing my taxi permit, so I set off walking to the police station. All officers were pressed into disaster duty. Suddenly homeless, I was directed to the Red Cross Disaster Headquarters, two miles across town. There, I found out about the Disaster Shelter at St. Luke's Methodist Church, which would become my home for the next three weeks. Still on foot, I traveled that mile and a half and checked in.

Some days after the bombing, I still felt confused and shaky. I wondered if it was more than "shock" (post-traumatic stress disorder?). Nearby, St. Anthony's Hospital was still in the disaster frontlines, so I went there. My examiner gave me a quick checkup, had me perform a finger-touch drill, and sent me on my way with little consolation: "You're still upset and disoriented from the event. It will settle out."

While the food at the shelter was good and the cots were tolerable, my stay was hell. I watched others receive visitors day-after-day, but I was alone. My twenty-five-year-old daughter paged me from Kentucky the first day. She had no idea of my one-hundred-yard proximity to the bomb. After a few days, a dispatcher from the cab company came by. This visit, while brief, was unexpected and pleasant. Later, I told a Red Cross worker how disappointed I was that no one from my church had called on me. I had been a member and regular attendee for three or four years. A couple of days later, the security officer at the shelter handed me a man's business card and asked if I would see him. I noticed that "Compton, Russ" was jotted on the back. I said, "Sure." This man had been assigned by the church to visit me. He shook my hand, said, "...that's too bad...," chatted a moment, and left. I've not heard from him or anyone else at the First Methodist Church since.

The cab company treated me decently. My taxi remained behind police lines for several days. The company gave me another vehicle to use, personally and professionally. I tried to drive a few times, but I felt incapable. The usual tariff of $175 per week—payment drivers make for dispatch and such—was never enforced or even mentioned. The bomb-shattered windshield I saw when I was finally allowed to retrieve my cab was replaced through the Red Cross.

I moved into a new apartment when the shelter closed. After many frustrating attempts to get back into the Kirkpatrick Hotel to collect my belongings, the police issued me an "entrance pass." I gathered some clothes and was pleased to see that my treasured camera had weathered the blast. I took the load of clothes to the car and headed back for the camera. A federal agent stopped me and escorted me out of the secured perimeter. Almost a week later, I was allowed back into the hotel. Unimpeded wind and rain had buffeted the interior of the building. I climbed the stairs and looked toward the table where my camera had been left on the last trip. There was no camera. A feeling of dread engulfed me—I knew I couldn't afford to replace the camera if it had been ruined, fallen, or been pilfered. I searched the floor around and behind the table. Still no camera. Feeling sickened, yet resigned to loss, I opened the case, hoping to find at least some of the accessories. An unidentified police officer had neatly placed each part of my camera outfit into its niche in the case, safe and intact. I wish I could express my heartfelt gratitude to him or her.

Several months after the bombing, I found myself sitting on the bed, doing nothing, for about two hours. I knew something was wrong. A dense fog was closing its grip over my life, and I was unable to see my way forward. Coincidentally, radio and television commercials were talking about National Depression Screening Week.

The results of my screening showed that I had many of the symptoms of depression. I then learned of Project Heartland that was set up as a clearinghouse for those who were affected by the bombing. After a few weeks counseling at Project Heartland, I was referred to the Community Counseling Center, where I still see a psychologist. Some months later, the Oklahoma City Fire Department published a disaster chronology. Reading through it, I discovered that an hour and a half had passed between the time I heard a low rumble and the time I hit the sidewalk. Perhaps a concussion has something to do with my faltering quality of life—I'm still not sure.

If I was to draw a graph of my life before and after the Murrah tragedy, the first part would be pretty even, almost tolerable, then there would be a steep decline. The counseling probably helped keep the bottom higher than it would have been if I hadn't sought help, but I'm still going downhill. My most optimistic outlook is schooling through the Vocational Rehabilitation Program to learn computer programming. I have already been deemed eligible and even have some knowledge in that area. The problem is funding, not for the schooling—Vocational Rehabilitation covers it when they have the funds—but my ability to earn a living while attending classes eight hours a day. The cab business isn't very good right now. It often takes ten to twelve hours of driving six days a week to make a decent living. Obviously, I can't continue doing that and go to school also.

Although things are not going well for me right now, I know it's important to maintain a balance. When one considers April 19, it's important to realize that a small handful of individuals did something terrible. From April 20 (up to today), the story changed. Through storms, floods, and earthquakes, never have the American people rallied so quickly or as solidly as they did here. Blood banks were filled, donations were boxed, and Red Cross warehouses overflowed thanks to the generosity of multitudes. The deeds done by many offset the evil done by a few. Yes, something undeniably good came out of April 1995.

Incident at 9:02 A.M.

Stephanie Cook

*A*pril 19, 1995, started no differently from any other beautiful spring day in Oklahoma—the sun was shining and all was right in the world. Little did any of us know that the peaceful morning would be shattered by a heart-rending explosion, leaving our lives changed forever.

I had gotten to work around 7:30 A.M. It was a slow morning at the Alfred P. Murrah Federal Building. Every Wednesday, the Property Disposition branch at the Housing and Urban Development agency where I work, had a bid opening for foreclosed properties at the Ramada Inn on 39th Expressway. My co-workers, Joan and Luciann, went every week. At that time of year, with income taxes almost due and people waiting for school to be out in May, we were not very busy.

I checked my basket for work that needed to be done and had everything completed and waiting for signatures. A few minutes before 9 A.M., I told Linda, our branch secretary, that I was going to the snack bar on the fourth floor and if my friend Freda called, to please tell her I had already gone down. That was the last time I saw Linda.

93

Stephanie Cook

I had just sat down with my coffee, when suddenly, frighteningly, the lights went out and debris began to fall from the ceiling. I sat there, stunned, having no idea what had happened. Inexplicably, I hadn't heard any noise. All at once, dust and smoke became so thick that I began to gag and choke. What's happening? I recall thinking it was as if the world had been turned upside down. At that point, I had no clue as to the extent of the devastation that the bomb had caused. When the air finally began to clear, I looked around and could see the outdoors, which was strange and confusing, since there should have been several walls and offices between me and the outside. I knew something terrible had happened; I could hear people all over the building screaming for help.

A stranger helped me over the rubble, and I decided to return to the seventh floor via the west staircase. The destruction was terrible. Debris and duct work hung from the ceiling; no phones worked; there were no lights; desk and file cabinets were in pieces everywhere; whole sections of flooring, walls and windows were gone. *People were gone.*

I worked approximately five feet from the north windows in the center of the seventh floor. My desk was gone. Suddenly, all the noises from the trucks, fire engines, and people ran together in a strange and terrible cacophony that only added to the confusion and chaos.

No one from my immediate area was there, but I did see Larry Harris and Cliff Cagle. Larry's face was covered in blood, and Cliff was lying injured on the floor. Larry was trying to decide what to do about Cliff, who appeared to be seriously injured and could not be moved. Larry didn't know which way to turn—whether to leave to get help or to stay until help arrived. I told him to go ahead, and I would stay with Cliff until the rescue people came.

I found time to think as I was waiting with Cliff and questions raced through my mind. What had happened? Who was still alive? Which of my friends and co-workers were gone? Will we ever get out of here? It was like a very bad dream as I looked around at what should have been there and was not. Chaos—papers and equipment were everywhere. The screams of sirens on rescue trucks mingled insanely with the sounds of people screaming and crying out for help—and Cliff was still on the floor. I kept talking to him to keep him alert because I was afraid he was going to die. My throat was so dry—there was no water available—but I saw a dented soft-drink can and cracked it open. I saw a phone and with shaking hands tried to call my mother to let her know that I was all right, but the phone was dead.

After what seemed an eternity, but really was only a matter of minutes, a policeman arrived, crawling through the debris and covered with a fine layer of dust. After seeing I was injured, he insisted I go down to the plaza. I didn't want to leave Cliff, but the officer assured me he would stay with him. When I arrived at the east plaza, I saw some of my co-workers, and, together, we began to look for other survivors. I saw Mr. Graham, and we looked for his wife, Jane. She was alive and had been taken to the hospital. I saw a man with a mobile phone and asked if I could use it. He dialed my mother's number, and I left her a message that I was all right. I found out later that the message had been a tremendous relief for her.

Within a few minutes, someone said there was a second bomb, and they moved us even farther from the building for safety. Time dragged—all of this seemed like forever. Things seemed to be going in slow motion, like a bad movie, and I was struck by how surreal it all was. To be jerked from one's routine, rudely and violently, by means of death and destruction, results in disorientation and denial. This can't be happening. I could see that thought registered on the faces of the people I encountered. But it was, and the stark reality was numbing.

Sometime later, they took me to Southwest Medical Center. I had severe bruises on my left arm and a gash on my head that required seven stitches. The hospital called my mother, and she came to pick me up, but the shock of it all was still there. Sandy Teel was there; Robin Parent was in surgery; and I went home to try to get myself together and cleaned up so I could go to school and pick up my son without frightening him. I hoped they had not told the kids about this and, thank goodness, they hadn't.

For the last three years, I have been trying to make sense of this ordeal. I have healed physically, and I received some counseling. I have 23 percent permanent disability in my left arm. But for the Grace of God, I could have died. I was one of the lucky ones who lived. The thought has occurred to me—why was I spared? Obviously, my purpose in life has not been fulfilled. God allowed me to live through this to finish the task he has set for me.

My Only Brother— Gone

Teresa Tomlin-Corrall

O n April 19, 1995, at 9:02 A.M. I lost my only brother, Rick Tomlin, in the bombing of the Murrah building in Oklahoma City.

It was a normal, busy day at the law office here in Akron, Ohio, on the morning of the nineteenth. I'll never forget the events that morning because they are etched so clearly in my mind despite the passage of time. I was up at the receptionist's desk talking with my secretary, Deanna, when Joe, my fiancé, called. As Joe did not make it a practice to call me at work, I was excited to hear from him.

My office was located near the back of the office so I chose to take Joe's call near our fax machine, which is located near the lobby. Joe asked me if I had heard from my mother that day and because of the tone of his voice, I got concerned. I said, "No, why?" It was approximately 11 A.M. when Joe told me the federal building in Oklahoma City had been bombed. I must have gotten a little loud as the attorneys and secretaries came to see what was causing me to get emotional. Immediately, I went to my office and called my mom who was living in Edmond, Oklahoma. It is still very clear to this day

97

Rick Tomlin with his sisters, Karen and Teresa

---

what my mom said to me: "It's bad!" Mom did give me a bit of hope, telling me that she thought Rick's office was on the other side of the building. She wasn't sure of his office location at the time of our first call. By my next phone call to Mom, she confirmed that Rick was in the building and in his office when the bomb exploded. Later, I found out that my brother was talking to Tina, his wife of twenty-five years, when it happened.

Since the Akron bureau of Channel 5 is located on the same floor as my office, I proceeded to their office as I knew they had a television. My co-workers followed. We were all in disbelief that something so terrible could happen here in the United States. A reporter and a photographer from Channel 5 asked to come home with me.

As I was trying to stay calm that day, I started reflecting on my last telephone conversation with Rick, which concerned finalizing my family vacation plans to Oklahoma to see my family. Rick would have been the one to pick me up at the airport…that day didn't happen.

My brother worked for the Department of Transportation and had a window office located on the fourth floor of the Murrah building. Rick was always traveling in his position as Special Agent. In fact, I always teased him about spending my money in his travels for the government. Rick loved his job, his office, and life. Rick was forty-six years old, married to Tina, and had two children, Richard, twenty-four, and Jeremy, twenty-one. He was happy.

Somehow I knew that Wednesday night when I went to bed that my brother was gone. I cried.

The morning after the bombing, Joe; my then two-year-old son, Carl; and I flew to Oklahoma City. I felt that they had already found my brother when I arrived at the Oklahoma City airport. (I found out later that I was right.) We drove as close to the building as we could, which wasn't close at all.

My sister, Karen, and her family arrived from Kansas that same day. My Uncle Jim and Aunt Lorene arrived from Cincinnati, Ohio. We then went to the crisis center which was set up at the First Christian Church by the Red Cross. A lot of Rick's family had already arrived. I was very impressed with how quickly the Red Cross went into action and how smoothly the place was being managed in such a short time. They had everything we could want and if they didn't have it, they would get it for us.

Each family was assigned an escort who was in charge of us and had to keep track of us. This was a big task considering that at one time we had thirty-plus family members at the crisis center. We had three hot meals per day, snacks, water, milk for the children, phones to use with no charge for long-distance calls, child care, counselors, and clergymen. Emotions ran very high. I don't really remember what I did, other than talk on the phone, to pass the hours in the day. The military was guarding us. The media was not allowed in the crisis center. I spoke to the media when outside or in another church building, and there were usually two military personnel standing off to the side, which was a strange feeling. The Red Cross director would come in and brief us twice a day. The medical examiner would also give us a report. I was at the crisis center for five days. A monkey, dogs, and rabbits were brought to the crisis center to help with counseling. Kirstie Alley from the TV show *Cheers* was there to sign autographs. She grew up in Wichita, Kansas, so this hit home for her, too.

Once you registered at the crisis center, they kept track of where you went. We usually did not leave the crisis center until evening, when we knew that Rick was not going to be identified that day.

My friends Mark and Janie came from Tulsa to spend Sunday at the crisis center with us and also to attend the statewide prayer service.

It was Sunday afternoon (four days after the bombing) when I was informed that Rick had been identified. I had just attended the prayer service and upon my return to the crisis center, I was grabbed by a social worker who asked me to come with her when at the same time my stepmother and stepsister informed me that they "had" Rick. I thought that I had prepared myself to hear the news that Rick was gone, but I didn't handle it well at all. I literally fell apart.

Rick was found on the third floor in the credit union area by two marines at approximately 10:30 the day of the bombing. This is about the time I found out that this tragedy had happened. The marines who found Rick told us that the reason they found him right away is that he wore cowboy boots that didn't come off when he was thrown from his chair. They could not move Rick right away as they were looking for survivors. Later, they could not move him because there was a woman right below him who had to have her leg amputated before being moved and they didn't want to risk any movement until she was safe. Rick was one of the first thirty bodies taken to the temporary morgue that was set up near the bomb site.

During those days of pain, the people in Oklahoma came together as one big family. Everyone wanted to help. My dad, Charles, took my suit and coat to the dry cleaner...no charge. While in Enid, Oklahoma, my stepmom, Blanche, went to pick up a prescription for my son and was told "no charge."

Rick's funeral was held in Hutchinson, Kansas. I did get to see Rick though I contacted a counselor before doing so. His head and hands were bandaged. We were not allowed to touch him. Under his suit was a plastic suit as we were told he was full of glass. The tie he had on was a Looney Tunes tie with the Roadrunner...that was Rick! It made me smile to see him then. He loved the Roadrunner and was restoring Roadrunner cars. There were highway patrolmen from Oklahoma at his funeral. Federal workers from as far away as Michigan attended. There were Rick's classmates and buddies from high school. It was an unbelievable turnout! There were patrolmen standing at attention at almost every corner on the drive to the cemetery. It brought tears to my eyes to see all the people who were there for my brother.

A lot has happened and continues to happen since the day of the bombing. I have new friends and acquaintances now that I wouldn't have had if this tragedy hadn't happened. I have been seen on television across the nation. One of my best friends in Phoenix, Louise, said that she turned on the television during the bombing coverage and was surprised when she saw me. We hadn't seen each other in two years. Louise said that what came to mind first though was that I looked really good. Relatives that had not yet been contacted regarding the bombing saw me on television and wanted to know if what they saw was really true.

The bombing had an almost immediate impact on my view of life. Joe Corall and I were married July 22, 1995. The decision to get married was made shortly after the bombing. We learned that you should not put off what you want in life.

My sister and I are even closer than before. We miss our brother tremendously. My parents are toughing it out, but then I can't even imagine losing my only son, my firstborn, as my mother and father have done.

Life goes on for all of us... as hard as it might be. A day does not go by that I do not think about the bombing, what has happened since, and what will happen in the future. The healing process will be very long for those connected in any way with the bombing.

Rest in peace, my brother. I will see you again.

You Can Do It, Mom

Cathy Coulter

I arrived at work that morning at my usual time, 7:25 A.M. I
work for the U.S. Department of Housing and Urban
Development (HUD) in the South Plains Office of Native American
Programs on the eighth floor.

I carried in two gallons of drinking water (the water in our
building tasted nasty) which got a big response from my co-workers,
Dave Burkett, George Howard, and Jules Valdez. Dave and George
wanted to know if I had turned into a camel. Jules asked me if I was
going to take a bath at the office. I laughed at all three of them. We are
a very close office, and this is how our mornings usually started off.

It was cold in our office, so I walked back to Sonja Key's desk and
asked if I could borrow her sweater. She said I could and handed her
sweater to me, along with an envelope. I walked back to my desk and
opened it. It was an invitation to her daughter Julie's graduation on
May 6 from Oklahoma State University. My daughter Jennifer's
senior prom was also to be held on that day.

I logged into my computer and started going through the mail
and the typing in my in-box. Then I started typing the rough drafts.

I had sat at my desk all morning and when I looked up at the clock it was just before 9:00. I decided to go to the restroom and then on to break.

I was coming out of the restroom stall when I heard this terrible noise that sounded like a sonic boom except it had to be at least one hundred times louder than I remember it sounded like. I covered my ears and screamed. I heard my co-workers scream also, and, then, there was silence.

The lights flickered and then there was total darkness. At the same time, the ceiling

Cathy Coulter

fell on me, knocking me to the ground. Dust and smoke filled the room—I couldn't breathe. All I could think of was that there had been a gas explosion. I had lost five members of my family in a house fire in 1987, and I thought, crying, I have to get out. I can't put my family through that horror again. As I lay on the ground crying, I could hear the words my daughter, Jennifer, had said to me a number of times when things were not going just right, "Suck it up, Mom, you can do it. You can do it, Mom, get out."

When the smoke finally cleared, I looked up and saw that there was a hole in the ceiling. I could hear someone on the other side of the wall, so I started screaming for someone to help me. I thought I heard someone asking me where I was, then there was silence.

I picked myself up and looked around, terrified. I had become disoriented and didn't know where the door was. I kept telling myself to stay calm—think! I looked around and saw that the toilets were behind me, which meant the door should be in front of me. The mirrors and sinks were off the wall, so I had to climb over a lot of debris to get to the door. Once out of the restroom (which was on the east side of our building), I made my way along the south walkway toward the elevator and headed toward the entrance to my office on the northwest side.

As I got to the office door, three of my co-workers, Wanda Webster, Carol Latimer, and Sherri Coleman, came out with blood all over their arms, faces, and clothing. I started crying and Sherri Coleman told me to "shut up and get out" of the building. Carol Latimer's face was cut really deep, and I knew we needed something to try to stop the bleeding, so I wadded up the sweater I was wearing and handed it to her. She grabbed my arms, and we started down the stairwell on the southwest side.

People were coming into the stairwell with bruises, cuts, bleeding, and in shock. I remember that we all walked down in an orderly manner to the plaza exit on the second floor on the south side of the building.

We walked out into the sunlight and saw that there was glass and destruction everywhere. Emergency crews were already there. People from our office and other offices in the building started coming out, and we all started asking, Have you seen this person or that person? It was a true nightmare.

The people who weren't hurt too terribly were helping other people, holding gauze to wounds, comforting the ones in shock. There was blood everywhere.

I remember a mother running up to us crying and asking if we had seen her baby. She tried to run back into the building, but we stopped her. The rescue workers started bringing a few children out at this time. The mother cried and cried. I don't know how long it was before I saw them carrying an Asian boy out, and I touched the woman, who was also Asian, on the shoulder and asked her if he was her son. She cried, "Yes," and started toward the rescue worker, crying, "My baby, my baby."

In the meantime, my other co-workers started showing up. We began compiling a list of the people we had seen, the ones we knew were out of the building for various reasons, and the ones we had not seen.

During this time, we were told there was another bomb in the building and were instructed to run down to the park area. I grabbed Collen Larney's hand, looked around to see where Sonja Key and Susan Hunt were, and we all started running. We ran and ran. Collen and I lost Sonja and Susan along the way.

We both knew we needed to call our families to let them know we were okay, so we headed for Oklahoma City's convention center. I still didn't know at this time what kind of destruction the bomb had caused to our building.

I called my house and didn't get an answer, so I called my brother's house and my mother answered the phone. I was crying by this time and whispered, "Mom, it's me. I'm okay," and she started crying, too. I asked her to pick me up, and she said I needed to stay put, that they were told that there might be other bombs.

I walked around the convention center crying. I decided I would walk to my brother's house, that I needed to see my kids, Jennifer and Matt. There was no telling who might be at my brother's house. I was heading for the door when I looked up and saw my son, Matt. I ran to him, crying. He put his arms around me, telling me how much he loved me. I looked behind him and there was one of my brothers and my daughter's boyfriend. They led me outside and said another brother was driving around looking for me. We walked outside and there was my brother, driving in front of the convention center. He stopped in the middle of the street, and we got into his car and drove to his house.

When we pulled up to my brother's house, my family ran out to greet me. It was a beautiful sight.

The television was on when I walked into the house. I still hadn't seen the full destruction of the front of the building. I couldn't believe what I saw. I could tell immediately that had I been at my desk, I wouldn't have been with the people I loved. I cried for my friends and their families whom I knew were in the blast area.

These minutes, hours, days, and weeks have been a nightmare that doesn't go away. We all lost count of the funerals we attended. We were unable to attend all of them because many of them overlapped and you had to choose which friend's funeral to attend, but our hearts and prayers were with all the families.

It has been over three years since that horrible day. I lost some of my hearing and more friends than any one person loses in a lifetime: Dave, George, Jules, Lanny Scroggins, and Don Burns, all from ONAP—a total of thirty-five friends from our office. I still have nightmares and hopefully one of these days I will be able to sleep with my light off. Loud noises, especially thunderstorms, make me want to cover my head and drop to the ground. These are a number of things that make me angry because they have destroyed my sense of security.

I want to thank all the rescue workers. I watched as they gently led my friends, co-workers, and strangers to safety. I watched them as they all worked as one unit, banded together to rescue the victims.

I also want to thank my friends and family who have been my rock to lean on. I love you all. God bless.

A Love Story

Lyle Cousins

---

or most of you, reading this is as close as you'll ever get to Kim this side of heaven. I, however, was truly blessed to know her personally, intimately, and spiritually.

Kim and I met the old-fashioned way, in church. Both of us were single and in our early thirties. I remember she caught my eye on my first day of Sunday school. She was beautiful by anyone's standards, and I even remember what she was wearing.

She and I were both very shy, though, and it took me eight months to get up the nerve to ask her out. When we began to date, we usually went on simple outings like the state fair, a church activity, sometimes dinner and a movie, but mostly dinner at her place, watching TV or going to one of her son Corey's games.

Within a month, I knew that I was hopelessly in love with her. I began to pray that she felt the same way about me. From our first kiss, I think both of us knew that we would someday be married. I never took her for granted. I called her every day and did so right up to the day before she died. I loved to send flowers just to let her know I was thinking of her.

Kim Dillow Cousins

Corey had become a big part of my life as well. I'm Corey's first real dad and I believe with all my heart that as much as God joined Kim and me together, He also took a boy without a dad and a man without a son and put us together.

After Christmas, I began to make plans to ask her to marry me, but it seemed all my romantic plans kept falling through. One Sunday afternoon, I couldn't stand it anymore. I drove to her house and walked into the bedroom where she was ironing clothes and asked her to marry me. She never stopped ironing and just said, "Well, of course." I guess that must have been the happiest moment of my life. We cried happy tears for somehow God had taken two lonely people and put them together.

On June 25, 1994, we became one. Our wedding was beautiful and many tears of joy were shed. I know that day will remain one of my happiest no matter where I go from here.

Some of the most beautiful memories I have of Kim are on our honeymoon in the Caymans. Even as I write this, tears come to my eyes. Such a beautiful woman in such a beautiful place. I will never go back there. Anyone who reads this and goes to the Cayman Islands, please go to the Holiday Inn at sunset and throw a pink rose into the sea for Kim.

After we returned from our honeymoon, we began to make plans for a house and began discussing having a baby, but this was not to be.

On April 19, 1995, my springtime allergies were giving me fits and since Wednesday is a slow day at work, I took my boss's offer to stay home that day. After talking to my boss, I had gotten back in bed and cuddled up to Kim and by that time Corey had joined us. So the three of us cuddled for another hour until Kim had to get ready for work. I know that last hour was a gift from God and one that Corey and I would remember as peaceful.

Kim then got up and got ready for work. Her last words to me were, "I love you."

At about 10:15 A.M. Marquita from church called and asked if I had the TV on. When I told her I had been sleeping, she said that I'd better turn it on, so I did.

At first I did not know what I was looking at, until I recognized the building. At first it looked like just the windows were gone, then there was a helicopter shot and I could see how much of the building was gone. There was a shot of the parking lot across the street and the first thing I noticed was my Chevy Blazer, destroyed and on fire. Corey's and my fishing poles were sticking out the back window that had been blown out.

This is when I got down on my knees and began to pray. It seemed like He was the only hope that Kim had. As much as I tried to remain calm, I learned what distraught really means.

Many people stayed with me over the next ten days, and it was comforting to know I wasn't alone. After ten days, our wait was over. Can you imagine going to two funerals every day for two weeks? I know people who did, but I went to one that I, in my wildest dreams, never thought would come. Just ten months earlier, Kim and I had stood in the sanctuary of South Lindsay Baptist Church proclaiming our love; now this would be our last time together at South Lindsay.

Our sanctuary holds over twelve hundred people and it was over half full. People I did not know were there and some I had only met the previous week. All with hearts as big as Texas and all of them broken. Corey and I sat together with the rest of Kim's family, with our eyes fixed on a baby blue casket that seemed to hold all our hopes and dreams.

Charles Reynolds, pastor of the church in New Mexico where Kim was saved, shared the story of Kim's salvation. He said one of the most profound statements that I have ever heard, that sometimes in death we affect more people that we ever could have in life and that Kim had done just that. Charles was right; through her death many have come to know Jesus in a personal way.

As I write the end of this story, I have found that I love her now more than ever and it seems like she has been gone only a few weeks. Her memory is still fresh in my mind. I see her face every day in the face of a young boy. He somehow keeps me close to her and I hope I do the same for him. They say time heals all wounds, but I have seen some people who are crippled by their wounds, and sometimes we feel a little crippled but we go on, because we choose to.

Corey and I, we survive not by that of our own strength but by the strength of He who is in us and by the strength of others that know the truths we know. We can ask why a thousand times and an answer that satisfies the human part of us will never come. The answer to that question must be heard in the spiritual part of us. We have to accept that God is in full control.

To Kim
Kris Knight

*A*pril 19, 1995, is forever etched in my heart and mind. On this day my life was truly changed forever.

You had a beautiful smile—that could light up a room.

You were full of life. I can still hear your laugh, for it was one of a kind.

You enjoyed the simple things in life.

Chocolate you loved.

Family was important to you.

Corey, your son, was the light of your life. He was your gift from God. He came at a difficult time in your life. Yet you took what was given to you. You now had a purpose. Your life was really only beginning at this point. Your love for him was immeasurable. What a great mom you were. It was not always easy for you being a single mom. You were mom and dad to Corey for most of his life. You did a wonderful job raising him. It breaks my heart that you were cheated out of a lifetime of watching him grow. You left us your legacy—Corey—he is you made over, his hair, his smile, and those eyes. I feel so much peace when I look into his eyes.

I am so proud of you for all that you accomplished in your life. You overcame so much.

Life without you has not been easy. At times, it's so overwhelming. It's been hard getting used to you not being here. I miss you so very much. I am not the same without you. The day you died, a part of me died too. I sometimes think that this is all a nightmare and when I awake you will be here. The truth is, I was awake all along. I have been told that time heals; maybe someday it will. It feels like it all happened only yesterday.

As time passes without you, I see how important you were in my life. You were not just my sister, you were my friend. You meant more to me than I ever thought possible. You and I shared so much together. Still, I am sad for all the things that were yet to come.

I always knew that I would be the one who was the "older sister," even though it was you who were the oldest. You counted on me to be your protector; even as little girls I knew this. I took the responsibility because I knew it was meant to be this way. Through the difficult times in your life, you knew that I would be there to fight for you. No one in my life will ever need me the way you did. I feel helpless at times because I can't help you anymore. You do not need me anymore. I have an emptiness in my heart that was yours. It will never be filled again. This is something that I have to accept and learn to live with. I feel you with me. You had faith in me, that I could somehow make things better for you. You are responsible in part for shaping my life and for who I am today. For most of my life, I thought I was the one who gave so much of myself to you. I know now how wrong I was. My strength came from you. You have given me a wonderful gift—strength. It will carry me through this. Thank you for giving me so much.

You could always be yourself with me. You didn't hide anything. You knew you didn't need to. You trusted me like no other. No one knew you like I did. I am so thankful that you knew that you could always count on me. This gives me peace. Our relationship, good and bad, was something special that was and will always be "ours." I hold all we shared in our lives dear. I will treasure them forever. I wouldn't trade one single moment for anything. I am grateful for thirty-one years of memories that I have. I am glad you're my sister and that I got to share so much of my life with you. You will always be a part of me. Death cannot take that away.

You are my first thought each day and my last before I fall asleep. I love you with all my heart and soul.

I will not say goodbye to you because I know we will meet again. Until then, I know you are taken care of.

My Smiling Child

Elcena Cummings

*M*y smiling child still smiles in Jesus' arms. On March 24, 1963, Christi Yolanda Buckner was born to me. The first time I looked at my newborn she smiled. She was a strong baby and quick to learn. Everything she learned, she mastered. She was a loving child who never made a lot of mistakes. Even as a child, she gave love and shared love. She was my fourth child out of six. She had a special bond with her sisters and brother. They were always close in sharing and love.

When Christi began school, she was very happy to feel big. She was very energetic. She would always do cartwheels on the playground and in the yard. She would get on top of the play gym to do tricks on the bar. She was a brownie girl scout. In junior high she was an average child, very physically active and knowledgeable.

Then motherhood began. Christi loved that very much. Her husband was Aldo Jenkins. Her firstborn was Shimar in 1979. He was our pride and joy. He was the first grandchild and she shared him with all of us. Then her daughter, Shawna, was born in 1980. Her son Shelby Christian was born in 1982; he was her smiling child. Then

Christi Jenkins

another son, Scott Christopher, was born in 1983 to complete her family. Whenever you saw them together or apart, they were smiling. They were a smiling family because they were happy people.

Christi united with God on December 24, 1989, and received the Holy Ghost. She enjoyed being a servant of Jesus and was not afraid to witness. Wherever she went that was her joy until her life ended. As she was driving to work that fateful morning, she was listening to a tape by Sister Dorothy Norwood. When the automobile was released to the family and the ignition key was turned on, the tape continued to play. The next words to the song were "I made it." That was our confirmation to us; I know she is still smiling with Jesus.

She dearly loved her husband; children; brother, Marvin; and sisters Marva, Marnita, Shermaine, and Tracie. She also dearly loved her mother, Elcena; her dad, Acie; and her church and church family.

Her motto was "Love in my heart is here to stay, love is not love until you give it away."

Her favorite Bible verse was "Favor is deceitful and beauty is vain. But a woman that feareth the Lord shall be praised. Give her of the fruit of her hands; and let her own works praise her in the gates" (Proverbs 31: 30-31).

We miss her more.

For Too Short a Time

Leslie Downey

*T*erry was always the "Little Mother" in our family. Cathy, Mitch, and I could always count on her for sound, sane, sisterly advice. Sometimes she was a little too persuasive, getting us to confess to "crimes" we hadn't committed!

Her love of travel must have sprung from family trips to Memphis for summer vacations and Christmas. We would all crowd into the car and make the best of the passing miles. When Terry fell asleep, her lower jaw would drop. Never one to pass up an opportunity, Cathy would stuff jellybeans into Terry's open mouth. Terry would awaken with colorful, sticky drool dripping down her chin. Good-natured about these tricks, Terry waited patiently for the right moment for payback.

We never knew when the family might grow by another furry canine member. Terry loved dogs and couldn't pass up a stray. We had a string of them: Tramp, Wormo, Knobby, and Ajax. Queenie, Terry's sheltie, was truly treated like royalty. She slept in her own double-size bed, under the covers, with her head on a pillow.

Terry could never be labeled "domestic." Once she asked me to

**Terry Rees
with her husband, Bob**

clean her house (for money, of course). At the time, Terry was single and was going to have an adult slumber party. "What's the matter, don't you want your friends to know you're a slob?" I asked. Terry replied, "Oh, they already know I'm a slob, I just don't want them to know I'm a filthy slob!" Her idea of cooking was to heat up leftovers prepared by someone else.

Everyone knew they could depend on Terry for quick wit, funny faces, and a good joke. Never hesitating to tell one on herself, she spoke of returning to Will Rogers World Airport in Oklahoma City after a business trip. She reclaimed her car, which was in the parking garage, and headed for the exit. While driving around and around for thirty minutes, she passed the same security guard numerous times. He finally stopped her and showed here the way out, after she admitted her embarrassment over getting lost at her hometown airport.

She and I would perform our special rendition of Janis Joplin's "Mercedes-Benz" for family gatherings. Her husband, Bob, was the video cameraman for these events. The films where Terry was the "star" were the best of all.

Terry let her siblings do all the work of having children, while she acted the part of "Auntie." My daughter, Allison, and Cathy's four children loved to play with her. She was a special friend to Bob's grandchildren. All the kids looked forward to her Christmas gifts, for they would have been chosen with great thought and care and were always unique.

Anyone would be impressed with Terry's collection of teddy

bears. She began acquiring them ten years before she died and had accumulated hundreds of them. When shopping, she was quite selective about which teddy bears would go home with her. They had to "talk" to her. She had a bear room whose creatures overflowed down the hallway and into a spare bedroom in the home Terry shared with Bob and their sheltie, Jasmine. They occupied tables, chairs, benches, and shelves that Terry had purchased for them at antiques and craft shows.

If there was a space left unoccupied by a bear, it was filled by a book. Terry loved to read and to work crossword puzzles. She couldn't enter a mall without visiting the bookstore, and she couldn't leave the bookstore without making several purchases.

Terry could be found in line anytime there was a call to help people in need. She donated blood and plasma regularly at the Oklahoma Blood Institute and joined with her co-workers in sponsoring charity events. Every Christmas Terry devoted time and energy to reach out to those less fortunate than she. During the last year of her life, Terry spent much time caring for her grandmother, Dinkie, who had moved to Oklahoma City in failing health.

A supervisor in the Office of Public Housing, Terry loved her job with HUD, her employer for eighteen years.

She brightened our lives for too short a time.

A True Friend

Stephanie Ellingson

---

*T*he loss of Claudette Meek has changed many people's lives. Claudette has been missed by her surviving fellow workers at the Federal Employees Credit Union, her church family, her friends, and her family. Many people have crossed my path who convey to me how Claudette's positive influence greatly influenced and impacted their lives.

The people Claudette worked with saw her as an excellent boss and example. Her boss, Ms. Rogers, thought the world of her and felt fortunate to have her as an employee. The customers of the Credit Union shared with me the exceptional job she had done when working with them. She treated her customers as very special people, which they appreciated.

Her church family expressed that her absence has been noticeable. She was committed and she believed in doing a great job in all her obligations, great or small. She was involved with the ladies group at church. She tried to make the ladies feel special in every way that she could. Since her death, the ladies have felt a huge void.

My sister had many friends. Somehow, she showed her love and concern for each of them. She was always available when they needed her and was a source of encouragement to them. She gave her time and talents to friends in the form of craft gifts.

Above all, she is missed by her family. She was the eldest of four children. She was the mother of two, Michelle and Robert. Michelle was married in January 1997 and found her wedding very difficult to plan without her mother.

Our parents have suffered a tremendous amount of pain. Her siblings no longer have Claudette to look to for wisdom. She always showered her nieces and nephews with love and gifts. There is a hole in all of our lives without her.

Claudette Meek

I describe my sister as a remarkable person. She had a unique laugh that spread joy to all who came in contact with her. The sound of her laugh is just a memory now.

My sister died on April 19 but we did not bury her until seventeen days later, on May 6.

Life has not been the same since that day.

Descending
the Ladder

B. H. Espe

$\mathcal{F}$or a day that began as many others, it was a day that the
nation and I will never forget.

At 9:02 A.M., I was working on a slide presentation to be given to
the graduating veterinarians at Oklahoma State University on the
following Monday. I was not at my desk but in the conference room
located at the southeast corner of the fifth floor.

The first indication I had of the bombing was a loud rumbling
noise and a violent shaking of the building. This was followed by the
falling of the suspended ceiling, light fixtures, wiring, pipes, etc.
Somehow I managed to slide partway under the conference table
where I had been working. This probably prevented me from suffering more than minor cuts and bruises.

After the noise and shaking stopped and things quit falling, I
crawled from under the rubble and began to look around to the north
where there had been a wall. I could now see the building across the
street and its parking lot where vehicles were demolished and in flames.
To the west, where there had been a wall, I could now see where most
of our office space had been. All that was visible was a five-story drop

B. H. Espe

where the floor had been. By looking west and upward where there had been four floors, I could now see blue sky.

What had happened? My first thought was an earthquake, but that is not realistic in Oklahoma. The second thought I had was an explosion, probably caused by natural gas. It wasn't until later that I learned that it had been a bomb.

The wait to be rescued from the building then ensued. There was no floor between my location and the stairwell. It was obvious that I would have to come down a ladder, and for one who has a fear of heights, this was of great concern. After waiting between forty-five minutes and an hour and a half, I was rescued by the Oklahoma City Fire Department. My climbing down the ladder in a rather unconventional manner was picked up on live television. In fact, it was through television coverage that my family learned that I had survived the Murrah building bombing

We lost seven dedicated employees and good friends in Animal and Plant Health Inspection Services that day. Our loss, while extremely great, is small compared to that of their families.

The response of the people of Oklahoma City, the state of Oklahoma, and the nation has been unmatched in history. We have received literally hundreds of calls, cards, and letters from friends, acquaintances, and even people we have never met, offering their support.

One of the most touching of the caring experiences occurred about three weeks after the bombing. We were visiting our son in Maine and I was contacted by Massabesic Junior High in Waterboro and asked if I would talk to the students and accept a donation to one of the various Oklahoma disaster funds. I made a short presentation to the entire school and accepted a check for over one thousand dollars to the Mayor's Relief Fund. It was not until later that I learned that the money had been raised by the students for their annual school trip, but when they heard of the Oklahoma City disaster, they decided to donate the money instead. While this is just one of the many acts of caring, this one from a group of students fifteen hundred miles from Oklahoma confirmed my faith that the American spirit is alive in future generations.

Now over three years since the bombing, not a day goes by that I don't remember fondly those who we lost.

That's My Girl

Constance Favorite

I love and miss my child so much. I miss her for her child and for her husband. I miss her for her sister and her family. I can't forget all of her friends who love her and miss her. I miss her for them, too.

I can remember her prom. Out of all her friends, Lakesha was the prettiest, at least Corey and I thought so. She wore a short white dress with flowers around the bottom and around the sleeves. I made her face up so perfect and her hair was all in place. Her legs were strong as she stood tall, and with all her confidence she stood proud.

God, I miss her so much! I remember her graduating from boot camp. As we showed up, she looked so happy. Her husband, Corey, was happy for her, too. It made him feel good to see her so happy, and as always I was proud of her and her accomplishments. Baby Corey didn't know what to feel. He hadn't seen her in a few weeks so he was a little upset but happy to see his mommy again.

She got through boot camp even though she didn't think she would. She called me to tell me she wasn't going to make it because she couldn't finish her laps within the required time. I think the time

Lakesha Levy

was two or three minutes and some seconds, but I told her she wasn't trying hard enough. She told me she was trying and I just didn't understand. I told her, "I know you, so try again and this time give it one hundred percent." She replied, "I did," and I said, "You didn't." She said, "Ma, you just don't understand." I told her, "I know what you can do and you can do this." She said, "Let me go." Before she hung up I called her name and she said, "What?" I knew she wanted to cry because she sounded as if she was trying not to let me hear it in her voice. I told her forget about the minutes and just do the seconds. She laughed and said, "Yeah, right." I told her to call me back and let me know if she made it. I told her I loved her and she said, "You too, bye." This was her last time to make it happen. I had no doubt she'd make it, she just had to try a little harder. She did just that, and she made it. I can't remember the day, but she did call to let me know she'd succeeded. I told her I knew she would. She was so proud of herself, she'd even done better than she thought she would. That's my girl!

Lakesha and I became so much closer. We realized how far away we were from each other and we knew we needed to continue to let each other know just how much we needed and meant to each other.

We still had our share of ups and downs but we respected each other's opinions, as always. That's my baby. She's spoiled to the root of her soul. I miss her so much!

Lakesha would call with something silly to say and I'd tell her she was so silly, all the while laughing at what she said. She'd talk about her family, Big Corey and Li'l Corey. Well, we couldn't end our conversations without her saying something about her life with Big Corey, like how much she loved him and how her baby was so smart. I would say here we go; I knew I had to listen and I did. "My husband is so handsome and he's getting muscles." "My baby knows how to go to the bathroom by himself." She would always have to say things along these lines and I'd jokingly say, "Do I have to hear this?" She'd say, "Yeah, you know it." I'd just laugh at her. I miss those conversations so much. That's my girl!

I'd call Lakesha disgusting and she'd call me disgusting but there's nothing we wouldn't do for one another. Many people didn't understand the relationship we had with each other but they always knew there was much love shared between us. Lakesha would worry me with all kinds of stuff. She'd ask for things knowing I'd say no but also knowing I'd turn around and say yes. When I needed my hair done I'd ask her, and she'd tell me I was disgusting with my hair but she'd do it anyway.

Oh, how I miss our fights! We'd argue with each other about many things, but it was always done with and out of love. She'd grown right in front of my eyes.

Our relationship was one like no other I'd known. We'd talk to each other like we were mother and daughter and we'd talk to each other like we were friends. She'd say, "Constance, girl, let me tell you this" and then she'd begin to talk. This didn't bother me at all because I knew this wasn't said out of disrespect. She knew her place and I knew mine. We both knew we had this mother-daughter-friend thing going on and it was good. In most cases we were a team and in other cases we greeted each other with friendly, cordial opposition. Our love was unconditional. I love and miss my big baby girl!

Every Monday morning Li'l Corey and I pass the cemetery where Lakesha is. One morning (November 11, 1996), I asked Li'l Corey, as I always do when we pass there, who was over there. He said, "Mommy Kesha." Then I asked him, "And what do we say to Mommy?" He said, "Good morning, Mommy, I love you." He then asked me if Mommy was brushing her teeth. I said, "Yes, she is brushing her teeth for you just like you do for her." That brought tears to my eyes.

Lakesha. My daughter. My friend. My confidante. My love. My life.

Lakesha...my daughter. We were together just the two of us when Lakesha was three years old; this is when we separated from her father. Lakesha was my only child until she was ten years old.

Lakesha...my friend. We talked and argued. We joked and laughed. We made plans with and without each other. We shopped and we wore each other's clothes. We planned and cooked holiday meals together and we also spent quiet time together just watching television.

Lakesha...my friend and confidante. We could talk about anything and there was nothing we couldn't tell each other. We shared our problems and our secrets. Lakesha is very special.

"IF GIVEN A CHANCE..."
ROSALYN WATTS

Lakesha was always making people laugh. She had a happy disposition that shone almost every time she was surrounded by those close to her. Kesha was also smart and had great potential. Though she was faced with a couple of setbacks, she never gave up hope. Though her dreams changed as she got older, she always tried to succeed at whatever she did. Kesha was spoiled but she wasn't rotten. She had ways to aggravate us all and even though we'd get upset with her in the process, we could never stay upset long. It usually lasted about five minutes, then chances are she'd do or say something that would change the entire atmosphere and she'd put a smile on our faces.

Kesha was very caring and she was strong, too. She stood up for everything she believed in regardless of the opposition and this signifies the attributes of a person destined for success.

We are a close-knit family: Kesha was more like my sister than my niece. Now that part of me is gone forever.

Losing Kesha is the hardest thing I've ever had to go through. My thoughts are mostly of knowing I'll never see or hear her again. The tears shed almost daily are tears of hurt, sorrow, and pain. The impact this tragedy has had on so many people's lives is horrendous but I can only speak for myself as for the feelings I go through. I must say I have some good days and some bad days even after three years. I know this will continue, this cycle of ups and downs, because I miss Kesha so much and my love for her will forever be strong.

Kesha was twenty-one years old, with her entire life ahead of her. She had a family of her own that she so dearly loved, but the life she had planned for them was cut short after only two years. Kesha was young, vibrant, smart, beautiful, and full of life, and she had massive dreams. If given life's chance, who knows what she would have accomplished.

Good Stuff, 2;
Bad Stuff, 0

Barry Fogerty

*N*othing—that's what I remember of the first nine hours following the Oklahoma City bombing. My first glance of the living world was from the intensive-care unit at Oklahoma Memorial Hospital. My co-workers from the Oklahoma Water Resources Board and those marvelous Oklahoma City firemen from the station at Fifth and Hudson have filled in the gap for me.

Mike McGaugh, a fellow board employee, regained consciousness some ten minutes after the bombing, asking himself, "Why are my feet in sunlight? Why am I lying down?" When he regained his senses, he thought of his office mates and put his concern into action.

Despite his injuries, he sought me out and found me stretched out across a drafting table with my legs pinned under me. He tried to wake and coax me out of the smoky, dusty building. Unsuccessful, Mike made his way to a large hole in the south wall of the building and shouted for help. He eventually caught the attention of one of the emergency workers who signaled back that help was on the way.

Soon a fireman, whom Mike described as an angel with the face of a human male, extracted me from the mess, braced my neck, and bandaged my head with a hood. Rescuers carried me down the hall in some sort of chair as I cried out from my semiconsciousness, "What are you doing? Put me down! Are you crazy?"

An emergency medical technician set to work on me from a make-shift unit in the parking lot north of our building. As he cut off my tattered and bloody shirt, I grouched at him, "Don't cut that… that's a good shirt! Can you save the buttons? My wife will be mad as the dickens!" It's a good thing these professionals don't take offense at shocked people who are likely to say anything.

Barry Fogerty

My self-appointed guardian angel of the day, Mike, rode to the hospital in my ambulance, gave authorities the information they needed, and stayed with me until I was turned over to the doctors. He then called a friend, who called my wife, Linda, a teacher at Bernard Elementary in Tecumseh.

Linda immediately left for the hospital. My daughter, Kristi, a college junior, heard about the bombing on the radio and found me. My son, about to graduate from Oklahoma University, also heard newscasts and searched me out.

Dr. Houck, an ear, nose, and throat specialist, handled my case at the hospital. He told me that a team of three doctors worked three and a half hours to cleanse wounds on my head and back, and repair them with thirty-six stitches. After that first day, I had two more surgeries to remove glass from my back. I also had hearing loss and balance problems, so Dr. Houck referred me to specialists to deal with those.

My good wife took me to Oklahoma Memorial Hospital for fourteen of the next sixteen days.

Linda has been my best friend for some twenty-seven years now. I don't know how she managed to juggle all of her duties those weeks following the bombing. Besides my injuries and her end-of-the-year teaching tasks, she was preparing for our son's college graduation and our daughter's August wedding. Just the paperwork relating to the bombing and subsequent medical attention must have weighed at least fifty pounds. I thank the good Lord for many things in this world; my family is first on that long list.

People I worked with, in my vocation and avocations, called and offered encouragement and help. Kids, now teens, I taught over the years in my first-grade Sunday school class called to say "thanks" and "best of luck" to me. The young girls I instructed as a Rainbow Dad expressed similar thoughts. I had been building a small, high-performance sport plane, and my fellow hobbyists in that endeavor called with their concerns. I never knew so much help could arrive—from lawn mowing to sorting through the paper jungle.

I'm able to do almost everything I could do before, though maybe a little slower. I can exercise, drive, and, best of all, fly a light plane.

Final tally: good stuff, 2; bad stuff, 0.

Footprints
Bruce Griffin

*I*t started as a normal day for both of us. We got up late that morning. I think we hit the snooze alarm one too many times. Ethel went on to work downtown, and I went to work in Guthrie.

We felt the jar from the explosion in Guthrie, some thirty miles away. We turned on the radio in the office, and started getting reports about a bombing at the federal courthouse. I thought, Boy, that's just right across the street from the federal building where Ethel works.

I went down to Personnel and saw on TV that it was actually the federal building. I told my boss that I needed to leave and search for my wife. A friend drove me. I hadn't smoked in over ten months, but about halfway between Guthrie and downtown I bummed a cigarette.

It was such a mess downtown. We ended up just circling the city due to the traffic. We were given emergency numbers to call at the Red Cross, but the lines were constantly busy.

When we finally were able to get to the downtown area, we walked within two blocks of the federal building. When I saw it, I thought, My God, nobody could live through that. I went numb.

You don't know what's what. My friend and I decided to go to the

Ethel Griffin

Red Cross, but we ended up in a traffic jam. We decided to go back to my house and start calling hospitals. We called all that afternoon.

I was in shock. You function, but you don't really know what's happening. I did a lot of praying, even though I'm not religious.

I contacted the kids and then it was just sitting and waiting. When the kids got into town they made a lot of fliers with the picture and description of Ethel, took these to the hospitals, and started passing them out.

I tried calling Ethel's cellular phone and got a busy signal. You would hear talk about pockets in the building where survivors might still be alive. I clung to hope; you hang on to every last thread. You know, hope against hope, because miracles happen. It was a miracle that anyone survived.

Several days later on Sunday, I got a call from the medical examiner's office. My kids had gone to church and I told him I was alone. He asked me if I could get someone to come down with me and I told him that I would call him back.

After hanging up the phone, I sat around for awhile and thought, Well, I really haven't been alone in this. The good Lord has been carrying me since this happened and if He has gotten me this far, He can get me down there and through this, too.

They were able to make a positive identification of Ethel because not only did they have fingerprints from the government, but also dental records.

I realized right away, especially after I got that call from the medical examiner, that half of my life had just been taken away. Ethel and I were very close. Everything we did, other than go to work, we did together. We loved to travel and she had me involved in crafts, going to various craft shows. We were married almost twenty-nine years.

I went back to work pretty soon and that was good for me, but you just get through strictly by the grace of God. I was kind of like a zombie, but with each day I got a little better.

For a long time, every time I was in the neighborhood, I had to go to the cemetery. I had to go. I still do sometimes, but not as often.

I came to the realization that life does go on and you have to make the best of it. I don't think my wife would want me to sit around and mourn her every day for the rest of my life. She was not like that. She had read somewhere that if you had a happy marriage, and a spouse died, you would probably get married again. I said for a long time that I probably never would marry again, but those thoughts have changed. Life is too short to try and go through it alone.

Today I certainly realize that life is a lot more fragile than most people think. It's been years and years since I've gone to church, but my relationship with Christ is a vital part of my life. He just took me in His arms and helped me through this.

It's like that story about footprints in the sand, where a man sees two sets of prints during the good times of his life, where the Lord was walking with him, but then only one set during the most diffi-cult times, and he wonders where God was during those times. But then the Lord tells him, "Those were the times when I carried you." And He has certainly done that for me.

I have really lived a very blessed life. I really have. Not that I did anything to deserve it, but I realize now just how blessed it's been.

I guess one of the things I have a hard time with today is that I can't believe an individual would purposefully do something like this. I've heard stuff like, "Well, they had a gripe against the govern-ment." But this hasn't changed the government one iota.

The victims were just regular people who went to work every day, to try and make a living and to try and help others better their lives. Really, this whole country was a victim of this crime.

Yet the only person who has any rights are the criminals. The victims and their families have no rights whatsoever. I do get angry at my tax dollars being spent so defense attorneys can run all over the world to defend perpetrators.

I guess for me there will always be a void until this comes to completion. Whatever that might be. I know my life is never going to be the same, but I do the best I can.

I Don't Want to Die Like This

Rhonda Griffin

I was in a hurry to get to work that day. At HUD, we can work credit time, and I was saving for a summer vacation. With a large enough tax refund, we could even go to Disney World.

I dropped my fourteen-year-old daughter, Jamie, off at school. As she got out of the car, I said, "I love you. See you tonight."

Continuing on to Vo-Tech, where my son, Charlie, attended, I asked, "Don't you think your mama is acting so much better?" I had come out of depression a few months earlier.

Charlie answered, "Yes, Mom. You seem so much happier. It's like I have my mom back."

I went on, "Since your Aunt Kay died, it has been really hard for me to get close to anybody. But, you know what? I have a lot of friends at work, and I can truly say that I love many of them. It's like we're one big family at HUD."

Once I was alone, I prayed, as I did every morning on my way to work. I asked God to watch over my family and then tacked on, "Oh, yes, Lord, please watch over me, too."

It was 8:45 when I arrived at the office. "Good, I can earn one

Rhonda Griffin

credit hour today," I thought.

I greeted Betsy, turned my computer on, and said good morning to Michael who shared a cubicle with me. My co-workers Robyn and Kim smiled and went about their morning tasks. I noticed that Bob was alone in his area. "Why has everyone deserted you?" I joked. He replied that some people were in a training session on the ninth floor and some were in the field.

"Rhonda, you have a good day," he said.

Rita rushed in from training for a moment to schedule lunch with me at 12:15.

I hurried back to my desk to help answer the phones because six people were out that day. It was unusually empty at HUD; there were about sixty people gone from the seventh and eighth floors. Thank God!

At 9:00, Glenda signed in, and I teased her, "It's about time you got to work."

Holding an envelope for mailing, I heard a "swoosh" and everything went gray. I thought my computer had blown up and instinctively threw my arms and hands over my face and head, then rolled my chair away. I felt things hit me. My first thought was that the computer had blown up part of the ceiling; my second thought was that I was asleep and having a nightmare. Finally, the bombardment stopped. I was at Glenda's workstation, four feet from mine. My desk and Michael's were gone. A huge concrete slab dangled in the space where I had been sitting.

Glenda remembered my asking, "What's happening to us? Our building is gone and we are still here." I thought it must be a bomb, worse than the one at the World Trade Center.

Smoke enveloped us, and we couldn't breathe. Glenda covered our mouths and noses with her skirt. We made our way to the windows and looked out. Everything was still.

Soon, people began running toward the building. Others were leaving. The streets filled with the bomb-squad truck, fire engines, police cars, and ambulances. People, covered in blood, cried and screamed as they were helped from the building. Others, unconscious, or maybe lifeless, were carried.

We couldn't get to the stairs and I panicked, afraid that the remains of the structure would collapse. I screamed, "Somebody help us!" We prayed for our friends and co-workers; we prayed for everyone who had been in the building. I remembered the day-care center. Looking at Glenda, I exclaimed, "Oh, my God, the babies!" We prayed for them. We prayed for ourselves.

There was a second bomb scare and an order to evacuate the area. A rescue worker told us to lie on the floor. There was so much glass and debris that we could only kneel and cover our heads with our arms. I knew I was going to die. I told the Lord, "I don't want to die like this, but I know that if I do, I will be with you."

A sudden thought came to me. If I stood up, someone might see me and help me. If another bomb exploded, I would be dead whether I was kneeling or standing. I asked Glenda if she wanted to try and jump to safety. She said no.

I turned my head and found myself face-to-face with a man. He had risked his life and disobeyed orders by coming into the building. He took each of us by the hands and walked us over a window frame to two police officers who were there to guide us outside. They, too, had endangered their lives, defying the threat of a second bomb. It was 10:35 A.M.

A few days later, I met again with the man who rescued us. He said that something told him that if he did not get to us, we would jump.

I lost thirty-five friends and co-workers. My life will never be the same. On the outside, I sustained cuts, bruises, and knots. But on the inside, my heart is broken into a thousand pieces. The Lord spoke to my heart about three weeks after the bombing, when I thought I couldn't make it any longer. He said for me to take it one day at a time. I know that with His help, I will heal. If it weren't for God, I wouldn't be here to tell my story. I thank him for all the people who helped, and are still helping, following this tragedy. I thank God for the off-duty police officer who first came and rescued us and for the other two who held our hands as we ran from the building.

We Were a Team

Rudy Guzman

O n April 19, 1995, I was in my apartment in California and happened to be awake at 6:45 A.M., which was unusual because I work the late shift for Federal Express. Around 7:00 I turned on the television and was watching the local news when suddenly there was a breaking report about an explosion in Oklahoma City. My curiosity aroused, I decided to turn to CNN to get further information. The first report was that the explosion had occurred at the federal courthouse, so I was somewhat relieved because I knew my brother, Randy, worked in the federal building. Still curious, I found Randy's business card and decided to give him a call. The phone just rang and rang, with no answer. Not knowing how close the courthouse was in relation to the federal building, I was still not alarmed. As I continued to watch further reports, the updated information said the building that exploded had been the Alfred P. Murrah Federal Building. Again, I tried to reach my brother at his office, and still no answer. Only when I saw the address of the Murrah building on television, and matched it to the address on my brother's business card, did I become concerned. I then called the

Randy Guzman

Public Affairs office of the Marine Corps, and inquired if my brother's office was in the Murrah building. They confirmed my fear that the Marine Corps recruiting office was in the Murrah building, but had no further information. I started calling everyone who knew Randy, but no one had heard from him. I decided to get to Oklahoma City somehow. I ended up taking a Federal Express plane, and arrived in Oklahoma City early Thursday morning.

I went straight to Randy's apartment and was contacted by the Marine Corps office. They told me to stay put and not to go down to the site. They would contact me as soon as they had any information about my brother. Later that day my parents flew in from California and joined me in the agony of waiting.

On the day of the bombing, I assumed that my brother was risking his life helping others in the rescue effort. As time went on, the assumption of Randy assisting others changed to hoping that Randy was alive. Our family prayed and recited the Rosary, hoping that Randy would be found and would be all right.

As the days slowly passed, the waiting became unbearable. It seemed as if time stood still. We wondered constantly if Randy would be found alive.

Monday, the twenty-fourth, was the day that changed our lives forever. That morning, we were preparing breakfast and heard a loud knock on the door. I answered the door, and saw Randy's commanding officer, a Marine Casualty Assistance Officer, and two chaplains. They wanted to speak to my parents, so I let them in. They sat down with my parents and I stood in the background. I heard the unbearable information, that they had found my brother and he had not survived.

I remember my mother screaming and yelling, and seeing my father crying. I broke into tears for a minute, and remembered Randy telling me if anything ever happened to him, to take care of everything. He gave me these instructions before leaving for the Persian Gulf War. I took out a notepad and started making notes about what to do. Randy had given me specifics about what funeral home to use and where he wanted to be buried. I tried to put my emotions aside and carry out my brother's wishes.

My brother, Captain Randolph Guzman, was a proud Marine. One of his tours of duty was representing our country during the Persian Gulf War. He dedicated himself to and risked his life for the liberation of Kuwait. And yet it was one of his comrades, who also fought in the Persian Gulf, who took his life. He was killed by a fellow American, who became an enemy of our Constitution.

As part of my duties, I went to view my brother, to determine whether the casket should be opened or closed. He was lying in his casket, in his dress blues, his uniform in tip-top shape, his ribbons on his chest positioned perfectly. Seeing Randy's face all swollen and battered was a sight I was not ready for. It appeared as if someone had used a hammer and inflicted hundreds of blows to his face. I tried to hold back my tears but I could not. I said all the good-byes on behalf of family and friends. I turned to the funeral director and asked him to close the casket. I did not want anyone to go through what I just had. I still have that horrific picture of the condition of my brother in my mind.

I escorted my brother back home to California, to his final resting place, along with fellow Marines. Our American flag draped over his casket and the sound of taps made me realize it was my final farewell to my big brother. I had fulfilled my duties as he had wished but I no longer could hold back the tears.

When I go to the cemetery I reflect on all the treasured memories of Randy and me. While growing up, we did most things together. We had the same friends, shared the same activities—we were a team. We were both altar boys at our neighborhood Catholic church, working together as a team. We both competed on our high school track-and-field team. Randy was a long-distance runner and I did the shot put and discus. We cheered each other on and supported one another in our respective events. Again, we were a team. We were both involved in student government, working on projects and activities during our high school life. During student-body elections one year, Randy ran for president and I ran for vice president, both campaigning together. We both lost the election, but we were still a team. On April 19, 1995, my teammate was ripped from my life.

Randy, I miss you. I always looked up to you for advice and guidance. But most of all I miss the things that we did together, because we always were a *team*.

Oh Boy!

Patti Hall

April 19, 1995, was a beautiful spring morning. I was the Visa clerk at the Federal Employees Credit Union. I went to pick up my Visa payments and performed my usual duties. At 8:59 A.M. we had a foul odor in the hallway and I went to get a can of air freshener. Members where going into the credit union. I started to speak to Nancy Ingram as I pushed on the nozzle of the air freshener—and then the bomb exploded. When I awoke, debris was on top of me and I could barely lift my head to ask what happened. A lady said it was an explosion. I calmly laid my head back down and the next thing that I remember was people walking on our faces. Nancy hollered out, "You are walking on our faces, help!" I remember the rescuers saying, "We can't see you, we can't find you." They asked if we could get our hands up to the top of the debris so that they could find us. I managed to work one hand through the rubble. I remember telling a rescuer, "Do not touch me. Let me put my arm around your neck and lift myself on the stretcher, because the pain is so tremendous." The next thing I remember is riding in a makeshift ambulance and being very concerned because there was

Patti Hall

no siren and I didn't want to go to the hospital they were taking me to.

In emergency, I was able to ask them to call my neighbor, to go to my mom and stay with her. The hospital contacted my doctor and my mom and arrangements were made for me to stay at this hospital because I was in very bad shape. That day, I was in and out of shock and did not know that our building had been bombed. I had discomfort and asked my friend Mary to lift my head and put a pillow under me. When she did there was so much blood that the nurse was called and she sent everyone with me home immediately.

I did not know the seriousness of my injuries until five weeks later when I came out of a coma, and the real test of endurance was to come.

"OH BOY!"

My legs, knees, and ankles had been crushed and were wrapped up in castlike bandages from surgery. I had bootlike shoes on my feet, for support. I was in and out of consciousness, and once I thought I was at the beauty shop and that they left me there by myself. I had a tracheotomy, was put on a respirator, and did not know that I nearly died. My right collarbone was crushed, pelvis broken, ribs were broken, left elbow broken, left heel broken. I had numerous IVs and tubes in me, and it was the *fight of my life to survive.*

I was not aware of how horrible the situation was for all of the people of Oklahoma City because the doctors kept any media and information from me, to help me concentrate on my recovery. Only when they thought that I was ready did they encourage me to try and talk about the bombing. I was unable to discuss much because I was not aware of what had really happened. One night there was a terrible storm. The thunder was so loud I screamed out, and the staff had to take me out of my room, because I thought it was the bomb. Yet to this day, I am not consciously aware that I ever heard the explosion.

When I was discharged, it was stated plainly to me that I would have to undergo intensive therapy, physical and mental, for a long time. The doctors almost had to amputate my legs from the knees down and also did not think that I would ever walk again. They encouraged me by pointing out that I was a fighter and that I would walk if I wanted to.

Going home was a mixture of joy, fear, the future, the everyday challenge to go through rehabilitation and socializing. Having suffered this type of trauma, I had to face the physical limitations and most of all the fact that my co-workers and employees of the Murrah building were gone. When you are incapacitated you have such a deep feeling of loss that it makes it hard to push every day and to fight! I did not have time to grieve or truly understand the extreme seriousness of this situation, therefore I was also faced with a deep-down concern whether or not I could pull through. I have been under psychiatric care and counseling. Three times each week I go to physical rehab. Discussion has been underway to replace both knees and to build me a heel to balance my walking and relieve the pain in my back. My mother is eighty-two and has had two emotional breakdowns over the change in our lives.

As an injured victim of this tremendous crime, I was not able to dress myself, bathe myself, brush my teeth, go places, and was totally dependent on others. Today, I can drive my car, shop, go to church, help others, and try every day to keep a good outlook on life. I am so grateful for God's grace to get me through this ordeal and for giving me the prayers and the strength of the nation to continue healing and to be able to say, *"Oh boy! Oh boy! I have made it this far!"*

The Luck
of the Draw

Tom H. Hall

$\mathscr{A}$pril 19, 1995, started like any other beautiful spring day. I got up, had breakfast, and sat around for a few minutes thinking of other things I could be doing, then realized I'd better snap out of it and get on my way to work. Now it was time to kiss the wife goodbye, let the cat out, and make a mad dash for work. While driving to work, I thought of all the things I had planned for the day.

The first and most important thing on the list was a meeting with the building managers and Bob Dennis, the court clerk. This meeting was held in Don Rogers's office on the first floor north side of the GSA building manager's office. The meeting lasted from about 8:30 until 9:00.

After the meeting, I stepped next door to Richard Williams's office to clarify something said in the meeting. As I recall, I was standing about ten feet from the north glass wall, approximately seventy feet from ground zero. I can remember talking to Richard one moment and then all of a sudden I felt like I was being electrocuted. I felt a hot vibration going through me that as my body contracted, there was no way possible to pull myself loose. I have been momentarily shocked before, but this was something I had never experienced. I can remember yelling "Turn it off!" to no avail. Finally, I heard the arching and popping sound that electricity makes when it goes to ground and then it quit. I have no way of knowing for certain how long it lasted, but it seemed like forever.

After the power went out, I recall trying to sit up and figure out what happened. I wasn't able to sit up because the ceiling grid, sheet metal, and other debris was on me from my upper waist on down. I must have had my mouth open during the electrocution because it was full of concrete and fiberglass and I was gasping for air. I remember running my finger through my mouth to clear out the debris and open my airway, which helped a lot. At this point, I tried to move the rest of my body only to realize that my left leg and hand were crushed and I was not able to free myself. As I lay there I called for Richard and all I could hear was some movement in the debris. Then I yelled for help and within about a minute I could see a policeman through a triangular-shaped hole in the rubble. I would later learn his name was Terry Yeakey. He said, "We'll get you out in just a minute." As I lay there waiting, I thought that the second floor above must have given way and fallen on us. At this point I thought that the damage was just in our immediate area, and that Richard and I were the only ones hurt since I didn't hear the explosion or know the magnitude of damage. Within a minute, rescue workers were there.

Tom H. Hall

Firemen Monte Baxter and Mike Shannon made their way to my rescue. I was not able to see well due to all the blood in my eyes. All I could see was red. As they removed me and started to carry me off, I remember that my leg was in more pain than I had ever experienced. The pain was so great that I would pass out and then awaken seconds later when my leg was in a more comfortable position, only to have the excruciating pain return again and pass out again. I remember telling them to look for Richard and that he was just a few feet from me. The firemen carried me outside and handed me to the police officer, Terry Yeakey, who took me out to the middle of Fifth Street. As he carried me out I saw a glimpse of black sky and heard what must have been the cars in the parking lot across the street, exploding.

The next thing I remember is lying on the street on broken glass with someone doing first aid. A local restaurant operator, Pete Schaffer, and police officer Gordon Martin started first aid. I can remember that they were trying to cut loose my tie from my neck to open my airway and that they were concerned that my neck and back were injured. I was fading fast. I could hear things going on around me but could not respond.

Moments later I was loaded into an ambulance and started telling the emergency personnel my name, blood type, phone number, and other vital information. It seemed like I had a sudden burst of energy and automatically told them as much information as possible. They were poking and prodding and checking me out as I started to fade away again. When I woke up they were loading another person in the ambulance. I couldn't see so I had to ask who was next to me. I heard a mumbled "It's me, Richard." When the ambulance started moving again, I heard them saying that we were going to St. Anthony's Hospital. About the time we arrived at St. Anthony's, I heard on the radio that we were being diverted to University Hospital. We turned around and had to cross some railroad tracks; being bumped around increased my leg pain and I passed out again.

Just like in the movies they raced me into the emergency room with all the bright lights and they put the mask over my mouth and nose and I was out. I was University's first bombing victim. Records show that I was brought in at 9:30 A.M. That's an incredibly fast rescue: From ground zero to hospital in twenty-eight minutes.

When I woke up later that afternoon after surgery, I could see only through one eye because the other eyelid was lacerated and had to be sewn back together. My head felt like it was swollen so large that it was going to burst. The first person I remember seeing was my wife, Joanne. Some of the visitors tried to explain to me that the building had been blown up by a bomb. This didn't make sense to me. How could something like this happen in Oklahoma City? But a lot of things were hard to comprehend due to the pain medication I was on. The next day they moved me to a private room with a TV, and all that was on was the bombing coverage. I recall lying there still mostly out of it and confused. I kept thinking this must be the longest dream I've ever had and when was it going to be over?

I began to get a steady stream of visitors and the most memorable were some co-workers who came and told me of the injuries that our staff received. I remember asking about Mike Loudenslager and Steve Curry, whose desks were on each side of mine. There was a hesitation, and then they said that they hadn't been found yet. I guess that this was about the time I realized that this was not a dream.

While now having hopes for some miracle that my two closest co-workers and the many others unaccounted for would be found alive, I also felt that things didn't look promising. As days went by I kept thinking that there would be someone found alive days later, but it just didn't happen.

It took a couple of days to assess all my injuries: a compound fracture of my left femur, a broken finger, a severed jugular vein, a lacerated eyelid, glass lacerations from head to toe on my right side, a concussion, and nerve damage. I received many stitches and staples and twelve pints of blood.

After spending ten days in the hospital, I came home. It was great to be home at our quiet country acreage near Piedmont. I have two daughters, Hillary and April, who were six and three at the time. They were glad to see Dad come home but were a little hesitant at first to crawl up in my lap because of all the bandages and bruises I had. My patient and caring wife and mother catered to my every ache and pain, which turned out to be a full-time job for them. Thanks to all the welcomed visits from family, friends, neighbors, and my Air National Guards unit, my spirits were lifted and my mind would be momentarily distracted from the pain and discomfort.

It was the special care that I received from Dr. David Teague, my orthopedic surgeon, and the in-home physical therapy from Steve Antel, a close friend since grade school, that left no doubt in my mind that I would walk again. Within days I progressed from a wheel chair to a walker and then weeks later to a cane. Although I still have a few aches and pains, it seems that physical therapy has turned me into a fitness nut.

Mental healing is a much slower process. As I write this (nineteen months after the bombing), I must say that I guess I'm still in denial because the emotional impact hasn't really hit me like it has many others, maybe because I have been so focused on physical recovery. I know that many things that were important to me before aren't now, and things I took for granted before seem more important now. When explaining your emotions to others, you don't think others thoroughly understand your feelings unless you're talking to someone who is also a bombing survivor. Almost everyone who survived the bombing says that, if they hadn't stopped for another cup of coffee or went to a file room or did some other routine thing, then they would have been where they would probably have been killed. If it had not been for the meeting, I would have been at my desk next to the glass and only twenty feet from the Ryder truck and would surely have been killed. When I think of how close I came to death, it sends a chill down my spine and makes me think that it must be the luck of the draw: when it's your time to go, you're gonna go whether it's the next second or the next year.

This Could Not Be Happening

Vicki Hamm

I awoke at 3:00 A.M. on Wednesday, April 19, 1995, unable to breathe. I could not catch my breath. I considered going to the emergency room. Instead I propped two pillows behind me and waited for the morning light to come. I debated if I should go into my office at the U.S. Army Recruiting Battalion. As the budget and accounting technician for twenty-four years I knew I had a deadline to meet. I decided I should go to my doctor, who is located in downtown Oklahoma City. I called his office and was told to be there at 8:30.

My doctor told me that I had bronchitis and possibly pneumonia. He was sending me to the X-ray lab on NW Tenth Street (across from St. Anthony's Hospital). I left the doctor's office and went across the hall to get my prescriptions. I had just finished paying the pharmacist when we heard this loud, earth-shaking explosion. The pharmacist said, "Something big has just blown," and we ran outside to look north on Robinson. We saw a gigantic cloud of smoke. Being familiar with the downtown area, I could tell that it was coming from the federal building where I worked.

I turned in a daze to walk back to my car. I stopped at a pay

Vicki Hamm

phone and called the office—receiving just the funny busy signal that indicates the phones are not working. I so much wanted to hear the battalion secretary say "Army Recruiting, Mrs. Gert." I walked in a state of numbness to my car and drove toward the federal building. I was stopped by a policeman and I told him I had to get back to work. He told me if I drove over the glass I would blow out my tires. I turned around and managed to drive to the radiology clinic.

I drove up Broadway to NW Tenth Street and turned west on Tenth. There was glass all over the street and sidewalk. I looked south toward where my office was and I saw the total devastation and the bombed-out shell of the office where I had worked the last eighteen years of my life. I thought the entire office was gone. I didn't see how anyone could have survived. There was a numbness in my stomach that remains to this day.

My heart began to ache and I felt a deep sense of sadness over the fate of the federal building and those in it. I felt a deep sense of guilt for not being there. How could this have happened to my office without me being there? It's not fair; I wanted to be with my co-workers. This could not have happened to them without me. What about all the friendships in the building that I had made over the last eighteen years? How could they be wiped from the face of the earth in just a few seconds?

I drove in a state of shock to the radiology lab and had the X-ray. I knew I should call our headquarters in San Antonio, Texas. I couldn't remember the area code and the phone numbers that I had called for the last twenty-four years of my life. I called the operator and she helped me get through. I told them there had been a bombing and I thought the whole office was gone. I then called my mother to let her know I was okay.

I made my way home. My plan was to get in touch with my husband. He works at General Motors and cannot be easily reached. As I drove home to Moore, Oklahoma, I kept watching for his red pickup truck. I had the feeling that he may be on his way to the hospital to look for me. I saw his truck parked near the corner of NW Twelfth and Santa Fe in Moore and I pulled up beside it. As he came out of the store he saw me and stopped. We looked at each other. I wanted to get out of the car so I could give him a hug but I wasn't sure I could stand up without falling. He cried and I cried as we hugged each other through the window of the car.

When I got home I called my supervisor's home. His wife answered the telephone and I asked if she had heard from Major Bain. She said no. I tried to remain calm but I feared that if she had not heard from him by that time he was probably dead along with the rest of the office. About fifteen minutes later Major Bain called. He had been in the building when the bomb went off. He took care of his people at the bomb site before he left the area. He asked me if I would go with him to St. Anthony's Hospital where a command post had been set up with a listing of the injured and what hospital they were in. I went with him and we made our way into a large room of dulled, shocked, tearstained faces. I'll never forget how being there did not seem real. This could not be happening!

Memories of a Sister

Ladonna Harris

⎯

*T*he spring sun glinted in the eyes of workers as they hurried to their businesses on that April morning, a lovely day! A noise—so loud it could be heard eighty miles away—changed everything. I thought it was a sonic boom. Most people went on about their tasks, ignorant for a few brief minutes of the significance of the sound. A newsman on the radio said there was an explosion at the courthouse. A gas leak? No such luck—and not at the courthouse. The Alfred P. Murrah Federal Building had been bombed. It was a day I will never forget. My sister, Linda "Coleen" Housley, worked as a loan officer at the Federal Employees Credit Union, located on the third floor.

Days of waiting were days of contrast. Numbness, shock, depression, and disbelief mingled with vivid memories of our childhood. We came from a low-income farm family. Our parents, reared during the Depression, worked hard for what they had in life. We learned early that nothing's free—you have to earn your way.

Coleen was three years older than I was. Pat, another sister, is seven years younger. Pat and I always thought that Coleen was prim

154

and proper, that she could
scarcely make a mistake.
Once we grew up, I found
out that Coleen thought
she had to be like a mother
to us because our own
mom was sick so often. She
cooked and supervised the
household chores while I
was Daddy's tomboy, help-
ing him farm the fields and
drive the tractor.

We were cleaning up
the yard one day, fighting
as sisters do, and Coleen
picked up a stick and
threw it at me. She did not
know there was a nail in it
until she saw it sticking out

Linda "Coleen" Housley

of my forehead. She ran in the house, crying and telling Mother that
she didn't mean to harm me. I think it hurt her worse than it did me.

Coleen had lots of friends, both girls and boys. I was the typical
tag-along little sister, and she didn't always want me around. There
used to be a way that you could dial a number to make your own
phone ring. When I tried to work my way into her plans, she would
dial that number and tell me to answer the phone. When I did, she
would run off with her friends. I fell for this ruse again and again,
heartbroken every time. We both laughed about it when we grew up.

When Coleen was about twelve, she announced she was running
away from home. Mother said, "Okay, where will you go?"

"I'll find a place," Coleen replied.

Mother helped her pack a suitcase. I couldn't believe it! There
was Mom, assisting her, while I was crying, not wanting her to go
away. Coleen made it about a half block. Mother and I were watching. I couldn't understand how Mother knew she would come back.

I needed a new dress for eighth-grade graduation. Mother

bought me a sheath style, but I found that the other girls were wearing full skirts with can-can petticoats. I had to be just like the other girls, but we had no money for another dress. I cried so hard that Coleen took pity on me. She told Mother that she would make me a dress if Mother would buy the fabric. This was just one day before graduation. Coleen stayed up all night sewing. I woke up and couldn't believe my eyes. It was the prettiest dress I had ever seen— pink and perfect. I felt like Cinderella going to the ball. I loved Coleen so much for working so hard for me.

Coleen met "Carl" downtown while we were buying school clothes. He was a shoe salesman, good-looking, charming, and a ladies' man. He swept my sister off her feet. When he asked her for a date, she said no. When we got home, Coleen told Mother that she really did want to go out with Carl. "Call him!" Mother instructed. This was the fifties, and girls didn't call boys. It was a terrible, brazen thing to do, but Coleen phoned Carl. She was almost sixteen, and he was almost eighteen. They were soon married in our living room at home. Shortly after the wedding, they moved to Fort Hood, Texas. I missed my sister terribly. We visited her, but it just wasn't the same.

She had three beautiful children. When I was divorced and had two children, she let me move in with her until I got on my feet. She took care of my kids as well as her own. I will always be grateful I could turn to her when I needed help. She was there with me when my two babies died. She went through the same things I did. She was always there for me.

Carl was an abusive alcoholic, and he stepped out with other women. I hated Carl for treating Coleen badly; she surely didn't deserve it. She stayed with him for about thirty-three years, then separated for two, and then divorced him. She went to Al-Anon, and they helped her find herself again. They gave her back her self-respect and the courage to do and say what she had wanted to for years. She was a different person—happy. We were close again.

Coleen had worked for another credit union for eleven years and was promoted to loan officer. Her boss, Gary, helped her go through a lot of bad times by being her friend. After her divorce from Carl, Coleen and Gary started dating. I had not seen her happy for years, until they fell in love. Over Labor Day weekend of 1993, Coleen and Gary tied the knot on a paddleboat in Grand Lake.

Because she had married her boss, Coleen thought she ought to find another job. At fifty-one, she considered herself too old to be hired. I told her she knew her stuff and was a good worker. It wasn't long before she called and told me she was going to work for the Federal Employees Credit Union. "They actually wanted me!" she said. I never had any doubts.

Everything was going so well for her; she was so happy. Then came that horrible, tragic day of April 19, 1995, the day that shocked the world.

We went to the church that was set up for the victims' families. We waited and waited to hear something. It seemed like we were the only ones going through hell, but, of course, we weren't. I thought maybe Coleen was just wandering around, not knowing who she was or where she was. I hoped someone would find her alive. I prayed as never before.

After the bombing, while the workers were digging through the debris, it started to rain. The rescuers had to work even harder, but they never gave up. I kept hoping that the rain would seep into the holes where someone could at least drink the water and stay alive.

The wait seemed like a lifetime. On the thirteenth day, May 1, the call finally came: Coleen's body had been found. We went to the church where the medical examiner told us they had a positive ID. Yeah, right, I thought. She's still alive, and you have someone else's body. Her body and another were the last two found before the Murrah building was demolished. They said we were lucky to have her at all.

I called the funeral home to pick up her body that night. We all went over there the next day. It was so hard and sort of a blur. I still didn't believe it was Coleen. Then they brought out her personal belongings—no doubt about it—they were hers. "Oh, my God," I said. "It's really true, she's really gone."

The funeral was the largest I had ever seen, 750 people and more flowers than a florist shop. I know Coleen looked down from heaven in awe.

She left behind a husband of nineteen months, a son and daughter-in-law, two daughters, two stepdaughters, nine grandchildren, two sisters, and many other family members and friends.

This past May, I fractured my back and had to stay in bed for more than a week. I felt someone sitting on the side of my bed, but I looked around and saw no one. I know Coleen was there to watch over me as she always had in the past. I was not afraid; I felt very comfortable. I knew she would not ever really leave me.

A Bond of Survival

Allison Hatton

'm still teaching at the YMCA day-care center. Although the center has moved a couple of miles up the road, we still have some of the same children and we share a special bond of survival. That April day, Desmond missed his mom, so I picked him up to comfort him after I had opened the curtains that covered the top half of the windows that ran floor to ceiling facing the Murrah building. We started story time early that morning. I held Desmond on my lap with *The Grumpy Old Rabbit* in front of us. The other children sat to my right and left, our backs to the window. Usually they sit facing me, but not that day.

It was the loudest noise I ever heard. A lot of people don't remember the noise, but we all remember the building falling in around us and the dust and smoke filling the air. I was the closest person in the YMCA to the federal building. I grabbed Desmond and Bradley, tucked them underneath me, and covered my head. When I opened my eyes, my first thought was, We have a heck of a mess to clean up. We had some air conditioners right outside the wall—I thought they had blown up.

Allison M. Hatton

At first no one realized the scope of the blast. Workers all over downtown thought it was just their building that was affected. Mitzi, my coteacher, came in and our eyes met.

I'll never forget that look. At that moment, something just took over and we snapped into action, scooping up children and carrying them to the front of the room. When I found Christopher, I couldn't even recognize him. His body was covered from head to ankle by a fallen fluorescent light and he wasn't moving. I was afraid of what I might find when I lifted the fixture. As I grabbed the corner to pull it away, I heard a cry. It was like music to me. He was alive!

The teachers systematically sent child after child to the front of the center. We had to lift them up and over a large piece of debris which blocked the path. Later, we found out that it was part of the Ryder truck which contained the bomb. I was used to seeing these little ones cry and fuss over slightly bumped heads or tiny little cuts. On that day, covered with blood and debris, they walked quietly to the sidewalk in the midst of massive destruction. Their cries would have comforted me; their dazed silence left me frightened and worried.

We had rounded up all the toddlers and were headed outside when I heard Linda call from the infant room, "The babies! The babies! Somebody's got to help me get the babies!" She had gathered all the infants in one crib. During our fire drills, we just roll it out the door to the street. But, with the ceiling crumbled at our feet, we couldn't even get the bed through the doorway. I grabbed infants, one in each arm, carried them to the front, and handed them to strangers, calling out, "Here—take this baby!"

Children, babies, and bystanders gathered quietly on the lawn outside the YMCA. I went back into the building to make sure we had everyone. That's when I saw James. I couldn't tell who it was because of the blood. From his trembling two-year-old body came a faint, scared cry. I ran and picked him up. He was seriously injured. Outside, the police moved everyone across the street because of the danger of more explosives. Some of the children were slipping in and out of consciousness because of injury or shock. James had lost an enormous amount of blood through lacerations on his head and neck. I held a towel to his head and shouted, "He needs to go to the hospital! He's losing a lot of blood!" A man came over and took him. I called out, "Wait, we've got to get his brother!"

The boys needed to stay together, not just for their mutual comfort, but also to make it easier for their parents to find them in the chaos. Another bystander was holding the four-year-old brother, William. He turned to us and we ran down the street to the ambulance. Because of the tremendous amount of rubble, no vehicles could reach the area around the YMCA.

As we ran, I was confronted by the magnitude of the catastrophe. I had been so absorbed in the task of rescuing the children that I didn't notice the destruction of the Murrah building or the blocks and blocks of collateral damage. Oh, my God! I thought. Is this Armageddon? I didn't know if Oklahoma City had been bombed, or if the damage was even more widespread. As far as one could see, there were bloody people wearing the tatters of clothes that had been blown from their bodies. I was totally unaware of my injuries.

As the paramedic worked on James, I comforted him and William, reminding them that everything would be all right, that their parents would find them soon. The ambulance driver radioed that he had four patients. I looked up. James, William, and a man were in the vehicle with me. As soon as I saw the man, I looked away. He was very badly injured; I'm not sure he survived. His arm was attached only by threads of muscle and he moaned in agony. It was then I realized that they counted me as a patient. My white shirt was soaked with blood and dirt from carrying the wounded children. My hair hung in wet, red strings.

I wanted to be with James and William, but the driver made me buckle up. "It's the law," he said. En route to the hospital, James lost consciousness. The paramedic unstrapped me.

"See what you can do, he's not responding," he said.

I just knew he was going to die. I prayed, "God, if you're going to take him, please don't do it now while I'm here. I've known this child all his life and I can't bear to see him die!" I pinched him. His eyes would open for an instant, then roll back in his head. I pinched him again as hard as I could, ordering him again, "Wake up!" I sang the Barney song... anything to keep him focused. I knew, because of his injuries, if he went to sleep, it would probably be forever.

We were among the early arrivals at the hospital. James and William were taken one way and I was guided another. Not a good patient, I argued, "No! I need to stay with the boys!" The staff insisted that I be treated, but I still considered myself uninjured.

As the doctor bandaged the cuts on my head and feet, he asked me questions about myself. When I mentioned the YMCA, he asked, "Did you see David?" His small son had been in our building. A tremendous wave of guilt washed over me. I didn't remember seeing David. I sobbed, "I'm sorry, I'm sorry." He assured me I had done nothing wrong, that he knew in his heart David was fine, but I felt somehow responsible.

By the time I was released, the corridors were full of bloody bodies in wheelchairs.

My mind wandered to my co-workers, to the people in the restaurants and other businesses I visited each day. Had they survived?

William and James were doing well, although James would need surgery. I went downstairs to see if I could spot their parents and other acquaintances in the growing crowd. I had been identified as a teacher in a day care. Strangers came up to me with pictures of their little ones and asked me, "Have you seen my baby?" It was only then that I found out that there had been a day-care center in the Murrah building. One by one, I watched the hope drain from the faces of anxious parents as I told them, "No, I was at the YMCA center." So much suffering.

My parents and husband arrived to take me home. They hugged

me and pulled immediately away, afraid they would hurt me, thinking that the blood I wore on my clothes was my own. I glanced at my watch and remarked, "Darn, I guess I won't make it to my 3:00 class today." They looked at me as though I had dropped in from another planet. Despite all that had happened, I could still think about the fifteen bonus points that had been offered for perfect attendance! (Because that was the only class day I missed, the professor deemed that I had a very good excuse and gave me the credit.)

April 19 was the easy part. In a sense, I died that day. My life has changed. I will never again be the person I was. My marriage is over. But, many changes are for the best.

I was a twenty-three-year-old who thought she was invincible. In the two seconds that it took for the bomb to go off, I learned life's too short to be unhappy and that you can't sit around and wait for things to happen—*you* have to make them happen.

My Superhero
Tom Hawthorne Jr.

$\mathcal{W}$hen I was five years old, my father took me to my first Cincinnati Reds baseball game. He told me what to watch for if I wanted to understand the game, told me some of the player's names, and, even more importantly, told me where we would sit to have a better chance at catching a homerun ball.

Dad was my ultimate hero, invincible and all-knowing. He knew just how to yell and raise his hand to summon a concessionaire at the game. He bought hot dogs and sodas, and he knew all the words to the National Anthem. After the first pitch was thrown, my father magically produced a new baseball glove for me. I don't remember much of the game, only that the Reds won, and, in the bottom of the fifth inning, Johnny Bench hit a ball high in the air. The ball just seemed to keep going. Dad gripped my wrist and brought my glove up. Then he let go and the ball went right in. This experience started a great love of baseball for me and was just one way in which my father taught me to enjoy life.

Dad would often wake us up on Saturday mornings to have breakfast on our front lawn. He would spread a blanket under our huge cottonwood tree, and Mother would serve us pancake sandwiches and juice. We would listen to the birds, and Dad would tell us what kind of birds they were. Then, after we had helped clean up, we would all have a game of tag or hide-and-go-seek. Some days we would get exhausted and lie on the grass and watch the clouds. Dad would tell us what he saw in the clouds, magically transforming cotton into silk.

**Tom Hawthorne Sr.
with grandson Dylan (*left*) and
granddaughter Hannah (*right*)**

You could see Dad's flair for life in our holidays. At Easter, we bought dozens upon dozens of eggs to decorate, often taking hours to color. After we came home from church, we would change clothes while my father hid the eggs. This was not your ordinary egg hunt! Dad relished the task of finding difficult hiding places. We would find them under the dog's food dish and in the tailpipe of the car. The eggs that were missed—and there were always a few—were left to be found by an unlucky sniffer a few weeks later.

Each holiday was different. On the Fourth of July, we had a family reunion with my mother's family. My dad shone at night, taking us to a fabulous fireworks show and then setting off on our own. He would dance along with us, sparkler in hand. On Mother's Day, he would help us make breakfast for Mom. When Halloween came around, he would help us make costumes out of old clothes and paint. Thanksgiving Day, he would have each of us make a dish and then he would rave at how good the food was. He loved to celebrate life.

The one holiday that stood out each year was Christmas. It seemed as if each Christmas got better. He would stay up most of the night on Christmas Eve, setting up trains and other toys. We would wake up well before sunrise and rush to see what Santa had brought us. Then, Dad would finally wake up, and we would open the other presents. Dad would hand them out, one at a time, and take the time to marvel at what Santa had given us. Mom and Dad never received any gifts from Santa. They got one gift from each of the children and that was all. I came to discover later that they had their own ritual on Christmas Eve. After they finished wrapping gifts and assembling toys, Dad would make them both a cup of hot eggnog, and they would exchange gifts, smile at their Christmas endeavors, and share joy.

My dad wasn't just a wonderful father, he was also a wonderful husband to my mother. They were truly best friends. They seemed like a couple of schoolkids, the way they relished life together. My father never had or needed a night out with the boys. He enjoyed being with my mother more than anyone else. He often gave her chocolate-covered cherries as a sign of his love and friendship. In a time where divorce has become a normal occurrence, my father savored his vows instead of regretting them. He reinforced our respect and honor for her also, telling us how proud we should be of her accomplishments. He taught us that a woman's place was wherever she wanted it to be, that we should hold equal regard for a homemaker and a lawyer. Even though he espoused many feminist beliefs, he also believed in the rites of chivalry. Mother never had to open a door for herself, and Dad taught us that we should always let her go through a door first as a sign of respect.

My father treated all people with respect. He told me once, "Anytime you disregard a person because of their religion, where they are from, sex, or lifestyle, you are only hurting yourself by eliminating a potential well of knowledge." He said similar things often but never included race because that was just common sense in our house.

My dad always seemed to have time for us. When we were young, he read stories to us before putting us to bed and always spoke with us about what the stories meant. There seemed to be a moral behind any and every story he read. He taught me that life isn't always fair and that we should all do the best with the cards we are dealt. I also learned from him that I shouldn't pout or complain when I didn't get all the breaks but should enjoy the challenges put before me. He never failed to have the answer to everything. On a Boy Scout fishing trip to Lake Michigan, the other men hired a boat and went on the lake in search of pike. My father knew a special reason for being there. He gathered all the boys together and bought nightcrawlers for us. He then guided us to a small fishing pier and watched with glee as we caught small perch after small perch. My dad was the hero of the day.

He was my hero every day and when it came to money, he was no different. I can't remember a single time where we shopped for clothes for him. He spent that money on clothes for us. He was only a blue-collar worker in a factory, but we never went without anything. When it was time to join the band, he was there to buy a trumpet. When I needed money for a school trip, he was there. He made a habit out of working overtime and wearing old clothes. It took me many years to realize this because he never complained. I truly believe he enjoyed going without because he knew that meant there was more money to spend on his children. That never stopped. Even after I was married and had a son of my own, he showered his grandson with love, gifts, and toys.

In recent years, I developed a great desire to give something back to my father. This desire created a dream for me of how I was going to make Dad's retirement years happy and carefree. I decided that, whenever the Reds made it to the postseason, I would buy two tickets for my father and me. We would go to Cincinnati and maybe catch another ball. My plan was to arrive at my father's house with tickets and travel arrangements in hand. That dream will never come to pass.

On the morning of April 19, 1995, a tragedy occurred and my father was caught in it. Someone blew up the Murrah Federal Building in Oklahoma City, and Dad was killed in the explosion. He was there to help a crippled, retired union worker get his Social Security

benefits started. He was there only to help someone else. He died as
he lived—giving. His death was probably a ripple in the ocean of
humanity, but it was a tidal wave to me. My hero was gone. There
would be no Reds World Series with Dad. I had thought that my
father would live forever. I lost a father, a friend, a role model. The
world lost a voice of reason. My father was a man who believed in
conservative values but also in liberal tolerances. He was my embod-
iment of all that is good and wholesome.

When planning his funeral, my mother and I both decided to say
a few words about him. We didn't discuss with each other what we
would say but ended up with similar orations. We both spoke of happiness, love, and hope. The funeral was not sad, instead it was full of
celebration. The people laughed at my mother's tales of Dad's
boyish antics and applauded at the end of each of our talks. It was a
true celebration of life. In the ceremony, I came to a revelation: I am
becoming my father, and this consoles me. I guess a good parent
never dies, they just live on in their offspring. You know, I think I'll
still go to that Reds game, and I'll still buy two tickets. My son will
need a place to sit.

God Will
Carry Me Through

Janet S. Helton

I spent the first hour of my day getting ready for a seminar that the University of Central Oklahoma's Small Business Development Center was sponsoring that morning. I went about my business making copies for the seminar. As I stood facing the south wall in our office, in front of the copier, I got the strangest feeling. This feeling told me I had to go to the training room. I did not pay much attention to it because I did not want to go to the training room and then have to return for the copies.

Once again, this same feeling came over me, only much stronger. It was a sense of panic, filled with urgency. Finally, the feeling was so strong, as if to say, "You have to go to the training room and do it now!" On any other day I would have stayed until the copier finished, but I decided to go to the training room, leaving the copier running.

While looking out a window in the training room, I looked at my watch; it was 9 A.M. Again, a sense of urgency came over me telling me to go to the front of the room and to do it now. The front portion of the room where the registration was to be held was a small room with a doorway into the hallway and an entry way from the

Janet S. Helton

smaller room into the larger training room. The training room was surrounded by windows on two sides. The "registration" room did not have any windows. As I later learned, this was one of the safest places I could have been in the building. I looked at my watch once again and thought, Maybe no one is going to show. As I walked back into the registration area, I heard two people coming up the stairs. As I processed their registration, a ceiling tile fell down, hitting me on the back of the head. Then it was as if everything stopped for a moment.

Everything moved in very slow motion. I remember debris falling from the ceiling and a sharp object hitting me on the left shoulder. At first I was not sure what it was, but I quickly figured out it was a light fixture. I knew that what happened was very serious and was not just in that room.

Immediately following this, the windows inside the training room exploded, followed by a muffled yet loud "BOOM!" I remember thinking and mentally preparing for the building to start falling down around us. My thoughts were, Okay, this is it. This is my time to die. Okay God, if this is it, let's get it over with and fast. My life was quickly flashing before my eyes.

As I concentrated on getting myself and the two other people out of the building, I was amazed at the destruction inside the *Journal Record* building. I was faced with going down a stairway with live light fixtures hanging down in front of us and though I briefly thought of what could happen if I touched them, I was determined to get us out or die trying.

Every corner I turned in the building brought more and more destruction, more and more people who were injured. The biggest shock hit me when I finally made it to the first floor and could see out what used to be the glass doors on the east side of the building. I thought I was looking at something from Bosnia or Beirut. I could not believe what I was seeing and never thought it was a bomb.

After getting outside, I began my way to Walker Stamp and Seal Company where my husband, Bob, works. I knew I was safe and felt assured he was safe, but never imagined what he would be thinking about me. Little did I know that he had gone inside the *Journal* building and through our entire office, stood at the window in our office, and looked at what was once the federal building. He had no idea where I was, what had happened to us, or that the blood he saw all over our office was not mine. We finally met up by the Southwestern Bell building, which was across the street from the *Journal Record*.

I then remembered my purse was at my desk. Ordinarily it would not have been that big of a deal. However, inside it was my glucose meter and all of my insulin supplies. Bob offered to go back inside the building to try to get it for me, but I said no. We were both out safe and I didn't want him to leave my side. We were both safe and together; that's all that mattered.

The memories of April 19, 1995, are of tragedy, loss, destruction, and tears shed by millions. However, many people remember it not only for the tragedy but also for the outpouring of love, kindness, giving, and caring.

I remember the day with a combination of sadness, loss, giving, receiving, and unity. Most of all, I will remember it as the day my life began to change forever. These changes did not happen immediately. It has taken two years for me to realize some of the changes I have gone through and am still going through. I often thought I would not stand up under a tragic event whether it be a flood, tornado, family illness, death, or accident. However, the events of that day showed me I am a stronger person than I ever thought I was.

The following days, weeks, and months were difficult. Many

days when I woke up in the morning I thought to myself, I can't do it anymore. I can't deal with this another day. The pain and numbness were so strong that many times I prayed that God would take away the pain and take me out of this world. I continued about the daily tasks of caring for my family and rebuilding our office, all the while feeling like I was carrying a thousand-pound brick.

In October following the bombing, my husband and I attended a concert at the state fair. I sat and cried through the entire concert. At one point the fans were making very loud noises, stomping their feet on the stands, making them vibrate and rumble. I nearly panicked because the rumbling stands brought back some very real memories and feelings.

I remember singing a song describing what Heaven would be like: no more pain, no more crying, and no more hurt. Only sunshine, happiness, and peace. I earnestly prayed to God at that point to take me out of this world. I longed for His promised peace and quiet, but obviously God was not ready to take me.

So many times I question why God watched over me that day and not all the other people who died. I have asked why so many times. For me personally, the why has made me a stronger and better person than ever before. Obviously the why will not be answered in this world.

I spent the year and a half following the bombing trying to hang on and all the while slowly slipping away from my family and friends. I existed but I was not living. I was slowly withering away, physically and emotionally.

After serious prayer and thought, I made a decision that would once again change my life. I quit my job, started my own business, and continue to teach at the community college part time.

People sometimes ask me if I hate those responsible for this event. I have not allowed myself to form an opinion. I have put it in God's hands. No matter what happens here in this life, justice will prevail in the very end.

I still struggle with many things related to the bombing. Each day, month, and year becomes easier and easier. However, I know I can give it to God and He will carry me through. Like so many other people who were in downtown Oklahoma City that day, I have sights and sounds burnt into my mind forever.

Fighting the Monster

Dot Hill

*A*pril 19, 1995, I was a very happy person. Life was good until 9:02 A.M.

I work for the General Services Administration as a purchasing agent. We were located on the first floor of the Murrah Federal Building. At 9:02, I had just gone to our break room to watch the first fifteen minutes of the *Live with Regis & Kathie Lee* show, one of my favorites.

Pam, from Goodwill, was cleaning our break room and walked out as I came in, asking me to leave the door propped open for her. I placed our large recycling can in front of it, turned on the television, sat down at the table, took a bite of my roll, and the next thing I knew the lights went out and I heard a loud BOOM! My body swelled, all the air was forced from my lungs, and almost immediately the ceiling started falling on top of me and dust was in the air. I thought the television had blown up, the air conditioning or something had fallen through the roof, a bomb had gone off—I was going to die.

I needed to inform Don Rogers, my boss. I opened my eyes and

Dot Hill

saw nothing but black. Dirt particles filled my eyes, nose, and mouth as I tried to breathe, making me choke. I am extremely claustrophobic and knew I would die, if not from suffocation, at least from trying to fight for air.

Just as I began to panic, Pam began screaming for someone to help her. I always thought I would be the type to panic in a dangerous situation. Maybe Pam's screaming is what saved me from panicking because I immediately called out to her that I was coming but could not see.

Finally, I reached her and grabbed her hand. We inched our way along the granite wall, tripping over debris and trying to reach the GSA's front door. We were still suffocating. You couldn't see in front of your face and had to keep your eyes closed. I was wondering if we would ever get to breathe again.

Suddenly we heard men's voices. Pam began to yell for them to come help us, and they responded that they were trying. When I felt another hand on mine, I opened my eyes to try to see who it was. Through all the "stuff" hanging in the air and getting in our noses and eyes, I saw Don Rogers. He had Bob Dennis with him and both were covered in white and black dust, almost like powder. I asked Don what happened. He didn't know but said we had to get out of the building.

When we stepped out onto the corner of Fifth and Harvey, my world fell apart. Don and I stood looking at the destruction, the smoke, the fires, hearing the popping sounds, and smelling something horrid. The whole front of the Murrah building was gone. Stuff was hanging off of it and smoke tumbled out.

Across the street, the Athenian restaurant was crumbled in and the cars in front were on fire, as well as cars in the parking lot beside it, and debris was everywhere.

I turned to Don and said, "What the hell happened here? This looks like Bosnia." Don couldn't reply. He was as shocked as I was. We just grabbed each other and hugged. For the second time that morning, I asked about the babies on the second-floor day care, and Don said they were probably all gone.

I couldn't stand it. My grandson, Tyler, used to be in that day care. I got to know the other babies when I would go play with Tyler. I visited them after he left there because I would miss him so much, and they brought comfort. Precious gifts from God, all of them. I felt terribly sick to my stomach.

By this time, sirens could be heard. A policeman came over to us, and I told him about the day care on the second floor. He turned and looked at the building with no sign of hope in his eyes. He asked how many children, and I said approximately twenty-five. He immediately got on his radio to relay the message, then turned and followed Sherman Catalon, an assistant building manager, who had started back inside where he had walked out only moments before.

It took me only a moment, and I was following. I made it to the door of the second-floor entrance, and it was blocked with chunks of cement and other debris. I looked up and saw people standing close to the edge of where the building had been torn away and became concerned about getting them out safely, too. There were other federal employees saving fellow federal employees' lives. With no hesitation they dived right in after their friends and co-workers.

To this day, I still feel that more lives would have been lost if the federal workforce hadn't gone back inside to help.

I began climbing up to help John Cresswell, our maintenance mechanic, and he told me to stop. A man placed a section of the fence from the day-care playground against the planter, using it as a ladder to get up to John. I pushed him to help him up, then followed.

John again told me to leave, that I didn't need to see this. He didn't know what I had already seen on my own. Again, I looked up at the building and saw a black man sitting close to the edge of the third or fourth floor. The man's head was bleeding profusely where his scalp had been torn, and he was looking at me with huge, dark eyes as if to say, "Well, are you going to come help me, or just stand there staring?" John told me not to worry; it was too late. I later learned his legs had been amputated by falling glass.

As I climbed down the planter, a woman came running toward the entrance of the second floor. I stopped her and told her she couldn't go in. She said her baby was inside.

I asked his name while leading her to a spot where we could sit. His name was Blake. I knew Blake. I then asked her if she prayed and she said yes. So we prayed for her baby boy, that he would be found safely. An FBI man walked up and told us we had to leave. I informed him about her baby being in the day care, and he took her away.

Later, tiredness hit me like a rock, and I just stopped where I stood and stared at the south side of the building. I encountered a co-worker who said he was concerned for his sister who worked on the ninth floor. I never knew he had a sister in the building. Funny the things we learn and how.

I headed back to the north side and on the way I stopped and thanked God for letting me live. It would be the last time for a long time that I would do that, or even talk to Him.

When I saw federal workers, firemen, or other rescue workers carry someone out of the building, I would go look at the body to see if I knew who they were. Most were unrecognizable as people, much less as individuals.

At a local motel the next day, I was stunned to see the headquarters GSA had set up. We did the best we could to keep our act together, but it was a strain. We mourned not only for the loss of dear friends but also for their families. We attended funerals, dealt with pain and suffering, and supported each other. We drew closer together as a family and as friends.

From the very day of the bombing, we all went right to work doing what a building manager's office does—taking care of others.

It became our crutch. Those who could, worked long, long days, for many months. We all carried a dark cloud overhead though: our common bond—memories, nightmares, and, the worst, guilt for being alive.

For me, depression set in and life went out the door. I could no longer sleep, eat, or function as a mother and wife, daughter, sister, or friend. Nothing mattered anymore but my need to die. That in itself added more guilt, since I felt any single family would let me trade places with their lost loved one if it were possible.

Death became my strongest desire, my only companion. I could no longer live with the guilt and the memories. It took eighteen months for me to begin getting a part of myself back, to care about my family, friends, myself. I will always carry the scars in my heart and mind, but for now, anyway, I am able to be productive again.

When the monster returns to haunt me more, I will fight harder to be victorious over it. I hope.

Unimaginable
Marla Hornberger

I work for HUD. About one minute before the bomb exploded, I picked up a travel voucher that I had been working on and walked into our administration office located in the southwest corner of the eighth floor of the Alfred P. Murrah Federal Building. I stopped in front of Freda Beene's desk to give her the voucher and was waiting to ask her a question. The next thing I knew, I had been thrown on top of something. I think it was the safe beside her desk, and I could feel glass from the window behind me going all over me. It was like being in the middle of a hurricane or a tornado with all the glass and debris hitting me. When it was over, I stood up and tried to open my eyes. The ceiling had fallen down, walls were knocked over, and wires were hanging everywhere. It was very dark from all the smoke and dust in the air. I heard Tom Ward saying that we needed to get out, and he was helping us climb over office equipment and debris. I remember looking down at the floor and realizing that you couldn't even see the floor anymore because there was so much debris everywhere. I started toward Tom, but, on the way, one of the wires hanging from the ceiling got tangled in my earring. Susan Hunt came up behind me and said, "Marla, we have to get out." I said, "I would if I could get loose." So she helped me get the wire loose, and Tom helped me climb over things. There were no doors where there had been doors, and walls were leaning over. I made it to the stairwell and started down. Most of the doors leading into the stairwell had been blown off their hinges, so all the smoke from the front of the building was pouring into the stairwell. The lower I went, the thicker it got. I had to use the handrail to feel my way down. I was

Marla Hornberger

beginning to panic because I couldn't breathe, and I thought I was going to die. I kept telling myself to breathe slower so that I wouldn't take in so much smoke. The exit onto the plaza from the stairwell is on the second floor, but, because of all the smoke and debris, I missed the exit door and got all the way to level B before I realized I had gone too far. Then I really got scared. I had to turn around and climb back to the second floor. By then, someone had the door open, and I found my way out.

Somehow, I got through the blast with only some glass in my hand, and sore throat and lungs from the smoke. I had glass in my hair and clothes but none of it cut me. For several months after the bombing, I would get little sores on my scalp, face, and legs from small pieces of glass working its way out. I still have trouble with one shoulder and both wrists.

There was an ambulance outside already and some of my friends told me to come get in, but I told them I was okay and started for the northeast corner of our building as if we were having a fire drill. As I got closer, part of my mind was registering that there was fire and smoke at the front of the building, so I turned around and started back down Robinson. It is eerie to remember that morning. I know there must have been sirens, exploding tires and gas tanks, and people crying, but I only remember silence. If a person spoke directly to me, I heard them but I didn't hear anything else. A lady who worked in the federal courthouse came up to me and asked if I needed help. I said I just needed something to drink because my throat hurt so much. She started leading me down Robinson, but we had to go several blocks before we found a building that people weren't coming out of. We went in and they got me something to drink, and I used their phone to call my husband. I realize now that I must have been in shock because when I spoke to my husband over the phone, I told him something had happened to our building. He said he knew (he had not seen a picture yet) and was I all right? I said yes, I thought I was, but I was on someone else's phone. I told him I needed to get back to work, so I would see him later, and I hung up on him. By this time, the police had set up roadblocks and wouldn't let me back up the street. About an hour later, I realized I was just wandering around downtown Oklahoma City and if they weren't going to let me go back to work, I should have Tom come get me. I went into a building, and they gave me a wet towel to wipe the blood off my hands. I called my husband and asked him to pick me up. I ended up having to walk down to the interstate to wait for him because they had the street blocked off.

I went to my doctor when I got back to Yukon, and I remember thinking that people were looking at me like I was a ghost. Of course, they had already seen the devastation on television that I was not aware of yet. As I was walking out of the doctor's office, my youngest son, Kenneth, was rushing up. He was a senior in high school, and they had turned on the television in his classroom. As soon as he saw the building, he knew that my area was no longer there. He and another boy in his class, T.J., whose father worked in the building, both jumped up at the same time and ran out to try and find out about us. Unfortunately, T.J.'s father didn't make it. My other son heard it on the radio at work and left to try and find out about me.

I didn't realize until later when I saw the front of our building on television just how lucky I had been. My desk was located right up against the north windows on the eighth floor where now there was nothing. The five employees who sat around me all died. If I had been at my desk, I would have died. So many times I have wondered what made me get up from my desk at exactly that time. I looked around and the three people who answer my phone when I am away from my desk weren't there (thank God), and I came so close to sitting back down to wait for Cathy to get back. But for once, I just left it unattended because I was only going to be gone a minute. That mundane decision saved my life.

The last year and a half have been difficult. We had all those funerals to go to. One day, there were ten funerals that I needed to attend, and you had to pick and choose; it was awful. Not only did we lose thirty-five co-workers, but there were so many people from the credit union and other agencies that we knew. No one can really imagine what that is like.

Heartache in the Heartland

Vickie Houston

*T*here was just a hint of cloud in the sky on April 19, the air smelled sweet, the birds were singing, and I had arrived early at my job at the Regency Towers. That was about the only unusual thing about that morning because I normally ran in right at 9:00. Mary and Julie had already gone down to the deli to pick up their morning Cokes, and I had poured myself my first cup of coffee for the day. We were standing in the front office deciding what our schedule for that day would be when we heard the most ungodly sound—thunder that seemed to last forever.

I was afraid to move at first. I didn't know what to think or do. The ceiling tiles above our heads started falling and wires and insulation came loose and hung over us. Not knowing what to expect next, I started to run out the patio doors. It was raining glass, so I turned to run the other way and encountered huge cracks in the walls. The girls and I ran to the phones to call 911. It was busy. I felt trapped. I was afraid that all the upper floors of the building were going to crumble around us and crush us—or worse, bury us alive! I thought I would never see my family again.

Richard, our maintenance man, came into the office and told us a car bomb had gone off. I still wasn't sure what had happened. I assumed that all of downtown was as devastated as our building, and we were surrounded by total destruction.

Two teams were set up to go into each apartment to evacuate the building. Our team, consisting of an Oklahoma City police department officer, a nurse, and myself, started searching on the sixth floor. Another team went all the way up to the twenty-fourth floor. We planned to meet on the eighteenth.

As we entered each apartment, I was amazed at the destruction. The officer advised me to check every room, even behind shower curtains. It suddenly dawned on me that our job was not just to evacuate but to find residents that were hurt, or maybe even killed.

When we got to the tenth floor, the electricity went out. The halls were so dark I couldn't see my hand in front of my face. Water pipes had broken, the floor was flooded, and "rain" from the upper floors fell on us. It seemed like we were in a tunnel. Fortunately, the police officer had a flashlight.

We had to kick in jammed doors on some of the apartments. Everything smelled like smoke and every apartment looked like a little bomb had exploded inside. Every window was broken out, cabinet and refrigerators doors swung open, and dishes were shattered all over the floor. Pictures, which had been decorating the walls, were now on the floor. Furniture had been shaken toward the centers of the rooms. In some apartments, the walls were gone!

I stopped to look out a window on the tenth floor. Until that moment, I had no idea what had happened. I couldn't believe my eyes— it looked like a war zone. The federal building, which once stood tall and proud, was now a pile of rubble lying in the middle of Fifth Street.

A voice came over the officer's radio as we inspected the sixteenth floor, "Evacuate immediately, there's another bomb!" I didn't want to die like this. I turned to the officer and told him I was too scared to go on. I wanted to leave the building. I ran down sixteen flights, afraid to use the elevator. Two police officers grabbed me at the parking garage and yelled, "Run! There's another bomb!" People cleared out for three blocks.

I sat on a curb and kept telling myself, "This must be a dream. Things like this just don't happen in Oklahoma." Helicopters circled the area so low in the sky that my ears hurt and my hair slapped my face. Ambulances lined both sides of the streets as far as the eye could see. So much had happened. I glanced at my watch; it read 10:30. I thought it must be mid-afternoon—had time stood still?

The clean, sweet-smelling air had turned dusty and smoky. The sound of birds singing was now gone, replaced by crying, sirens, and moans of agony. People walked around like zombies, hurt, bleeding, and scared. Some were getting their wounds stitched up right there on the street. At the other end of the block, people were dead and dying. Blood and glass were everywhere. Cars were burning and half of the Murrah building was laying in the street.

I decided I had enough and told Richard that I wanted to go home. That wasn't as easy as I had hoped because the FBI had taken over the Regency Tower and its parking garage. I finally got my car back after three weeks.

The Regency Tower security tape showed that the Ryder truck, which held the bomb, parked in front of the apartment building and pulled away at 8:56—just six minutes before the explosion. Richard parked his car in the spot where the truck had been. Flying sections of the Ryder vehicle destroyed it. Trash from the bomb was found inside the Regency Towers, and a tire and bumper from the Ryder truck landed on top of the building.

My life, as well as most Oklahomans', has been forever changed. On May 23, 1995, at 7:02 A.M. the remains of the Murrah building were demolished. Part of me was glad to see it go; yet another part hated to see it leave. I know the biggest part of that empty shell symbolized hatred, yet another big part of it was a symbol of the love that Oklahomans have for one another.

My Long Search
for Answers

Perla B. Howard

My husband, George Michael Howard, had been gone from our California home only eighteen days when the bomb exploded. I was at work in San Francisco's financial district when a friend called to inform me of CNN's breaking news about an explosion in Oklahoma City.

"Isn't that where George was transferred?" she asked. "Yes, but there are many federal buildings in major cities," I said. It was my first attempt at denial.

The second attempt, I see it now in hindsight, was when I packed my clothes that night for an emergency flight to Oklahoma City. I purposely did not put a black dress in the suitcase, telling myself that I wouldn't be needing one. I did, after all, because I received his body four days later and a memorial service soon followed in his hometown of Dallas, Texas.

I've long wondered what transpired between 9:02 A.M., Wednesday April 19, and 4:30 P.M., Saturday, April 22. Did he die quickly, or was he in pain for a long time? Where was he in all that rubble? How long before they found him?

George Michael Howard

The answers did not come right away. With much pain in my heart, I was forced to set aside the task of grieving over my husband's violent and untimely death, and to muster physical, mental, and emotional energies I never knew I had to fight a legal battle with my father-in-law. He sued me in Oklahoma federal court after he tried to claim the insurance proceeds and was denied.

On July 4, 1995, I decided to attend the raising of the flags from half staff to full mast at the Oklahoma State Capitol. During an hour of meditation at the open-air chapel near the bomb site, I was approached by two volunteers from a nearby church. One of the women told me that her husband was among the fist rescuers in the torn-up building. "He must have pulled out thirty bodies," she added.

"I'd like to meet your husband," I said. "Maybe your husband was the one who helped my husband. My husband's hands were folded on his chest, so his body must have been limp when recovered. Here are his pictures, maybe your husband can recognize him," I implored, showing her a sheet of eight by tens.

"I'm sorry, my husband is at home," the woman said. "He still cries because he could not save anybody. He won't be able to recognize anyone from pictures; he told me that all the faces were covered with soot.

"However, it's very possible that my husband helped your husband. I want to assure you that members of our church wrapped each body individually in a blanket and kept them in the basement of the church, and prayed over them until the medical examiner's office came to transport the bodies."

In October 1996, while staying at the home of friends in Littleton, Colorado, I started to read a book in their library. In *How We Die,* Dr. Sherwin Nuland wrote about the final moments of accident victims in very clinical but utterly humane terms.

> ... the time is probably no more than four minutes.
>
> ... there are the eyes to consider. If open, they are at first glassy and unseeing, but if resuscitation does not commence they will in four or five minutes yield up their sheen and become dulled, as the pupils dilate and forever lose their watchful light.
>
> ... the agonal phase merges into clinical death and thence into the permanence of immortality.

My healing from this emotional trauma has been long in coming. The months after the bombing have been marked by many sessions with a psychological therapist and countless pills to regulate my sleep and calm my emotions. I long for the day that I can triumphantly tell myself, "I am well now."

When that time comes, I want to revel in that I had a few good years with George M. Howard who, when I first met him in the middle of a tropical ricefield, wore his blond hair in such thick curls that I had to say, "You look like some Greek god!"

Our Faith Pulled Us Through

Bill and Melony Howell

O n January 3, 1995, at the age of twenty-six, I began working for Hogan Information Service as a computer technician. My office was on the north side of the building but I often walked to the south side to look out the windows during my breaks. I worked from midnight until 9 A.M. on the fifth floor, facing the south side of the federal building. I would often watch the children come into the Murrah building day care.

The children were my first contact since they would arrive at 7 A.M. Melany says, "He would often come home and say that he was missing his boys, since he had been watching the children at the Murrah building."

On April 19, 1995, at 2 A.M., I observed a Ryder truck drive by the Murrah building. About 5 A.M. I saw a figure standing directly below me by the dumpster on the south side of the building. The man had a white piece of paper and he kept looking from the paper to the federal building. The man did not look like a homeless person.

Between 5 and 5:30 A.M., I walked to the west side of the Water Resources building, then returned to my work. At 8:55 A.M., I started

Bill Howell with sons Peyton and Mason

to leave my office, but was stopped by Shawn Mayer, who needed help with a printer problem. I fixed the problem, but Shawn continued to talk. Shawn always talked a lot, but for once I was glad he did. Suddenly I felt a tremendous vibration through my body. I did not hear anything, but only felt the vibration. Shawn looked terrified so I said, "Let's get out of the building." I had served several tours of duty in the military, including Desert Storm, so I immediately went into my "training mode." I began helping the injured out of the *Journal Record* building.

Once outside, I noticed my car, which was parked on the north side of the building. The car had a sunroof. Shards of glass from the sunroof had been driven into the driver's seat, the back seat, and the two infant seats. If I had not been stopped by Shawn, I would have been sitting in the driver's seat and probably killed by the glass.

Returning to the building, I went into Mark Johnson's office, which is located on the south side of the building. Mark saw the flash of the bomb and his body had been thrown against the wall. He had suffered a head injury.

I continued to assist others and render first aid. "Everyone said Bill kept his cool and helped a lot of people," Melony stated. "Looking at Bill, he seems uninjured. However, he seems to be dealing with survivor's guilt," she added.

I wish I had gone over to the federal building to help with first aid. I still beat myself up for not helping more.

I've noticed that I have become more irritable with the children. The survivor's guilt seems to be leaking out even though it's been over three years now. "It was the scariest day of my life," Melony stated. "I thank God that Bill is still alive."

On April 19, 1995, Melony's sister called her from Monaco, France, where she was studying. She could not get through to Oklahoma City. The phone recording said, "The lines are down, due to a national emergency." As news of the Oklahoma City bombing reached France, people of France often cried publicly as they watched the news. "On April 19 the world had been touched by this bombing," Melony stated.

Sometimes we go to the Memorial Fence and I think about the children who died, that I use to watch arriving and playing at the federal day-care center. That's been the hardest to deal with. My wife has helped me recover. "We have become a team," Melony said. "Our faith has pulled us through."

Sparkling Blue Eyes

Miranda Ice

I hated first hour choir at school. Sometimes I would sit there and wish something would happen so I wouldn't have to go for a while. I would never want what happened to my family to happen to anyone else, yet it happened to 167 other families. April 19, 1995, changed my life forever.

Unlike others who heard or felt the bomb, I didn't. I thought it was a normal day. When I got to my second hour, the TV had been turned to the news. The newscasters were talking about a bomb that had blown up the federal building. I began to worry because my dad worked downtown. My best friend, Erin, kept reassuring me that everything was okay. I felt better until my counselor got me out of class to go to her office. I tried to page my dad, but he never returned my call.

I went back to class and about ten minutes later my counselor came back with news I didn't want to hear. She said that my mom had called and told her it was my dad's building that had exploded. I cannot describe what I felt at that moment. Feelings of total empti-ness and numbness consumed my body. I knew things would never be the same again. I felt as though in that short thirty minutes I had aged thirty years.

I went home at lunchtime that day. My mom had called the Red Cross in an effort to find my dad. My sister was already there. She had felt the bomb at her home in Oklahoma City. It seemed like days before the Red Cross called us back. Finally, late that afternoon they notified us that Dad was at St. Anthony's Hospital. I felt so relieved that there was a chance he could be alive. We immediately got in the van and drove to the hospital. When we arrived, we went to a large waiting room with the other families.

Paul Ice

There were counselors there and all kinds of food donations. We saw Dad's name on the wall under the list of survivors who had checked into the hospital. All we had to do now was locate him.

After four hours of waiting, we could not understand why they wouldn't tell us where my dad was. I was so mad that I couldn't even speak. I just didn't understand how a hospital could lose a patient. A nurse walked over to my family and told us that Paul Ice had already checked out that afternoon. They also told us that the Paul Ice who had checked out was fifty-seven years old and had a different social security number than my dad. My dad was only forty-two. I couldn't believe there were two Paul Ices! I can remember at that time all the hope I had felt was gone. I knew that I would never see my father's smile again or watch his big blue eyes sparkle. As we stood there in the waiting room, we overheard a nurse talking about someone named Priscilla upstairs in ICU. The only person named Priscilla we knew was Priscilla Salyers, who worked in the office with my dad.

My mom and sister asked the nurse if they could go upstairs and talk with her. I stayed in the waiting room for any news of my dad. When they came downstairs, Mom told me it was Priscilla from Dad's office. She told my mom that she and Dad had been talking to each other when the bomb went off. She said the last thing she saw was my dad's blue eyes. And she told my mom she didn't think my dad made it. We waited for a while longer but decided to go home and wait for the Red Cross to call us.

From that day forward we sat in front of the TV and next to the phone. For eight long days we never left the house. It was strange to see the world carrying on when our lives stopped for so long. At 4:30 A.M. on Thursday, April 27, 1995, we got the call we had been expecting and dreading. My dad's funeral was two days later.

In that one moment at 9:02 A.M. on April 19, 1995, our lives changed forever. Not a day goes by that my sister and I don't think about my dad or wonder, What if things were different? I have learned not to dwell on things that never will be. I know my dad would be proud of who Sarah and I have become, and I know he watches over us and cheers us on from Heaven. When I get really depressed or discouraged about something, I close my eyes and in my mind I can see Dad smiling at me, his blue eyes sparkling, giving me his favorite thumbs-up sign!

A Future Lost

Laura Kennedy

*S*teve and I knew Blake was special from the first day he was
born. He was such a good baby. I know people think we say
that about him now because he is gone, but he really was very good.
He was just one of those kids who was never any trouble. He was
only one month old when he started sleeping through the night, and
from then on he very seldom woke us up. He weaned himself off the
bottle. It was as if Blake knew instinctively when it was time to go on
to the next phase of development.

He was always very happy. Everyone in our family loved playing
with him and everyone made a fuss over him. He liked to play with
balls and he liked to dance to his Barney tape, "Rockin with Barney."
He was just so unique and so good, as were all the kids in the day-
care center in the Murrah building.

We put Blake in that day-care center because it was a two-hour
drive each day to and from work, and this allowed us to spend time
with him. I worked in the Murrah building so I was able to be with
Blake whenever he needed me. Blake was just getting old enough to
play outside on the playground at the day-care center and the Friday

194

Blake Kennedy

before the bombing I had watched him go down the slide for the first time. Blake just loved day care. All the kids were happy there. It's hard now because I think I shouldn't have had him there. As parents, we feel we should have known, we should have been able to protect him, but how could anyone have known it was dangerous?

We were notified on Saturday that Blake had been identified. We were told that he died instantly and did not suffer, and that knowledge brought us some comfort. The shock and numbness of those early days immediately following the bombing carried Steve and me through the funeral. We thought we were going along pretty well for a while, but slowly the shock wears off. Steve went back to work three weeks after Blake's death and that's when it really started to hit him. I was in the building when the bomb exploded and have had some physical injuries. I have chosen not to return to work but instead to allow myself time to grieve. I have also had physical problems from stress such as not being able to sleep and stomach problems. At times, it is hard to know what problems are caused from my physical injuries and what problems are from the stress of grieving.

The pain is so great. There is so much anger and so many emotions. At times it seems nothing helps and no one understands. It is so hard to meet people now who never had the opportunity to know Blake. You can describe him to people but it isn't the same as knowing him. I feel bad they never knew him. He really was a good little boy and I wish everyone in the world could have known him for a little bit of time.

Our lifestyle has changed so much since the bombing. Prior to April 19, we lived at a fast and busy pace. And now, after the bombing, it has gone on so slowly. Blake was only eighteen months old when he died and it seemed such a short eighteen months. Now it's been eighteen months since the bombing and it's been the longest eighteen months of our lives. We wish we could trade these last eighteen months for Blake's eighteen months of life. It's unbelievable how time flies.

We wish we could have spent more time with him.

Our house used to be filled with so much activity and joy. Blake was our only child and now the house is so quiet, where once it was filled with his happy chatter. He was just getting ready to start talking. We could hear him trying to form words, and now our house is silent. The quiet is so painful. It makes it so empty now that the life is gone from our home.

Blake's room is across the hall from ours, and it is still the same as he left it. I used to lie in bed and listen for him in the mornings, but very rarely would he cry. Instead, I would go in there and find him standing happily in his crib. It's so hard now to look into his room and to see his crib and his toys. It's so empty.

Christmas is so hard. It's hard to know what to do to get through it. It seems the holiday lasts so long and so much of it is for kids. There seems to be no reason to put up a tree or to wrap presents without Blake. With every birthday, with every Christmas, we wonder what he would be doing and what presents we would be giving him. We miss out on so much.

What is most painful is the future things that were lost. We face a whole lifetime of grief as we wonder what he would be doing at each birthday and each holiday. We will never see Blake off to his first day of school. Steve will never be able to play sports with Blake. We'll never see him become a daddy. You never expect to not see your child do all these things. With all the kids in the day care, there was so much potential lost.

All of us are coping the best that we can. People think you're strong if you've made it this long.

It's not that you're strong, it's just that somehow you've managed to make it. Just because family members and survivors are doing things, it doesn't mean they are strong. They are just trying to survive. It's a struggle for the rest of our lives. It's a painful journey we will walk now that our lives have been changed forever.

The Two Longest Hours

Sonja Key

———————————————————————

I went to work at the normal time, about 7:10 A.M. It was a pretty spring day. The sun was shining, but the temperature was cool.

I worked at my desk that morning and did Garry Tillotson's HUD-25 Request for Travel. We were going to Louisiana to the Coushatta Indian Housing Authority to set them up in management for their units.

Sherri Coleman and I talked about the Windows training I was scheduled to go to in Room 911 at 9 A.M. I had signed up for the wrong course, the beginner's, but we decided I should go anyway. I printed Garry's travel request before the class and took it to Marla's desk to be processed just before time to go to the training.

Jules Valdez had been bantering with me all morning—just picking. I left my desk about three or four minutes before 9:00 and walked upstairs to room 911 to the computer lab that had been set up. Sheila Shick, the trainer, asked, "Why do I have you scheduled for today and tomorrow?" I told her I wasn't sure I would be able to be here today, so I also signed up for the makeup class. I told her if she had room, I'd stay and get it out of the way. She said okay.

I sat down in the front row next to Jane Graham. I was against the north wall of room 911. Before we logged onto the computer, Sheila asked if everyone had logged off their computers before coming to class. I said, "Oh, no, I didn't." I just did Garry's travel order and I forgot. I told her I needed to run down and log off. She said, "That's okay. I'll go in and kick you out under my administrative access."

Sonja Key

I sat back down and was visiting with others as they came in. Juroy McGuirt was the last one to come in and sit down. He sat next to the south wall in the row I was in. I remember asking him if he thought he was "Mr. Astor" and could sit on that side of the room by himself. "Why, of course," he said.

The next thing I remember is a total blackout, an explosion, and being thrown to the floor on top of Jane Graham with the walls and ceilings falling down on us and the floors under us buckling. Then, I remember trying to clear my head to think, and I could hear the crumbling and crashing of the building shattering all around us. I remember thinking, It's coming this way; we have to get out. We were instantly engulfed in thick black smoke and a horrible cloud of awful dust. You couldn't see or breathe. The smell and taste were unbelievable.

I looked up and saw the twisted and mangled steel studs, heat vents, and wires from the ceiling and, through the dust and smoke, the blue sky. Again, I remember thinking, We have to get out of the building.

Sheila started yelling for everyone to get under a desk. I said, "No. We have to get out of here." I remember saying that my husband was a fireman, and we had to get to the stairs.

Robert Roddy said, "I like Sonja's idea." We began to climb out of the rubble that had fallen on us and to make our way out. Jane Graham was knocked out, and I began shaking her, saying, "Jane, Jane, you have to get up." She said she couldn't, and I said, "Yes, you can and you will. Come on and I'll help you." We made our way to an opening and out into the hallway. A door had blown sideways and was lodged in the wall and against the water fountain. Rubble was solid beneath the door. We couldn't budge the door or get under it so we decided we would have to climb over it.

Somehow we made it to the stairwell and started down. Glass and debris were everywhere. I kept telling everyone to stay together and keep coming. I have no idea how much time elapsed from the time of the explosion until we made it to the plaza-level door. I remember the door having either something against it or being jammed and yelling that if anyone was there to push. The door opened, and we began to stream outside.

We were stunned and in shock and looked around aimlessly for a minute or so. I began searching for my friends, asking if anyone had seen them come out.

I don't know how long it was before I saw Sherri Coleman, Susan Hunt, Cathy Coulter, and my other co-workers coming out of the building. Some of them were horribly injured. Carol Latimer was bleeding from the top of her head all the way into her shoes. Cathy had been wearing my sweater that day and took it off and wrapped it around Carol's head to try to stop the bleeding. It looked like Carol's ear was nearly cut off. We sat her on the curb to wait for help. I was standing by her, shaking uncontrollably from shock and cold, and she was trying to give me my sweater. I kept saying, "No, Carol, you have to keep holding it to your head, you are bleeding very badly." Calvin Moser came up then and took off his suit coat and put it on me so that Carol would keep the sweater around her head. Calvin took off his shirt for us to wrap someone else who was bleeding badly. I took off my slip for us to use on someone else.

Ann Banks was sitting on the curb with her wig on crooked and blood was streaming out from under it. I told her we were going to have to take it off to see how badly she was hurt. She took it off and laid it beside her on the curb. Her head was cut in back.

I remember Larry Cook bleeding all over and the ambulance putting him on a stretcher and me holding his hand saying, "It's going to be okay, Larry. It's going to be okay."

Ruth Heald was led out by V. Z. Lawton and Ken Altizer. You could tell she had lost one eye, maybe both. She was cut and bleeding so badly all over that it was hard to tell exactly how seriously she was hurt. After we got Ruth in an ambulance, Ken stayed with me. He could not see because his glasses were in the building. He asked me not to leave him because he couldn't see. I told him not to worry, I wouldn't leave him.

They brought Patty, from the credit union, out, and she looked hurt so badly I didn't think she would make it.

I remember Carol Latimer's sister searching frantically for her and stopping me to ask if I had seen her. I told her yes, that she was okay but had been taken to a hospital because she was hurt badly; I didn't know which hospital.

Jane Graham's daughter came up and asked if I had seen her mother. I told her she came out of the building with me and was okay, but I didn't know where she had gone.

A small Vietnamese lady came running up to Sherri Coleman and me and asked Sherri if she had seen her baby. She was nearly hysterical. Sherri told her no. She was going to go into the building, and we held her and told her she couldn't. We told her they were bringing the children out. About that time, a fireman came out carrying a little boy. Sherri asked if that was her baby. She screamed yes and broke lose and ran to him.

Carol and Sherri were taken to the hospital in the ambulance with Patti from the credit union. They had Sherri hold the little Denney girl.

Bob Chumard walked to the office supply and bought a notebook and pen so Susan Hunt and I could list everyone we knew who were out of the building so we could try to determine who was missing.

We had been on the south side of the building all this time. After we had listed everyone we could remember seeing, I said, "I'll go see if anyone came out the front of the building." I walked around the west end of the building to the front and just stopped, frozen. I walked back and only told Susan that no one came out that side.

While we were making the list, police and firemen came running through telling everyone to evacuate, that there was another bomb. We were all moved down the street to the parking lot behind the IRS building near the crystal bridge. We were all scattered so badly that we couldn't help anymore. We began looking for a phone to call home to let someone know we were okay. All the buildings downtown had been evacuated, but we finally found an attorney's office that still had employees there. They let us in to use the phone.

I called home and my son, David, answered the phone. He said, "Mom, Mom, are you okay?" I told him yes and asked if his dad was there. He told me had gone to look for me. I told him I would page him.

Harold, my husband, had been working at a construction site where he was building a house. He was on his way home to his office to use the phone when he got two pages from friends back-to-back. He tried to call them when he got home and the lines were busy. He started to make some of the calls he had come home to make, when the phone rang. It was his sister. She asked him if I was okay. He said, "I guess so, why wouldn't she be?" She said, "Oh, my God, you don't know, do you?" He said, "Don't know what?" She told him the building I worked in had exploded. He didn't know until then.

He was quickly changing clothes when the phone rang. It was Glenda Russell, one of two friends who had tried to page him. He asked her if she would go with him to look for me. She told him both of them were waiting for him, so come on.

They started downtown but the entrances were already blocked. The radio was instructing relatives to go the Red Cross office on Lincoln. He was at the Red Cross listing my information when he heard a television broadcast behind him. He turned around to look and that was the first time he saw the building. He turned back to the man taking his information and said, "She's gone. Her desk sits on the north wall, and it's gone. She couldn't have survived."

He went to Presbyterian Hospital after he left the Red Cross to check their list. He was in the chapel at the hospital when I paged him. He didn't recognize the number and would not go call because he was afraid it was a page to tell him they had found me and he needed to come identify me. Our friend, Glenda Russell, took his pager and made the call. When she realized it was me, she ran down the hall yelling, Harold, come quick, it's Sonja and she's okay. Harold came to the phone and just stood there and cried with me. I asked him to come pick up Susan and me and take us home. We agreed to walk to the post office at SW Fifth and Hudson so they could get in to get us. Ken was having Berta pick him up there.

Julie, my daughter, attended Oklahoma State University in Stillwater. She saw a group of professors standing around watching television. She asked what they were watching. They told her the federal building in Oklahoma City had been blown up. She began to cry and told them her mother worked in that building. She went to a phone and called her sister, Lynn, in Dallas, to tell her before she saw it on television. They all knew where my desk sat and from the pictures on television, none of my family expected me to be alive. If I had been at my desk that morning, this story would have been written by one of them instead of me. I am sure from the events that took place that day that I had a guardian angel that worked very hard that morning.

We checked the time on Harold's pager later that day and determined it was 11:07 A.M. when I paged him. My family told me that was the longest two hours of their lives.

A Legacy of Love

Marsha Kight

*M*any nights I stay awake until the wee hours of the morning thinking about you. A flood of memories wash over my soul. I think back to when I was carrying you, and I remember the wonder of feeling you move for the first time. I think of the autumn day you were born and the joy of finally seeing your precious face. I can still feel the warmth of that moment when I first touched you and held you in my arms.

Visions of your childhood are so vivid and clear, like photographs in my mind. I can see you take your first steps and hear you speak your first words. Holidays, birthdays, and school days form an endless stream of memories that are now both bitter and sweet. I see you with your favorite blanket that is now tattered by time and by use. A blanket that you only relinquished temporarily when you married but reclaimed once again on the day your own daughter was born.

I remember your wedding day like it was yesterday. I complained at first when you wanted to get married at home, but, sometimes, I can still see you standing in front of the fireplace as you did on that special day. You were so beautiful, radiant, and happy. I recall you laying your

Frankie Ann Merrell and her husband, Chuck

wedding dress on your bed that day and the two of us sitting there together reminiscing about your childhood, as the tears flowed down my face. You then handed me your treasured blanket, telling me to put it in a special place. Sometimes I hold it now to comfort me.

The day your daughter, Morgan, was born was the happiest day of your life and a day that I was privileged to share with you. I remember being on one side of you while your husband, Chuck, was on the other side. I will never forget looking into your eyes and seeing my little girl become a mother. Watching you hold your child wrapped in a blanket that you so cherished brought back such fond memories of the day you were born. Your passage into motherhood seemed to make you whole. You were such a wonderful mother to Morgan. It was as if you found your life's purpose in loving and nurturing your daughter. I can still see you playing with her and calling her "girlfriend." All the pictures of her displayed on your window at the credit union spoke of your love for her without saying a word. How tragic for Morgan to have lost the kind of care that so few children are given. How unfair that she doesn't have you and how unbearable at times for all of us.

April 19, 1995, at 9:02 A.M. is the moment you became a glorious angel in heaven and the moment that my life was forever changed. I remember stepping out of the shower and hearing a thunderous explosion, followed by the horror of turning on the television and seeing the building where you worked reduced to rubble. The fear, the agony of waiting, and then the knowing that you were gone—all are unthinkable even now. Those days were like being suspended in an unending nightmare from which I could not wake. The day we were finally notified that you had been found, the president and Rev. Billy Graham came for a memorial service. The message given was "let the healing begin." I had only begun to grieve. The prematurity and absurdity of such a message, as well as the political posturing, only served to widen the hole in my heart. I no longer understood anyone or anything.

Your memorial service was a celebration of your life. The music was "Circle of Life," "I Believe," and "No Man Is an Island." My husband, Tom, spoke of the last night he shared with you, as well as emphasizing the importance of saying "I love you" at every opportunity. The preacher also shared what you would have said, a celebration of your life and a powerful message to all.

How I wish I could go back in time and it be real again instead of this heartache. I would give everything, all that I have, if I could have you back again. I have never known such pain. At times, I have wanted to reach inside of myself and pull out my heart because the hurt was too great. I have known heartache, but this is one that never goes away. I will never comprehend such an act of hate. Part of me went with you that day and part of you dwells within me, moving me down a path and into an awareness that I have never known. I feel your strength within me, propelling me onward.

My life and the lives of our families were changed forever on April 19, 1995. The bomb ripped through our family, tearing at its very core. I truly believed Grandmother died a week later of a broken heart. Her saying "I die now" still echoes in my ears. We are struggling hard to survive and overcome the evil that took you away from us without it taking any more.

You knew adversity and heartache in your own life and in you these experiences produced strength, courage, and a tender heart. Pain could have made you bitter but instead it made you better and stronger. Everyone who knew you speaks of that warm smile with which you would greet them, how you would always go out of your way for others, and the ability you had for making everyone feel special. You lived your life with integrity, kindness, compassion, and goodness. These are the gifts you have left behind as a legacy to all of us. It is said that love does not die, only people do. So, while your spirit freely soars in the heavens, your love remains with us. We hold that love close to our hearts to give us comfort, just as you once clung to a special blanket not so long ago.

TREASURE LOST
H. TOM KIGHT

Dear Morgan:

This letter that I am writing to you today is for when you are older and are able to understand about life. I began this letter when you were just two and a half years old, now you are four, and yet I wonder what you really understand about what happened on April 19, 1995.

You tell Poo-Pah that your mother is an angel in heaven and that she lives in the house of angels. Yet every now and then you will say to me or to Nana, with tears in your eyes, that you want your mommy and even now you occasionally call Nana "Mommy."

Morgan, I wish I could work miracles and bring back Frankie, your mother, whom I also loved and miss very much. I promise you that you will see her someday with God and all the other angels. Know this Morgan, that your mother loved you more than anything in this world and because she brought you into this world, she still lives through you. Her love remains in you.

I now want to share with you that last night before the bombing. I had a date with you and Frankie for a pizza dinner and then the three of us went to a Walt Disney movie. We laughed a lot that last evening together, you spilling your first box of candy and Poo-Pah getting you another one. After the movie, we went back to Poo-Pah and Nana's house where your mother and I helped you work several of your favorite puzzles. You were staying the night with us, so when it came time for your mother to go home, Frankie gave us each the best gift a parent can give to a child or a child to a parent and that is a hug, a kiss on the cheek, and an "I love you."

I shared that at your mother's funeral with the other parents and asked them that tonight, when they put their children to bed, to give them a special hug, a special kiss on the cheek, and a special "I love you." And for those whose children live apart, to give them a call and tell them "I love you." I then asked all who were there at the funeral, over six hundred persons, to say a prayer that night and to remember our Frankie and all the other victims, for we are all someone's child, and Frankie could have been their child.

In the days immediately following the bombing, twice we were told your mother had been found. Each time our hopes would soar, only to be crushed when we found out it wasn't her. The first time we were told they had found Frankie, I went in to a hospital room to see if it was her and as I realized that it wasn't, I remember thinking that this was someone's Frankie, that this was someone's child.

Morgan, I wish in a way that I could keep you just as you are today. For a small child's love is the purest form of love that exists. A child's love knows no boundaries or limits; all it seeks is to love and to be loved.

You are already starting to sound like Nana. The other night when you and I were watching a Mickey Mouse tape in bed and I fell asleep, you woke me up and said, "Poo-Pah, you snore!" "You sounded just like Nana," I said.

Now to the more serious side, Morgan. As you grow up there is a little prayer I use quite often called the Serenity Prayer and it goes like this:

God grant me the serenity to accept the things I cannot change,
The courage to change the things I can,
And the wisdom to know the difference.

Also, as you grow up you must learn to deal with life on life's terms, not your's. This is not easy but it will help you understand life's journey.

Regarding the death of your mother, we are never ready to lose anyone we love or care about, but especially a child. Morgan, I lost my mother when I was a senior in college, much older than you are now. We, too, had gone out to dinner that last night, and when we got home she went to bed and I went out for the evening. I came home early the next morning to find a policeman standing in my driveway who told me the house had burned down and my mother had died in the fire. I hope because of your age you cannot feel the pain that I felt then.

Morgan, two of the greatest gifts a person can truly possess in life are love and compassion. Through this tragedy I have seen more of both than in all my fifty-six years of life. Your mother had gifts of both love and compassion in abundance in her own life, a rich legacy she has left for you as you grow.

I know how much I hurt as a husband, a father, and a Poo-Pah. Yet, I cannot even begin to feel the pain Nana feels, for as a man I will never know the special bonding of a mother who carries a child for nine months and brings it into this world. I pray that God gives Nana all the special strength to get through this.

Morgan, Poo-Pah will always be there for you in good times and bad times. You are the angel of my eye.

I love you,
Poo-Pah

Spared for a Purpose

Carol A. Latimer

I work for the Office of Native American Programs, Department of Housing and Urban Development as a financial analyst. My desk was on the eighth floor of the Alfred P. Murrah Federal Building toward the west end. I was sitting facing east.

I heard a popping sound like bullets and felt something hit the left side of my face in the ear and jaw. The force bent me over the top of my desk. I thought it was an atomic blast and that my life was over. I continued to be doubled over my desk, feeling glass and debris hitting me, but I do not remember feeling much pain. I did not loose consciousness as far as I know.

After debris quit falling and I realized I was still alive, I began clearing off the debris that had landed on top of me and heard Sherri Coleman, who was sitting in front of me, calling for help. I thought perhaps she was trapped, but by the time I cleared off the debris from on top of me, I saw Sherri coming toward me and I was glad she was not trapped. I looked up and saw lots of what I thought was smoke and so thought the building was on fire. We then saw Wanda Webster, and we all made our way first toward the southwest side of the building. All the windows were blown out and the walls were down. Everything was different as far as how we could find a way out. Sherri called out asking if anyone else was there, but we did not hear or see anyone.

We tried another route and located the doorway to the hallway leading to the southwest stairwell. As we came out into the hallway, we found Cathy Coulter coming toward us. She was wearing Sonja Key's black sweater which she took off and I held to my head since I was bleeding profusely. We all walked down the stairs. There were other

Carol A. Latimer

people in the stairwell but I do not remember who they were. They were not screaming or hysterical, but were all relatively calm. When we reached the second-floor plaza level, someone was opening the door inside the building saying he needed help and that people were trapped inside, but we walked out onto the plaza. There I saw Ivan Wisely and he assisted me to a bench on the south side of the plaza.

We were then told we had to get off the plaza and from there we were pointed to various locations. I ended up seated on the curb of Fourth and Harvey, Ivan still by my side. I was amazed that policemen and ambulances were already there. They asked all the people who were not injured to move back off the curb, so Ivan had to leave me, but by then a co-worker, Joe Chicoraske, was there beside me. A police or medical person was distributing gauze and assessing our injuries. He said I would have to wait a while to be taken to the hospital since my injuries weren't that extensive, and I told him that was fine.

I remember noticing them carrying out an infant who I did not see moving and assumed was dead. Not long after, an emergency worker said he had two seats in his vehicle, so Joe and I climbed in. There were two stretchers with women on them. They were Patti

Hall from the credit union and Arlene Blanchard from army re-cruiting. A woman brought a two-year-old girl and wanted someone to hold her so that she could go back to the building; Sherri Coleman came along to hold the child.

They took us to Southwest Medical Center. When we arrived, they directed us to examining rooms. Don Bewley was in one. Don came out and said for me to take his place because he thought I needed to be seen worse then he did. I didn't argue with him. While I was waiting, I asked Don to notify my sister, Marguerite, and let her know I was okay and at Southwest Medical Center. I believe it was around 10 A.M. by then.

Surgeon Dr. Thomas Vogel began the task of stitching my cuts. (I was in the ophthalmology room and not a regular emergency room bed.) They were working on my shoulder and I told them I did not feel well and could not hear them. I almost passed out because my blood pressure had dropped severely; they lowered the chair so I could rest for a while. When they tried to raise the chair again, it malfunctioned and would not stop going forward, almost tipping me out. Then it kept going forward and backward giving me a wild ride before it finally stopped. It took them a long time to suture all the cuts on my left shoulder, jaw, ear, head, and hand (approximately five hours). Everyone was very kind to me. My sister, brother-in-law, ex-husband and his brother were all there, I was told. They X-rayed my jaw because it was becoming very sore, but it was not broken.

Marguerite had gone to buy other clothes for me since my shoes were blood-soaked and they cut my knit top off. She did not have to pay for the shoes and jacket after she told the store the situation. She brought me home around 4:30 P.M. and stayed the night with me.

I did not know how extensive the devastation to the building was until arriving home and seeing the television pictures. I was so happy to see names of people who had called. I knew they were okay, espe-cially my carpooler, Lori McNiven, who worked for Social Security on the first floor, and Jim Cook, who was actually in the parking garage when the bomb exploded and was uninjured. I was on the phone constantly and was later told of the five people from Indian Programs that were still missing. It broke my heart that Lanny

Scroggins was one of them. When Jim Cook called me around 10 P.M. and said Lanny's wife had called to say they found him alive, I was so relieved. We learned the next day that was not true, that they had not found him.

I spent the next day and night at Marguerite and Tom's house. The day was spent mostly on the phone canceling credit cards since I had not retrieved my purse from my desk before leaving, and also talking with friends, co-workers, and relatives who called to check on me and assure me of their prayers.

My left hand began swelling and by evening it was very swollen. Marguerite and Tom were very concerned and thought we should call the doctor. The doctor subsequently called in another prescription for infection and told me to put a heating pad on it. When Dr. Vogel called the next morning to check on me, the swelling was greatly reduced.

We had a meeting of Indian Programs employees and a separate meeting for all HUD employees, both on Friday. It was so great to see and hug the survivors and so sad to hear about the thirty-five still missing. Cheryl, Lanny's wife, was there and told me they had tentatively identified his body. I had hoped he might still be found alive.

I came home and found John and Karen, my brother and sister-in-law from Texas, there to spend the weekend with me. Karen counted the number of stitches, around 126. I later learned from Dr. Vogel that I had lost between one-third and one-half of my blood supply.

My car had been parked in the underground garage adjacent to the building and it was unknown whether it was okay or not. The insurance company was ready to settle, but I asked them for a little more money since I checked on the value through the credit union. During the time the insurance company was considering more money, I received a call from a HUD worker telling me my car was okay. I got my car on April 29.

During the next week I got my purse, everything was still in my wallet except $30 which I did not mind was missing. I was just happy to have my purse and the personal items in it. Later, I also got three pictures of the boys and me that had been sitting on my desk, and a satchel that I used for a briefcase that had been sitting on the floor behind my desk. It was in perfect condition.

I am so thankful to God that he spared my life but also so sad for all those people in the building who lost their lives. Not only did we lose thirty-five HUD employees but there were eight from the Department of Agriculture, Veterinary Services, most of whom I worked with previously. I was especially heartbroken that Adele Higginbottom was one of them.

So many people—family, friends, and complete strangers—expressed their prayers on my behalf and I am grateful for their caring. I have felt the wonderful aura of all those prayers, like someone's arms surrounding me and giving me a hug. I have never experienced that before and it has been a wonderful, peaceful feeling.

Gone...
Everything
Was Gone

V. Z. Lawton

I never heard a boom, only a rush of air, then the lights went out and debris from above fell on my desk. There was an eerie feeling in the air. I wondered how I ended up on my hands and knees, covering my eyes with my hands. Something must have hit me in the back of my head and knocked me down, I told myself.

Dust from Sheetrock™ and cement and fiberglass particles floated through the air, drifting through smoke. The smoke didn't make sense—there was nothing in the building that would burn and make that much smoke. I struggled to breathe.

As the air cleared, I stood up, facing south. There was an unusual amount of light in the building. When I turned around, I found out why—the north half of the building was gone. The people who had been sitting in front of me were gone—their desks, chairs—everything was gone.

I heard a familiar voice. Ruth Heald called out, "Is anyone near me?"

"I'm here!" I replied.

"Don't leave me, I can't see!" she pleaded.

V. Z. Lawton

I found her under her desk, her face covered with a mat of blood about an eighth of an inch thick.

We heard Ken Altizer calling out, "Is there anyone else on this side of the building?"

"Ruth and I are here. She's bleeding pretty badly. Are the east stairs still there?"

Ken said the stairs were still navigable. He waited for us as I cleared a path through the desks, chairs, filing cabinets, and trash, which littered the floor.

Two metal doors separated us from the stairs. The first one was jammed. I bruised both shoulders trying to open it. Finally, we kicked the door free, squeezed through, and started downstairs. They were clear down to the fourth- or fifth-floor landing, and then they ended in a pile of rubble. A rescue worker met us. Ken and I eased Ruth over the rail to him. As soon as we climbed over, we guided Ruth through the courtyard and down the block to waiting medics.

Ken had lost his glasses and was having trouble seeing. A couple of ladies took him to call his wife, who picked him up and took him to the emergency room.

I'm not doing anybody any good just standing around filthy, dirty, and bloody. I'll go shower at the YMCA, I told myself. I walked across the courtyard again and over to the corner of Fifth and Robinson. The YMCA building, next-door neighbor to the federal building, was trashed—no shower.

I turned and glanced back at the Murrah building. It was unbelievable. I could look right up and see the desk where I'd been sitting. How did I ever get out of there alive? I wondered. I knew there had been a BIG BOMB. It looked like Mannheim, Germany, in the 1945 war zone.

Someone announced that there was another bomb. I ran and sheltered myself on the east side of the YMCA. There was no second explosion. It's time to get home, I thought. Going a round-about route, I found my car where I had parked it next to the Water Resources Board building. It was totaled.

I'll call my wife from the post office, I reasoned, and headed off again. When I got there, I found yet another destroyed building. I also found a Good Samaritan who let me use his cellular phone to call home. My wife was very concerned—it was 11:20 A.M.—almost two and a half hours after the blast. I thought it was only about 10:00. My sense of time did not come back for another week.

Some elevator servicemen, who happened to be at DeVilbiss Brake Shop, delivered me safely home at about 1:30 P.M.

Angels
and Ghosts

Eric Littlejohn

*I*f I had been in my room, I'd be dead. I was lucky that day
because usually each morning I would walk down the street
from where I was staying at the YMCA to the street in front of the
Murrah building to wave at my aunt who worked there. But that
morning everything was making me late.

I dropped my toothbrush, my hair wasn't done yet—a lot of little
things. God was telling me, "Don't go there this morning, Eric, don't
go there."

I was standing in the bathroom on the fifth floor just brushing my
teeth, when KABOOM!

I felt this tremendous rush of wind, like a tornado, and it pushed
me all the way back to the door and broke out the windows.

I saw this guy ahead of me covered with blood, and he asked me
what was going on. He went with some other people down the elevator, but I took the stairwell and walked out into the street. I looked
back toward my room because I wanted to go back and get some
clothes out, but it was on the front side of the building and that part
was destroyed.

Outside I saw glass and smoke, and I started toward the Murrah building to see if my aunt was okay. When I got there, I thought she was dead, because normally she would have been right there in front of the building where I waved to her each morning. Actually, she had gone to the back of the building at that time for something, and two days later I found out that she had been injured, but survived. They had even put a tag on her foot because they thought she was dead.

When we all got together later we talked about how our family would survive, because we are strong. But I will never be the same.

I had a bunch of cuts on my back and still have back pain, and my mind and my nerves are not the same. My nerves are shot. I can't sleep like I used to. I could not sleep for a couple of months in a row at first. I'd have night sweats, and sometimes during the day, too.

I'm trying to catch my breath all the time, because whatever they had in that bomb affected a lot of people's lungs.

I can't relax now. I've always have to be doing something. Loud sounds tense me up. I don't eat as much as I used to because I just don't have an appetite. When I need to go out to a public building, I won't go if I think I will feel trapped. And if I do go, like even to the bank, I wonder, Well, if I go, am I going to come back?

Despite all of this, I am thankful for what I do have. People in Oklahoma City are cool. A lot of them helped that day and since. And I still have a lot of love for God. It's always been that way for me. This wasn't God's fault. He helped me out, I'll tell you that.

He turned me in the right direction, put me in the right room. My sister is always telling me, "God has got something in store for you." I believe that.

The hardest thing now is when you see all this about the trial on the news. I know somebody helped those guys do it, but we'll never find out who else was involved. They're the ghosts. Why would somebody kill kids, kill people, because they're mad? I think about it when I'm by myself. Just let justice be served.

Whether or not it is though, you've got to go on. If you get stuck in life, you are going to lose it all. Be strong, because life is short. Make a difference. If anybody, all cultures, would just grab onto one another and walk together—that is what I saw on April 19. I saw bad things, too—blood running off the curbs, fingers with rings on them—but what I remember the most is that we all got together and were united. I've never seen anything like that in my life, everybody helping each other, not being selfish, not thinking of themselves.

It's the way it should be.

Thank You, Oklahoma

Sharon Littlejohn

*J*ust a small note to express my heartfelt appreciation for the kind words, thoughtful acts, and Christian love demonstrated during my recovery.

Oklahoma, you are truly special. You have touched my life, brightened so many dark days for me, and lightened my broken heart. Yes, I have bad days, but I can hold on to the love you have brought my way and find strength to endure the pain.

I will never truly understand the events surrounding April 19, but I look to verses in Proverbs which state: "Trust in the Lord with all thine heart; and lean not unto thine own understanding. In all thy ways acknowledge him, and he shall direct thy paths."

Again, thank you so much for everything. Please keep me in your prayers. God bless you and God bless the state of Oklahoma.

Respectfully,
Sharon Littlejohn

**Sharon Littlejohn
with son, Marco**

I waited patiently for the Lord: and he heard my cry. He brought me up also out of a horrible pit, out of the miry clay and set my feet upon a rock.

The Remarkable Providence of God

Sharilee Lyons

I was sitting in a computer class at the U.S. Department of Housing and Urban Development (HUD) Headquarters in Washington, D.C., on Wednesday, April 19, 1995, when our federal building in Oklahoma City was bombed. I wasn't really suppose to be there. The training was not directly related to my job, but my supervisor thought the experience would be good for me. The class was divided into two sessions of one week each. My supervisor let me pick which week to attend. I don't know why, but I chose the week of April 19. My supervisor took the first week of training. Because of my choice, I wasn't at the office on that dreadful day, and therefore lived. My supervisor was at work that day and was killed.

For some reason, my name was not on the list of class attendees at HUD Headquarters Training Academy. Friday, April 14 arrived and I had not received any travel orders to leave that following Sunday afternoon. I could not go to training without a Travel Authorization Number.

I became frustrated with the whole situation and decided to forget about going and just stay home. John, my supervisor, probably

Sharilee Lyons with co-workers (October 10, 1997)
Front row: Pat Findeiss, Stephanie Cook, Sharilee Lyons, Kathy Silovsky,
Mary Anne Weaver. Back row: Paul Staeheli, Gene Timmons

would not have had a problem with my decision. After all, the training *wasn't* essential to my job. Nevertheless, I called the Training Academy at 3:00 Friday afternoon, but they still hadn't found my name on the participant list. They said they would keep checking and call me back before 3:30, my scheduled time to go home. I never received that phone call. At 3:30, I phoned the academy once more, and although my name was never found on any list, I was instructed to go to the training anyway.

The next day, Saturday, April 15, a co-worker (Caren) and I put in eight hours of overtime at the office. We played Christian music tapes on Betsy's cassette player while we worked…Betsy was killed. We spoke to Jim McCarthy, HUD's Director of Housing, who came into the office with his family…Jim was killed. That Saturday was the last time I saw the Alfred P. Murrah Building "alive." I remember putting my Bible in my desk drawer that Saturday, locking my desk before I left, and putting the desk key in my purse. I still have that key.

On April 19, 1995, it was 10:02 A.M. in Washington, D.C., where four of us from the Oklahoma City HUD office sat in a computer class completely unaware of what was happening to our building and our co-workers. My classmate, Gene, tried to call our office to check on the daily routine of things there, but no one answered the phone. This was not normal, for we had voice mail. He then called his wife at home and she gave him the grim news of the bombing. Gene reported the news to our class, and at first we thought he was joking. I even laughed. When the news was confirmed minutes later, I felt my heart drop to the pit of my stomach. My very first thought was, Lord God, You spared my life!

Our class was excused for the rest of that day, and the four of us from Oklahoma City were escorted to the HUD Secretary's Conference Room to watch the whole horrible thing unfold before us on a big-screen television. It was a living nightmare. It was also the beginning of a nightmare that would last for days, months, and even years in all our lives.

My computer training ended that Wednesday at 10:02 eastern standard time. A group of the other women in the class took me into their care so I wouldn't have to be alone. We went to Arlington National Cemetery, and even saw the changing of the guard at the Tomb of the Unknown Soldier. It was comforting to be with someone and to sightsee a bit, but it didn't eliminate the shock and extreme turmoil I was feeling.

The Training Academy let the four of us return to Oklahoma City the next day, and we were given credit for the class. There was no way we could continue the training and concentrate after what had happened at home. I remember that last night in Washington as though it were yesterday. I turned on the TV in my hotel room to get more news about the bombing and I saw Rhonda, one of my closest friends, standing on a ledge on the seventh floor, where HUD had been located. It was a close-up view of her, and the horror I saw on her face caused me to burst into tears.

"Oh my God! That's Rhonda!" I cried. "Rhonda! Rhonda!"

Then I saw Glenda, another co-worker, standing on that same ledge. Then I saw Carole wrapped up in a blanket, sitting on the curb along Fourth Street. She, too, was my co-worker and good friend.

It was a sleepless, nerve-wracking night for me as I lay in the hotel bed crying, praying, wondering how many more of my beloved co-workers were alive...or dead.

To be so very far away from home as I was, and to hear of the massive tragedy that occurred in Oklahoma City without me there was like being on vacation and while gone, learning that my home, all my belongings, and all my family members had been destroyed. The Oklahoma City federal building *was* my home away from home, for I had worked there for over seven years. My co-workers *were* my non-blood-related brothers and sisters who I loved very much. So many of my belongings which I held close in my heart *were* in my work area, and I lost everything...everything, that is, except my Bible and my life.

God put His protective shield around me and kept me safe, so that I stayed alive.

The Lucky Ones

Vicki Madden

_I_ was typing at my computer on the first floor of the *Journal Record* building, straight across the street from where the Ryder truck was parked in front of the federal building. My chair was on plastic on the floor to help it roll more smoothly.

Suddenly, there was this loud explosion and my chair rolled back about three feet. My first reaction was to grab my ears, like when firecrackers go off. All I could see was white smoke all around. It was almost like being in a tornado, the blowing back and grabbing my ears. I was just in shock.

I jumped up and screamed out, "What is going on?" I looked around and saw ceiling panels hanging down and smoke all around. The smell reminded me of gunpowder.

My next reaction was to get out. I looked at one of my friends who was sitting there with the phone in her hand and yelled to get out. I pulled open my desk drawer to grab my purse and started looking around to see who all was still there.

One of the salespeople had just walked in front of my desk prior to the bomb to get a Coke and had asked me if I wanted one. As she

Vicki Madden

was walking down the hallway, the explosion literally picked her up and threw her to the ground.

There was yelling, screaming—pain. Yet, at this time, we didn't know what was going on. I actually thought maybe something had blown up downstairs. This was a very old building, after all. It had the old water cooling system, and I didn't know if something down in the basement, maybe one of our presses, had a problem or something. I really thought at that point it was something related to our building only.

I saw people I had worked with for years who were severely cut and bleeding. On the way out we climbed over some debris that had fallen into the stairwell and walked out onto Sixth Street. There were ambulances; fire trucks; people running down the road, their clothes in tatters. I still didn't know what was going on.

My next thought was about my friend Nancy who was pregnant with twins. She always got to work at 9 A.M. and I wondered, Where's Nancy? I was pacing back and forth across the street on the sidewalk, talking to people and still trying to find out what had happened.

I saw Nancy running down the sidewalk, and we went around checking on people who worked with us and who were really hurt.

Suddenly, the police started running down the street and yelled for us to run north, saying, "They think there's another bomb!" That's when it hit.

We said, "Bomb?" They said, "Yes, the federal building has been bombed." A bomb? That was the last thing on my mind.

I thought, The federal building? I do printing for those people. I know people in the Federal Employees Credit Union. I debated whether to look in that direction, but I had to see if this was right.

I walked down the street where I could see around our building and that's when I saw the federal building. I looked one time, and I looked away; I couldn't look again. I couldn't believe all this was happening.

I was able to contact my husband and parents and get word to my eight-year-old daughter that I was okay. The next day, some of us from work got passes from the FBI to go back into the building to get personal items, and it was shocking to see all the debris. I didn't remember it being like that because my main focus was to just get out. You forget a lot of things when you're in a panic like that. To have to take a hard hat, flashlight, and gloves to get into the building where you've worked the past six to seven years is very strange.

It took a long time to let this filter through me. Shock really helps you with self-preservation. It took me a long time to really break down because I thought, Here I am, a mother; I'm supposed to be strong. It just took so long to accept, even though I knew it had happened and was real; it was as if I wasn't allowing it to sink in.

When I think of the victims, I think of the people who lost loved ones, or friends who were directly hurt because I was more fortunate than that. There were people who lost their kids, grandkids, and their wives or husbands, and they are the ones who are truly the victims. I was one of the luckier ones.

You never know how long you'll have your life. You read the news, and you hear about people being killed. All those years I worked in that building, that would be the last thing on my mind.

I am more cautious now, and I try to be aware of what's going on around me. I'm more apprehensive about things, yet I try not to be paranoid every day of my life. It's made me more appreciative of things. You just never know.

You hear someone say "Life is short," but now when I hear it, I hear it differently because now it's real.

The worst part of all of this is just knowing all those innocent people lost their lives that day. They were going about their normal routines, the children were playing, and they had no idea of what was to come. People lost their lives, which is the ultimate terrible situation. There are also people who lost jobs. There are people who have really had some problems getting through this.

As for me, I don't want people to look at me as a survivor, like, "Poor Vicki," because I was fortunate enough to have been spared. I have my life, and I have all of me. My daughter still has a mother. My husband still has a wife. God was watching over me that day.

I'm very, very fortunate.

In Memory of Our Loving Daughter

Vickie Mathes

Through the years of her growing up, she never met a stranger. In her early days she was always fascinated by different people.

She touched so many with her kisses and hugs. She put everyone in happier spirits than they were before they met her. We had taught her to respect her elders, and to help those in need, for you never know when you may need help yourself. She learned this lesson well, for she never refused to help someone in need along her way.

She had many hobbies that she enjoyed: rollerblading, skating, sewing, and crafts. She was a cheerleader in school and a trainer. She taught aerobics, and managed a clothing store and a tanning salon. She would help decorate other peoples' homes for Christmas. She was a teller in the Federal Employees Credit Union in Oklahoma City.

Our daughter was our world. She lost her brother at the age of two. His name was James Robert Mathes. I could have only two children. They were very close and loving children.

When we heard of the bombing of the federal building, we hoped that maybe she didn't go to work that day, but she did. We had

Tresia Jo Mathes-Worton

talked the night before, prior to my leaving for work. She was so happy. She had three days left before moving back home. She was to get married in July to Travis Jobe of Big Springs, Texas.

It wasn't long before we were in Oklahoma City. We stayed at her apartment. We gathered at the church with everyone who lost someone. Hopes and prayers were in the air. It seemed like one big family as we talked, held, and helped each other. We had more family coming in to stay with us.

Losing Tresia was so bad that the world around us almost came to an end. She was Daddy's girl. Where Dad went, she went along. Dad lost his girl, his fishing partner, and his best friend.

As for me, Tresia's mom, I lost a daughter and a friend I could talk to. She loved to shop, and there were times that we would shop and visit with friends all day. She had one girlfriend who was jealous of our friendship of mother and daughter. She told me this since we lost our daughter. She wished that her mother and she could have the love and understanding that Tresia and I had.

Some people really don't know what they have until they lose it. Parents, love your children, and children, love your parents, because when they are gone, you can't bring them back. You just have memories, and I hope and pray they are good ones. God gave us a gift and He can take them away, but God has them in His care.

Our family is still having a tough time. Dad and I keep working, and keeping busy in order to fill each day. They say time will heal all wounds, but it doesn't kill the pain. When the day is over, you want the phone to ring and to hear "Hi, Mom" or "Hi, Dad" in reply to your answer, but it doesn't happen. It's sad when you don't hear your child's voice anymore.

She was home the week before Easter that year. We went apartment hunting. We hid Easter eggs for the kids at church on Easter Sunday, before she left for home. We had lots of fun. The neighbors had a big rabbit, and she played with it and with the kids. It wasn't long before she had to leave to go back to Oklahoma City.

To us nothing will ever be the same. Our loss is God's gain. We know they're in good hands, but will always be missed.

There Is Still Good

Brenda Maxey

—————

"Hi, Mom," I said, calling home to check on the kids before they went to preschool.

"Good morning!"

"Are the kids up and getting ready for preschool?"

"Yes, slowly but surely."

BOOM!!! WHOOSH!!! RUMBLE!!!

I still get chills when I recall the sounds. I've had auditory flashbacks that put me in tears.

I was sitting at my desk at the Oklahoma Water Resources Board. Before the bomb, I could barely see through the dark windows of the federal building directly across Fifth Street to watch the children playing in the day-care center. On April 19, I was not watching the children. I had my back to the half-wall-size window in my office. At 9:02 A.M., I thought I was dead. Something had hit my head with great force. No, wait, I was alive. I put the phone back up to my ear to ask my mother for help. Nothing. What happened? Where is that black smoke coming from? What was that rumbling sound? Where did this four feet of rubble come from? Where is the door? Wasn't there a wall here? There's Paul Ricciotti.

"Paul! Get me out of here! Get me out of here! Get me out of here!"

I was white-knuckling his jacket. My hand had been cut and was bleeding so badly that when he got home, he thought he must have been injured, but it was my blood that had soaked through his jacket and shirt.

We went down the fire escape on the north side of the building. A man came running, shouting, "There's another bomb! Run!" I ran north as far

Brenda Maxey

as I could (a couple of blocks), glass crackling under my feet, one foot bare because I had lost a shoe when my foot slipped down through the rubble in the building. I was freezing. Blood was spurting from my head and my hand. A fireman told me to sit down. He wrapped me in a huge blanket, but it didn't help. Just then, a silver Lincoln pulled up, going the wrong way on the one-way street. The driver asked the fireman how he could help. The fireman responded that he could take me and several other people near me to the hospital. He frantically loaded me and three other people into the car and drove quickly to St. Anthony's Hospital. On the way, another passenger told me it was a bomb at the federal building. Why?

As I got out, I noticed I had bled all over the leather back seat. As they were wheeling me into the hospital, I met eyes with the driver and mouthed the words, "Thank you." I never thought I would see him again.

In the hospital, the doctor pulled a piece of glass the size of a slice of bacon out of my head.

After the doctor finished my head and hand, he thought I could go home. As I was getting up, I felt very sick to my stomach. The doctor decided to check me in overnight for observation. When he came to check on me the next morning, all my spinal fluid had leaked out onto my pillow. A CAT scan revealed that the inner portion of my skull had been shattered. I needed surgery.

Friday, another doctor removed a portion of my skull and a blood clot on my brain and put three metal plates in my head. (No, they don't set off metal detectors.) Sunday, I was ready to go home. As we were driving home, the back of the Blazer loaded with flowers, I noticed that everyone had their headlights on. It was amazing. It was the middle of the day and everyone had their lights on. My husband told me it was to honor the victims. I cried.

Today, after at least fifty doctor appointments for my head, hand, jaw, and back, and, of course, my psychologist, I can think about it and not cry. I still hurt daily, both emotionally and physically, but I am learning to cope.

A year after the bombing, I was at a memorial service and found out that the man in the silver Lincoln was an attorney. I called the bar association, and they instantly knew who it was, David Donchin. I had been searching for this man for a year. I couldn't believe it was all finally coming together. I called his office to talk to him, but I hung up because I started crying. I wanted to be strong. A week later, I mustered up the strength to call him again. At lunch, we talked forever. He was so humble. "Anyone would have done it," he said. But it was you, David. I will never be able to thank you enough.

I think of the precious future I have with my five- and seven-year-old boys, and I try to be positive. There is still good in the world, you know. You just have to look harder for it.

I Go On

Melissa McCulley

$\mathcal{W}$ednesday, April 19, 1995, was a day that started out like any other day. I was twenty years old, working for the General Services Administration, which was located on the first-floor northwest end of the Alfred P. Murrah Federal Building, and a junior attending full-time at the University of Central Oklahoma. I was working so hard to not only get my Bachelor's of Business Administration, but to finish in four years. I could finally see the light at the end of the tunnel. In less than one month, I would finally be a senior. Life was going well, then in only a few seconds, my life would change drastically.

I arrived at work bright and early that morning. I had been working on various projects trying to finish them up. A few minutes prior to 9 A.M., I received a phone call from one of the guys out in the field. He was requesting some supplies. I told him I would get them out to him today. I then proceeded down the hall to our break room where we kept our supplies. I gathered all the items requested except for one which we were out of. As I headed back to the office, I stopped at the front desk.

There I grabbed a piece of paper to write him a note to tell him what we were out of, and that I would send it to him just as soon as we got it in. Then all of a sudden everything went black. I felt an enormous amount of pressure, like I was being sucked down in the ground. I didn't know what was happening. I didn't even know if it was real or if I had blacked out.

Then it was over. Everything stopped and it was pitch-black and I was buried. I tried to get out but could not budge the debris. I began to panic and yell for help.

There was no response. At first I thought it had only happened to me, and that surely someone would help me. I waited a few more minutes. I was really beginning to panic. Okay, calm down, I told myself. You're alive.

Once again I began to try to move the debris. Finally, I was able to move enough to create a small hole and pull myself out. I could now see light where offices once stood. My first reaction was to get up and run, but I couldn't. My left leg would not move and the pain was severe. I tried again but I could not walk, and debris was piled too high to crawl over. I sat down on a pile of rubble and decided that I would have to wait. No one was in sight. I remember that when I first freed myself I could hear some of my co-workers' voices, but they were now gone.

I felt alone. Then I remembered Pam Briggs, a co-worker who was sitting at the station directly next to where I had been sitting. I yelled her name and she responded.

I think I next asked her if she was okay. A few minutes passed and then I saw Pam crawling over a pile of debris. She had managed to crawl out from under a pile and came to where I was sitting. Scared, we waited together for someone to help us.

We then heard a man's voice asking if anyone was there. I yelled, "Yes, there are two of us." He asked if we were okay. I said, "Yes, but I can't walk." He said to hang on, they would be there in a minute. He was a firefighter, but I could not see him. After a few minutes we heard the sound of rustling debris, then two firefighters and a policeman appeared. The policeman, who I later found out was Terry Yeakey, assisted me. He asked me how to get to the day care. I told him it was down the hall and up the stairs. He then put my arm around his shoulder to assist me out of the building. One of the fire-fighters assisted Pam and they followed behind us. The debris was so high and the pain so intense that I couldn't walk out even with Officer Yeakey's help. He then told me to grab hold of his neck from behind. He carried me out piggyback, while he moved and climbed debris as we went.

We were now at an opening of the building were once stood an office. There, two firefighters took me to the northwest corner of the building where they laid me down on the street. I never turned around to look at the building. I wasn't sure of what the building looked like until later that day.

As I lay in the street, two of my co-workers, Kathy Brady and Dot Hill, came to see if I was okay. I think it was at this time I felt extreme panic. I think I was crying, and I remember being so cold. I begged them to put my leg down because it hurt so bad. They told me that they should not move it, but did not tell me why. Later, I found out that I had a large gash right below my left knee. I was told that my knee cap was exposed, but I didn't see it for days later, when they took the bandage off. Come to find out that wasn't even what was causing the pain.

I next remember a stranger asking if he could call someone for me. All my family lived out of state. I said, "Yes, please call my boyfriend." Mike would know how to reach my parents. Whether or not that person called, I will never know.

After several minutes I was loaded on a stretcher and moved to where triage was set up to wait for an ambulance. The day was get-ting colder. I was given a blanket, and a splint was placed on my leg. I lay there and stared into the sky and waited and watched people pass back and forth frantically in front of me. I am not sure how long I lay there, but it seemed like an eternity.

I was loaded into an ambulance along with another woman. We were transported to Southwest Medical Center. As they took us into the hospital, I remember rows of people lined up staring at us. I did not know why. At the hospital they began to examine me and hooked me up to machines to run tests. I asked one of the nurses to call my boyfriend. She did but could not reach him. I did not know where he was. I did not think he knew what had happened. I then asked her to call my dad who lived in Houston. She told me that they could not do that right now.

Once I was told that I was going to be transported down the hall to have X-rays taken.

Once I was there I asked another hospital employee to call my dad. She said that she would and I heard her explaining to my dad where I was and that she thought I would be fine. She then handed me the phone. I began to cry as I talked to my dad, and it sounded as if he were crying, too. He asked me if I was all right. I was surprised that he knew what had happened. He told me that they had turned on CNN and it was plastered all over the networks. He then told me Mike had gone to look for me, and that he would try to reach him to let him know where I had been taken. Then he said, "I am on my way and I will be there this afternoon."

After hanging up, my dad tried to reach my mother who lived in Missouri. He was able to reach my grandmother who said that they had heard the news and that my mother was on her way to Oklahoma City. Two hours after Mom had left Missouri, she stopped to call my grandmother, who told her where I was and that I was okay.

The doctor returned and told me that my hip was dislocated. He said, "We are taking you to surgery to put your hip back into place and repair your knee." After surgery they transported me to my room. I was dazed and confused. When I got to my room a friend of my mother's was waiting. She knew that I did not have family here. She had come so that I would not be alone.

Mike and his mother arrived at the hospital. He had gone downtown to look for me, so no one was able to reach him. He finally called his office and they gave him the message that I had been taken to Southwest Medical Center.

I lay in the hospital room glued to the TV. I was shocked at what I saw. It was the first time that I had seen the building. It did not seem real.

Late that evening, I was able to reach a co-worker, Joanne. I wanted to know the status of everyone I worked with. She proceeded to tell me there were some in intensive care. She then told me no one had heard from Mike or Steve.

The next day I was released from the hospital. Luckily, besides the dislocated hip and the staples in my knee, the extent of my injuries were minor cuts and bruises.

Over the next few days, I remained glued to the television and awaited word of Mike and Steve. They had been killed. It was a horrible feeling, but at least the not knowing was over. That meant that the hope was as well.

I decided that I needed to go on with my life. My teachers all worked with me so that I could complete the semester. For me, it was important that I go on so that whoever was responsible for this horrible act did not take more. After a couple of weeks I returned to work. It was so different. It would never be the same.

Whoever did this took so much. They took my security, my friends, and life as I knew it.

I am still working for the GSA. I graduated from college in four years. Though I have managed to go on, there is not a day that goes by that I don't think of April 19 and those we lost.

Shattered Glass, Shattered Lives

Doris Morava

---

eavy feelings and dark imaginings of impending doom had haunted me for months. I felt as if I were being warned that something terrible was going to happen. I felt the urge to flee, but how could I have known what the future was going to hold? Yet, on the morning of April 19, 1995, these thoughts were far from me. It started routinely, as so many days before it. The sky that morning was a brilliant blue, and the sun was shining, heralding a beautiful spring day. Bill asked me if I would like for him to draw back the heavy drapes in our living room window to allow in the warmth of the morning. For reasons that I still don't completely comprehend, I strongly resisted, and insisted that the drapes remain closed. We live in the Regency Towers, and from our window we could see the Alfred P. Murrah Federal Building.

Bill was getting ready to leave, but I couldn't shake the feeling that I shouldn't let him go, so in my hesitancy, I asked him to pick up a few things at the store for me. His route that morning would have taken him right past the federal building. It was 9 A.M. I went to my purse for some money, and as I was about to pass it to Bill, my hand poised in midair, what seemed like a mighty gush of wind blew in the windows. The money disappeared from my hand, some to be found later in odd places, some to never be seen again. An unseen force scattered glass everywhere. Thick black smoke filled the room and made it difficult to see and breathe. We thought it was a tornado, but how could that be when the sky was so clear? In my hysteria, I ran frantically around the apartment, oblivious to the glass that was shredding my bare feet. Bill

Doris Morava

tried to calm me, and he, too, had a shard of glass penetrate his foot through a slipper.

The destruction happened without warning and ended as suddenly as it began. I recall seeing the drapes blown straight forward, and in only a few moments they seemed to crawl back to their original place. Our home was filled with many beautiful but also heavy antiques, many of which could have proved deadly if they had fallen on us. I believe leaving the drapes closed that morning may have saved our lives.

Still not knowing what had happened, Bill looked out the bedroom window that faces the federal building. He could see nothing but a thick black spiral of smoke swirling toward the sky. A neighbor began breaking our door down, and we were told to leave, as it was feared our building could collapse. Out on the street, we saw police on horseback, rescue crews, firetrucks, and so much glass. The street was now a sea of glass. We were told there was now another bomb threat, though we were unaware that it was a bomb in the first place. To this day, neither of us can recall hearing the explosion. From there, Bill and I were taken to a bakery, and then I was later transported to St. Anthony's Hospital, my feet covered in blood from all the glass.

Bill Selanden

We lost our home that day, and spent the next seven months at a motel. As time went on, we learned we lost far more in the blast. There were the physical injuries, of course, but it is the emotional and mental scars that seem to have no end. I started having nightmares, screaming for help in the dark but waking with no memory of the terror. Noises that were once common-place now fill me with horror. My nerves are on edge all of the time. Bill is extremely nervous and fearful. We wonder if life will ever be normal again. People say we should get over this and get on with our lives, but how does one move on from a never-ending nightmare?

After seven long months in a motel, we were finally able to return to our home in the Regency Towers. One of the first nights we were back, Bill was restless and unable to sleep. He kept asking me if I heard "them"? I listened closely, but heard nothing. He said, "Can't you hear the people? They're groaning, crying, and screaming for help." It wasn't long before I heard it, too.

Many people in the building reported hearing such tormenting sounds. They say it was the wind through the windows.

We lost many treasured possessions in the bombing. Beautiful antiques shattered and splintered, but our lives shattered in ways far worse. I can no longer leave my home nor do I desire to leave. My memory has been greatly affected, both short term and long term. Much of April 19 is still hidden in the recesses of my mind, yet to be recalled. We both live in great fear of the present and the future. If it happened here, we fear it could happen anywhere. Everything requires efforts of heroic proportions. I used to be very active, now simply walking is a monumental task. My doctors say I will recover, but I wonder when that will be. The bombing of the Murrah building robbed us of our safety, our security, our way of life, and we will never be able to forget the horror and devastation of April 19, 1995.

We Who Remain Will Carry the Hope

Calvin C. Moser

*G*ray, windy, blustery fall day. One year, six months, and twenty-eight days have passed as I write, though the events of April 19, 1995, are vivid in my mind.

I awoke to the jabbering of the radio announcer. I hit the snooze button and lay still for a few more minutes. The jabbering returned, so reluctantly, I got up and started my normal routine. The drive to work was uneventful. It was a nice day with not a cloud in the sky as the sun crested the east horizon with bright yellow orange and light to deep blue the higher I looked.

I parked in my usual place and walked the block or so to work, cutting across streets through the parking lots up the alley behind the post office and across the street, down to the corner of the Water Resources building. As I diagonally crossed Fifth Street, the sun was shining bright and I felt a light, brisk breeze. A clean aroma filled the air. I thought how much I would like to be sitting on a lake or pond bank fishing and enjoying the waking of nature in the woods.

My thoughts quickly switched to the bright yellow Miata as it

Calvin C. Moser

turned east onto Fifth Street. I reached the Murrah building entry as the car pulled into the first parking space next to the front of the Athenian restaurant. A short elevator ride, through the office door, down the hall and aisle. I could hear Jules Valdez in his area as I passed his work station.

Seven o'clock or so and another workday was underway. As I started working on some correspondence, I looked out the north glass wall. Looking down I could see the bright Miata; it was a pretty day.

My wife, Ginny, had given me the hot potato salad recipe that morning which JoAnn Whittenberg had asked for, so there it was in my briefcase. Knowing JoAnn got in early, I headed off to give it to her. Every time I saw her for the past two weeks, she would give me that look, "I know you forgot again." Without a word, I knew what she was saying. Now I went to the seventh floor and to her desk. I found JoAnn typing. "Here, you see I did remember! By the way, this is a very special recipe as it came from Ginny's grandmother." JoAnn said she was glad to get it and, "You give Ginny a big hug for me and a special thanks. I hope I can make it half as good as Ginny does."

Back to the eighth floor and to my desk. The office was filling as from my back corner I heard greetings and normal office conversation. Another day and lots to do. About 8:30 the phone rang. The voice stated, "Moser, I'm starving!" My buddy Dave Walker was here. I relayed that I was working and would be ready in about thirty minutes or so. "Moser, you're never that busy. Let's go!" I responded that I was busy and would be ready in a few minutes. "I'm going around the corner and I'll be at the elevator in ten minutes, so meet you there and don't get on the phone!" "Okay, Dave, see you there."

Down to "B" level and across to the federal court building snack bar. Greeting to the federal guards. Through the metal detector and into the snack bar. Dave ordered. I got my hot tea. We sat down along the south wall, second table. Several patrons were in and out. Dave ate and I got a refill. Ted Allen came in, got some coffee, and came over to the table. We offered a seat. He said he needed to get back right away; had to get ready for some meeting.

Dave said that Lil Perry had called last night and had some concerns about environmental things. We talked about her concerns, then the conversation turned. Dave said he had something he wanted to show me. We headed back to the office arriving at the eighth floor. I said, "Oh, I should have stopped at the credit union and cashed this check. Oh well, I'll do it later." Dave said, "Yeah, I want to show you the boat light Janet got for me. It's a really good one."

Arriving at Dave's desk there was the box with the light. Dave said Janet got it on a clearance aisle somewhere. I told him to call her and ask if they had another one. Dave called, then getting off the phone said, "Well, you're out of luck. This was the last one." I picked up the light and as I stepped away, I declared, "Don't worry, I'll keep this one for you and you can borrow it anytime you need." Dave was quick to reply, "Moser, put that down!" As I did he said, "What are we going to do for lunch?" "Come on, Dave, you just finished breakfast. We'll figure that out later. See you." And off to my corner I went, passing Lanny Scroggins, Don Burns, George Howard, David Burkett, Cathy Coulter, Carol Latimer, Joe Chicoraske, and Ann Banks. Arriving at my desk, I picked up the phone and called Ginny at work. She wanted to know why I was calling early. It was only 9 A.M. and I usually called her at 9:30. I told her that Dave was hungry and we had gone to break early. "Just wanted to say hi, talk to you later, and I love you. Bye." I hung up the phone and sitting in my chair, I turned from the desk and rolled to face west and my computer.

A flash, bright bright, like an ark weld flash with deep blue around the white flash. This white flash also had something blue in it. Then a crack like a shot from a rifle or a firecracker. High pitch, not a low-pitch crack. I felt the force against my body. My eyes closed at the sight of the flash. I felt dirt or something in the corner of my eyes; it felt like sand or grit. A loud deep roll like loud, loud thunder is all I could hear. I was on the floor and things were on top of me. What the heck was that? Something blew! The glass was out of our building. It was all over the place.

I got to my feet pushing debris off my back and head. I looked east. Ceiling tile, wire, flex duct, and a thick, choking gray-brown dust was in the air. Breathing was hard. I couldn't see very far east in the building, too much in the air. I looked out north where just moments before everything was tranquil, a beautiful bright clear-blue-sky spring day.

My mind was racing. What happened? I thought a gas line behind the Athenian restaurant where a service tap had been may have blown. No, that part of the building was intact but the front southeast top corner was gone. Why was that part of the building gone? The corner broke off like breaking the corner of a brick and it was all on top of that cute little yellow Miata. It was buried under the brick with only the back end driver's side showing. Maybe it had been a car bomb in the parking lot. A van, yes, a van was on fire—maybe that was the cause. Why and where did the huge concrete blocks, about 2 ft. by 4 ft. by 8 ft., come from?

I hit the metal vertical framing which just moments before was holding the glass window. The frame seemed to be secure. I grabbed hold with my left arm and leaned as far out of the building as I could. Then I saw! Then I began to realize how much devastation had just occurred in the split seconds prior. I heard not a sound, no one on the streets, just brick and concrete chunks, no paper. Then I felt a rush of air coming out behind me, out of the building, and papers began to fill the air and float down to the street. Smoke from the parking lots began to fill the air. Black, thick, choking smoke. It looked as if most of the center of the building was gone. Just a few feet east and from there on the floors and all else was gone to the east wall. A concrete beam was laying on the street. A big gray pile was on the street and where the building once stood. I thought, What has happened? Who is left? Who is hurt? Can I help? Does someone need my help?

❀   ❀   ❀

Yes, it's a gray, windy day. Grandma was ninety-six this October 1996. It was a nice funeral for her yesterday. Funerals, tears, hugs, meeting, memorial committees, counseling, hopes. Yes, life goes on and emotions like a roller coaster still roll. The memorial will be. We who remain will carry the hope.

A Letter to God's Angels

Ginny Moser

Dearest Little Ones,

I do not know you except for April 19, 1995. At 9:02 A.M. you became angels. I did not want you to become angels. I wanted to keep you here with your families. When I walked up to the south side of the Murrah building onto the plaza with blankets and first aid supplies, I did not know I would meet God's angels. Four tiny, broken, bloodied bodies wrapped in sheets and blankets, gently placed on two park benches. And all I could do was gently pat each of you as though I were patting you to sleep like a restless, sleepless baby and say, "It's okay, sweet baby, it's okay." I knew it was not okay, but usually Mom can make it better, but that day I could not make it better.

Then I saw you, sweet little baby boy. When the firemen brought you out on a stretcher you were hurt real bad. We tried to save you and I remember the doctor saying, "It's too late," and yet we did not want to give up. Someone yelled for another doctor, a second opinion. There was no time for second opinions that day, yet another doctor working next to you came to check you, too. The answer was the same, "Too late, he's gone." Every time I close my eyes, I see this little boy with his big brown eyes. Yet, they were not full of life, but full of death. Desperately trying to breathe. No, that was me willing you to breathe. There was no air for you to breathe, only blood in your mouth and in your nostrils and running down your face. No air to breathe in your lungs, only a hole blown through you where lungs for air should have been.

All there was, was a hole filled with blood covering your lifeless body. We covered you

Ginny Moser

with sheets and wrapped blankets around you. The doctor asked me if you had shoes on. My reply was no. Your little foot was tagged, and I touched you one last time and said, "It's okay, sweet baby, it's okay." Another one of God's angels left us. No time to grieve or think or cry. I remember thinking to myself when I saw you, how could anyone do this to another human being?

I remember you because you were older than the other babies and I wondered if perhaps you were in kindergarten or first grade.

No time to think or let my mind wonder, here comes another body. A young lady, probably a day-care worker or young mom leaving her child at the center. A pretty, young black lady with her eyes wide open and part of her face and head blown away. I tried to be strong and lift her off the stretcher with another worker, but she was so heavy, although not a very big person.

Someone had to help us remove her from the stretcher unto a blanket. I was drained of energy and working like someone or something had taken over my body. Was this crazy? Yet, it had to be done.

The firefighters, the police, and everyone worked so hard, and there was nothing I could do to save anyone. Check vital signs, check if body is intact. Do they have shoes on? Shoes? Most of them did not have feet or arms or part of their heads. An ear gone, an eye gashed out, and all I could do was check to see if they had shoes on so they could be tagged for identification later.

John Doe, Jane Doe, Baby Boy, or Baby Girl? Helpless is how I felt. Worthless is how I feel.

Dearest little ones, it still hurts so bad and I feel connected to each one of you. Everyone who was murdered that day was someone's baby, no matter what their age. Angels were there April 19, 1995, to take you home, and all I could do was pat you and say, "It's okay, sweet baby, it's okay."

It has been three years since that terrible day and I still cannot say goodbye. I still want to make it all better. My husband, Calvin, survived the bombing that day, and is still recovering from his injuries, mainly a broken heart. The cuts and bruises have healed, the hearing he lost is irreversible, yet we know how lucky he was to survive at all. His office was on the eighth floor, north side of the building. No one knows how he lived through this. People say there is a reason he lived. Who can determine who will live and who will die?

I still have nightmares, and can barely make it through a day without crying. The sight of a Ryder truck sends shivers through me, and I often have to pull off the road if I am driving. My grief is different than those whose loved ones died. Yet it is no greater or less. You cannot compare grief. I am still mad at God. I know He did not cause the bombing, yet I know He could have stopped it. I am trying to work through this as best as I can. Sometimes it makes me mad when people tell me to put it behind me, and go on with my life. Don't they know that is what I am trying to do? I know I cannot change what happened that day, and I am trying to live my life as best as I can. Loud noises and sirens startle me and I often have flashbacks to that day.

The holiday season is fast approaching. I am thankful for my husband and my children, yet I am also very sad. Sometimes I go downtown to the fence surrounding the site of the Murrah building and I cry. I then read the notes that people have left on the fence and look at the flowers and stuffed animals and T-shirts others have brought. It makes me feel somewhat better to know that people remember. I don't want anyone to forget what happened that day. I don't think we can totally heal. We cannot allow this to happen again!

The Unforgettable Day

Laura Ann Oak

*A*pril 19, 1995, started out like any other day. I woke up around 6 A.M. to get ready for work and what a great day I thought it was going to be! I was six and a half months pregnant and I was going to wear my new, black maternity jumper dress I had been waiting to grow into. I arrived at work at Water Resources at approximately 7:30 A.M. and began to work on my assigned projects. My husband, Mark, who works the midnight shift at Will Rogers Air National Guard Base, called about 8:30 A.M. We talked for about five minutes and wished each other a great day.

I guess it was pretty close to 9 A.M. when a sign-up sheet to bring goodies for a co-worker's going away party made its way to my desk. On the sheet I noticed our executive director, Gary, had signed up to bring chitlins. I had no clue what chitlins were so I called out to anyone who was listening to tell me what in the world chitlins were? Bob Chipman, who worked in the cubicle to the left of me, hollered to Paul, who worked to the right of me, to explain what chitlins were. Paul said he didn't have time and Bob would have to tell me. Well, Bob stood up and started to tell me what chitlins were when the most devastating explosion interrupted our conversation.

Although I cannot recall everything that happened immediately following the blast, I will try to explain some things I do remember. Although people could hear the actual explosion from miles away, I do not remember hearing it even though I was right across the street.

Mark, Laura, and Carly Oak

I do recall feeling a strange sensation rushing through my body. The first thing that went through my mind was that I was losing the baby. I cannot say exactly what happened during those frightening moments, but when I looked up and saw the massive destruction to my building, I was sure it was the end of the world.

At the time of the explosion, I was sitting at my desk with my back to the windows looking out onto NW Fifth Street. The injuries I sustained from the blast included two cracked teeth caused by the force of the blast slamming my face into the top of my desk. I also received several lacerations on my back, head, face, and left arm. Due to my proximity to the explosion, I also sustained permanent hearing loss. I truly believe that the only thing that saved my unborn child was that the chair I was sitting in had arms on it. The chair arms prevented my stomach from being jammed into the desk.

I assume the explosion knocked me out for a few moments, but when I came to I knew I had to get out of the building. I could hear Paul yelling for help, but I could not see him or anyone else for that matter. I could not see out of my left eye and I could taste blood. I pushed a cubicle panel out of my way and took off running. I was in the stairwell leading to the first floor when I ran into my boss, Joe. As we went through the front lobby I remember seeing the receptionist, Kelley, still sitting at her desk. Joe grabbed my arm and we ran out of the building.

Joe kept telling me not to step down with my right foot because I had lost my shoe and there was glass everywhere. I'm not sure if I did not hear him or if I just did not care at that point. I remember asking Joe if I still had my left eye because it felt as if it had been blown out. Joe said he did not know and gave me a handkerchief to put over it. A man stopped his car right in front of our building and ran over to us. He was going to help me across the street but Shelly, a co-worker, told him she would take care of me. I remember being so scared and I was shaking from the cold and from the loss of blood. I thought for sure I was going to die.

Due to the possibility of another explosion, I was moved to the corner of NW Fifth and Hudson. Clytie, a lady who was in the post office at the time of the explosion, held onto me while Shelly tried to make some phone calls. I recall some lady coming up and she started praying in tongues. The lady really scared me and reinforced my belief that I was going to die.

I had only been on the corner of NW Fifth and Hudson for a short time when a fireman came over and looked at my eye. Shortly after that an ambulance pulled up and emergency medical technicians began to work on me. They put a C-collar around my neck and laid me on a backboard. I guess they did not see all the cuts on my back because the backboard was really hurting my injuries. The EMTs cut my clothes off and asked me how far along I was (which I couldn't remember), and if the baby had moved since the explosion. The baby had not moved at all since the blast.

I barely remember the ambulance ride or what happened once I arrived at University Hospital. Luckily for my baby and me, they took us up to the Labor and Delivery Unit. Several nurses and doctors began running tests and cleaning me up. I gave them my husband's work number, which was a miracle in itself, because I could never remember it. My husband arrived a short time after the hospital called him. Mark said he arrived just as they were finishing up the X-rays and the initial assessment of my injuries. My husband felt really bad because he had to stop for gas and park about one mile away from the hospital, which delayed his arrival.

The next few hours took forever, but after numerous stitches and staples, they put me in my own room. I was exhausted and the sound of the baby monitor with the sound of my unborn child's heartbeat was very soothing. I spent three days in the hospital before I was finally released to go home.

I feel very fortunate to have ended up at University Hospital. They took great care of me and my unborn child. There were so many people who helped us through this ordeal, including my and my husband's co-workers, friends from my church, Catholic Charities, and the Gray Eagles from Will Rogers Air National Guard Base. I would especially like to thank my husband, for it is from him that I receive my strength and courage.

It has been a long healing process which is still not over. Although the pain from my physical injuries has subsided, the pain from the emotional scars varies from day to day. The whole incident still seems like a terrible nightmare.

Carly Ann Oak was born on August 3, 1995. She is truly a miracle.

Blasted Unto a Pile of Rubble

Clark C. Peterson

---

*G*od gave me a miracle on April 19. Out of 154 workers in the exploded north side of the Alfred P. Murrah Building, I'm one of five survivors. I'm the only one left from my fourth-floor office—Advertising and Public Affairs—a section of the U.S. Army Recruiting Battalion.

Running late, I rushed my usual five-to-seven-minute walk to work, making it by 8:58 A.M., with two minutes to spare.

I sat three feet from the north windows listening to my supervisor's final project instructions. Had I looked down upon NW Fifth Street, I might have seen a Ryder truck parked in front of the building, but I was too involved with my new assignment to notice anything outside. I returned to my desk, twenty feet from the windows, and heard my supervisor's last words, "That's all right, Clark. You can use the computer."

At 9:02 A.M., an electric spark shot from the left side of my computer and everything turned black. White-lit objects raced throughout a coal blackness. Sounds of moaning metal surrounded me. The bass pitch of the aching noise geared up half an octave as objects flew by too fast to recognize, except for a computer monitor and typewriter.

I glimpsed a woman, face full of terror and arms straight up, ten feet from me. Both of us were falling, although I did not realize it until half an hour later. The sight of her was so fleeting and faint that I could not identify her. She yelled, "Ah!" as if there was not enough time for her to inhale. My memories are so vivid, it's hard to grasp that only a few seconds had passed.

I thought I was calm and conscious through the whole ordeal, but later, eyewitnesses told me I was unconscious for about thirty minutes.

Clark C. Peterson

All the while, exploded cars across the street blazed with thick, black smoke. Because the smoke covered the destroyed part of the Murrah building, I was probably not visible to anyone.

When I came to, I thought that the raging black wind had instantly changed to floating debris, as quick as the blink of an eye.

I heard sirens and wondered what this was all about. As the cloud of dust cleared, I noticed that the armchair where I thought I was still sitting had been replaced by a 3-by-5-foot flat ceiling tile perched on top of a three-story pile of rubble. A few feet under was a pile of three-to-four-foot wooden spikes. Some used to be table legs.

The north half of the Murrah building was gone, except for the east and west walls. My location was ten feet in front of the remaining structure, about level with the third floor. This has to be a bomb! I thought, and a twenty-foot crater below confirmed my suspicion. Across the street in a parking lot, two of about fifty cars remained on fire, but I could not see any fire coming from the Murrah building. From where I sat, I could not see anyone else in the smashed remains of the building.

I asked myself, How could I possibly be alive when five tons of floor above collapsed, leaving nothing but air and the sky above?

A jagged three-by-four-inch bloody slab hung almost straight out above my right eye. I thought it was a piece of my head, but it was just debris stained with blood from a laceration on my head which later required two stitches. I swirled out my arms and was glad they both worked. My legs bent properly without noticeable pain. Still seated, I opened a cardboard box next to me and discovered papers used by our operations department. My body seemed to be all right, so I stood up.

From what used to be the ninth floor, I spotted a coarse one-yard ball of concrete suspended from a shaft of rebar. If a beam hit it from the west, the gray ball would fall and crush me in an instant.

I moved closer to the seemingly stable skeleton of the building by climbing a pile of debris topped with a flat board. Here, I figured, rescuers could reach down and pull me up to the fourth floor. Then I could help search for people under the rubble. I stood up on the small board, surprisingly steady upon the rubble heap.

Several muffled cried of "Help!" came from a woman, possibly under the remains of the third or fourth floor, and not more than forty feet away. It would have taken a twelve-foot standing broad jump to breach a gap in order to search for her.

People from the street below saw me. A fireman yelled, "Sit down!" I tried to shout back, but my mouth was full of dust. I did my best to communicate, "Others need help more than I do. Help them. I can stand here for a long time."

A short time later, another fireman said, "We'll get you out." I nodded and gave an okay signal to indicate I understood.

My thoughts were focused on getting out of my predicament and then digging for the injured among the rubble. Rescue workers arrived on the building's skeletal floors. A fire truck's extension ladder reached to the fifth floor. I watched a fireman climbing the ladder. Penny Turpen James took a photograph which showed my right eye colored by bloody debris and my hair flattened by gray dust and blood.

About this time, my aunt from Aitkin, Minnesota, saw me on CNN. A camera zoomed in on me as I moved about in the center of the bombed-out area. She cried out, "My God! Is that you, Clark?" as she recognized the shirt I wore.

My attention turned to a man on a stretcher being extracted from the fifth or sixth floor by the fire ladder. His bloodied upper and lower left leg appeared connected by thin fibers of skin. Many people would comment about the overwhelming odor of blood, but my nostrils were clogged with dust and I could not smell anything.

Fifteen minutes passed from the time I regained consciousness until my rescue. It seemed more like thirty minutes because my memory became like a tape recorder with nothing left out. Perhaps a chemical in the brain made recall easy and this chemical was secreted in large doses. Two men grabbed my wrists. I was pulled to the fourth floor and directed to get immediate medical attention. I eased down the crushed material, afraid that bodies might be underneath. The only recognizable objects were table tops from the snack bar.

An identifier was attached to my left wrist indicating that my injuries were probably not severe.

I reached the southwest corner of the block and sat on the curb, numb and in shock. No one spoke, but everyone around knew that an extremely high death count was imminent.

An ambulance took me to Children's Hospital where Dr. Tyson found multiple injuries: cuts, scrapes, and bruises over my head, hands, and arms, including lacerations which required fifteen stitches. Glass was found in my right elbow and I had a sprained back.

I asked a social worker to contact my folks in Hinckley, Minnesota. They had been watching television all day and trying to call me at the office and my apartment. I was released after four hours.

After six months of living in a motel, I was able to return to my apartment in the Regency Towers, finally renovated after heavy damage from the blast.

By mid-January 1996, I returned to work full-time at our new location. My three fellow office workers are gone: Karen Carr, Peggy Holland, and John Moss. The excavators said that their deaths were instant, a crushing blow lasting about two-hundredths of a second. I still remember that terrified woman with her arms straight up—it seemed to take longer than that. Whatever the blast-to-death time frame, I hope it was quick enough so that nobody felt a thing.

It was nothing short of a God-given miracle that my life was spared and that I wasn't more seriously injured. Since I was only seventy feet from the bomb, there was a 60 percent chance that both of my eardrums had ruptured. One week after the blast, my ears and hearing tested normal, but I had to have a piece of glass removed from my left ear, next to the drum. Also, falling fifteen feet and landing on a level ceiling tile was nothing short of incredible. Underneath was a pile of wood spikes and table legs which could have sliced clear through me. The flat board on the higher pile of rubble was also a miracle.

As a survivor of the worst domestic terrorism in our nation's history, I have come to two conclusions. Any place can be a target because good people can be found practically anywhere. Also, it has been said, "We're not guaranteed the next day." I say, "None of us is guaranteed the next second."

Babies in a
War Zone

Jamie Pratt

My husband, Jimmy, and I had just moved from Alabama
and I had applied for a job at a loan company on
Robinson just down the street from the federal building.

I accepted the position at 4:30 P.M. on Tuesday, April 18. The
woman told me to be there the next morning at 8:30. Jimmy had just
gotten a job, too, and it was wonderful. We were feeling good about
everything.

It was a really beautiful, brisk morning. It felt like a fall morning.
The sun was shining prettily, like it does on downtown. I knew it
would probably be warmer later, but I wanted to dress nicely, so I
wore a pretty silk blouse with a lot of red in it and a black skirt. I was
feeling good, everything was fine, and I didn't even get caught in
traffic.

When I arrived, my supervisor introduced me to everyone and
they all seemed nice enough.

I didn't know exactly what I'd be doing because I had never
worked for a loan company before. I didn't think much about this job
before I took it. All I knew was I was supposed to dress nice, and I

Jamie Pratt

knew I would be working with people, and I was used to that.

My supervisor put me with a co-worker who was going to train me. I was sitting facing Robinson and I could see part of the federal building. I was sitting in a chair with rollers on the bottom, filling out some paperwork. The woman told me to go ahead and sign in on my time sheet and I remember looking at my watch and writing down that it was 9:02 A.M.

The blast occurred and it was like everything went into slow motion. Before anything hit me, I remember thinking, Dear God, does this happen here often? It was really a bad first day of work! In that split second I was thinking it was a drive-by shooting, or maybe a natural gas leak. It's like I saw it coming, but I couldn't do anything. I remember coming to and it had knocked me back and out of my chair, because the desk was way up there covered with stuff.

Everybody was helping me up and saying we needed to get out of there. I thought, I'm fixin' to die, and I don't even know the first person in here. I was scared to look up, and when they grabbed me it jolted me and I bit my bottom lip all the way through. It had swollen up to the size of a baseball and it burst open and bled all over everyone. I could see all these strange women looking at me, yet it felt like I had known them forever. One woman's hand was hanging by a thread of skin and I wanted to ask if she was okay, but I couldn't.

I must have looked a sight with my blonde hair all bloody, glass in my head and back, and a cut on the back of my leg. We went back through to the back door and it was blown off its hinges. It took forever to get it open and to get out. We were thinking it was just our building, and that something else was about to explode.

We stumbled out onto the street and I'll never forget the faces of people who drove up. One woman kept saying, "We've got to get Jamie to the hospital." I was really freaking out about dying without anybody there because I was that scared. When you are scared, you really think you're going to die. We were all bleeding and we didn't have any towels, and these people who pulled up in their cars were looking at us, horrified.

People started coming out of the *Journal Record* building and the Southwestern Bell building.

Men were bringing babies out into the street. This young, very handsome blond-haired gentleman stands out in my mind. He had on what once I'm sure was a crisp, starched white shirt, a tie, and a nice pair of black slacks—a businessman. He had a baby on each hip and they were bleeding really bad, and they were not crying, and he was saying, "Do these babies belong to you all? Do you know where they came from?" And there was just blood all over that crisp, starched white shirt.

You could smell blood. It smelled like iron down there, it was so strong. You didn't look anywhere where there wasn't blood.

Finally, this woman got out of a car and took off her white vest and put it up to my head. She told me she couldn't take me to the hospital because all the roads were blocked off, but that I should wait for an ambulance.

We wandered around like crazy people. Burning cars were up and down the road and it looked like a war zone, except for the babies and the frantic mothers. It just didn't seem like there should be babies and mothers in a war zone.

They put us in an ambulance, then took us out for more seriously injured people. This old man, I don't know who he is to this day, had a towel to his head and he said, "I'm a Christian man and I've never been with another woman in my life besides my wife, God rest her soul. If you don't mind my blood, you can have this towel." He took it down from his head and he didn't have an ear. He didn't even know. He said, "I don't think I'm hurt that bad."

I wanted to say, "You don't have an ear, mister," but I realized he didn't even know. You don't know the horror we saw down there.

A policeman finally took us in his cruiser to St. Anthony's Hospital before people started arriving in droves. The doctor put stitches in the back of my leg without using an anesthetic and told me that if I could live through a bomb, I could take a few stitches.

I screamed a scream which came from the depths of my being. It was like a scream of release, so gut wrenching, like I was letting something out of me that I had to get out. It was such a scream that people came from everywhere to look into the room.

I got a ride home and I was so confused I could hardly remember how to get to my house.

Jimmy was at work without a car and had to hitchhike downtown because his boss wouldn't let him even call to see if I was okay. He walked all around and was tired and freaked out because he couldn't find me. Someone told him that some of the women at the loan company had been killed. When he found out I'd been taken to the hospital, he just sat down and started crying in the middle of the street.

A cab driver took him to the hospital, and when he saw on the list that I'd been released, he said he felt like he'd been born again. He had never felt so thankful in his whole life.

The hardest thing now is thinking about it. I can't turn it off. I think about it all the time. I don't think I'll ever be the carefree, "nobody's gonna hurt me, sleep with my windows open" me again. It's like I'm not supposed to forget.

I'm very paranoid. I don't go anywhere without locking my doors and rolling up my windows.

I have bad nightmares, even now. My husband sleeps on the couch sometimes because I kick him and wake him up with my screaming. We went home for Christmas, the first time we'd been anywhere since the bombing, and I woke everybody up in the house screaming, "Get the babies, please get the babies."

I wouldn't make it without the grace of God and my counselor, and I'm not even the kind of person who goes to a counselor. I was a heroin addict for twenty years, and I'm telling you, I've been through some raunchy stuff, being an addict. But I've never been through anything that's left me so weak and vulnerable. I have nightmares about people wanting to kill me.

You think about airplane crashes, tornadoes, and accidents, and you feel for those people and kind of accept that things like that happen. But when somebody intentionally does this, it's so crazy.

I've had such a hard time with guilt. All these babies died and here I am a survivor. I remember that a rescue worker put a baby in a woman's arms and the baby instinctively reached out and grabbed her and cried, "Momma," probably thinking she was its mom because of the feel of a woman's body. And she just said, "I'm here." I'm sure that baby thought it died in its mother's arms.

I believe life is too short. I feel like I've wasted so much of it. I can't make up for the twenty years I was an addict and hurt everybody who ever cared anything about me. Now, I don't think I'll ever do drugs again. I want to be aware of every minute. I don't want to miss out on anything. I don't want to waste my life anymore.

We Remember

Dennis Purifoy

$\mathcal{T}$he first rescuers were the survivors themselves. Before other heroes forged through the tangled debris of the Alfred P. Murrah Building, those already inside encouraged the injured and gave solace to the dying. They removed rubble and led or carried their fellow workers outside. Some made the hazardous trek more than once.

Sometimes we think, when faced with a basic survival situation, we would operate on an instinct to save only ourselves. For the bombing survivors, there was something else: concern for fellow humans without even the tiniest consideration for personal risk.

Sometime after I got out of the building to a sidewalk, an emergency medical technician stuck some gauze on my bleeding ear. Later, an office worker brought by a cup of water. No drink ever tasted so good! The explosion had caused a fierce storm of dust and I was hoarse from yelling. Another EMT warmed me with a small medical blanket.

I ended up at the Oklahoma City Clinic for treatment. Prepared for scores of casualties, the staff gave the few of us lots of attention and care. My shoes and socks had been soaked from the pooled water on the ground floor of the Murrah building; they were replaced by surgical booties and a blanket. Besides two stitches, a tetanus shot, and some patching of my cuts, I received a soft drink and some counseling. My wife, Cassie, came to pick me up just as a nurse brought me a sandwich.

Dennis Purifoy

"For I was hungry and you gave me food, I was thirsty and you gave me something to drink, I was a stranger and you welcomed me, I was naked and you gave me clothing, I was sick and you took care of me" (Matthew 25: 35–36).

As a Christian, I knew that I should take these verses to heart in service to others, but having these acts done for me made them real to me in a new way.

The enormity of the evil done on April 19 became apparent to me as time passed.

The good that was done in response to it was immediately evident. So many people gave selflessly. The good is what I choose to remember.

At Fifth and Robinson, April '96

It is an old tree,
Not well-shaped, more than plain,
It twists this way and that:
Trunk leans hard to the wind,
Limbs bent back from the wind.

No grace save for its growth,
Not planned or cared for,
No dirt at its trunk,
It grew on a blacktop lot.

Then that day last spring
A blast ripped its leaves
And flames roared about;
Too much to bear, in spring.

Yet it still has life,
Buds grow new green in spite,
One more spring comes back.
It tells of luck and life,
It tells of strength and hope,
It says, "I am still here—
You killed too much, but not all."

We lost too much too soon,
But we and spring are here;
We lost too much, but not all,
And we are yet alive.

There were memorial services at the Murrah site in the morning and later at the Convention Center. What really stuck with me was the walk, from one service to the other, down Robinson Avenue.

Families of victims, survivors and their families traveled the six blocks together. Just the act of walking expressed our common hurt and healing to that point.

The police, firemen, and other law-enforcement personnel who flanked Robinson Avenue held their hats over their hearts. A bank hung an immense American flag between buildings. But what made the walk extraordinary to me were all of the downtown workers who lined the sidewalks in quiet respect. On an overhead walkway, more workers watched. They had posted a simple banner that said it all, "WE REMEMBER."

Day of Miracles

Manon Ragland

$\mathcal{I}$t started out as a regular working day. The only premonition I had that it would be different was when I was mentally going over a checklist of what I hoped to accomplish at work that day. A spark flicked through my mind that something was going to happen to impede my plans. It lasted only an instant, and I pushed it away as a part of my persistent pessimism.

I arrived at my office at the YMCA slightly later than my usual 8:45 A.M., between 8:50 and 8:55 A.M. This most probably saved me from death or very serious injury. I laid my briefcase and my new white cape on my desk and checked the messages in my voice mailbox.

As usual, I went to the ladies' lounge before starting my work, taking only my office keys with me. I had just entered one of the booths when, literally, hell broke loose.

First, there was the unbelievably loud, terrifying blast of a bomb—the worst sound I had ever heard. I clapped my hands over my ears and screamed. Then, simultaneously, it seemed that the floor, ceiling, and walls started shaking, and I experienced a feeling

271

**Manon Ragland,
with her husband, Ray**

of almost unbearable pressure over my entire body. It was as if the air itself was a tangible thing that was trying to compress the life out of me. I had trouble even getting my breath. I looked up and saw the ceiling cracking and falling.

My first thought was to wonder if this was an earthquake. Never having experienced one, I didn't know if the terrible blast precedes the earth shaking, as the sound of a roaring train precedes a tornado, or if the shaking and destruction caused the noise.

I opened the door of the ladies' lounge and stepped out into an environment so familiar and yet so drastically changed that there was a surreal feeling about it. It seemed almost like a disaster movie set. My impression was that all color was muted by a pale, soft gray shimmering fog.

I looked across the lobby and saw everyone from the business office coming out. Someone was screaming that it was a bomb, "They're bombing the YMCA." One of the women was screaming and crying in hysterics, and I saw our CEO with blood streaming down his face and his white shirt almost completely muted by the gray. In fact, the gray seemed to make it stand out even more.

I wanted to leave. I was afraid there might be another explosion, but I was also concerned about the people in the other two offices at the end of the hall. I looked back down the hall and saw the other three staff members coming toward me, so I started toward the stairs to leave the building. There was debris all over the floor—ceiling tiles, lighting fixtures, glass. The glass doors that lock the elevators off at night were shattered. All I could think about was getting out.

All the alarms were going off in the building, making a terrible noise. I will never hear that sound again without a strong physical reaction. I could already hear the sirens from emergency vehicles outside the building.

As we started to leave the building, I turned and looked back. I saw one of the day-care workers with several children, little toddlers, behind the turnstiles separating the lobby from the entrance to the Health Club. The turnstiles weren't working due to the loss of electrical power. I turned and went back to help her get the children over the barrier and out of the building. The children were all dazed and bleeding. Most were too stunned even to cry, but none appeared badly hurt.

One particularly poignant incident that will always haunt my memory and my dreams is of a beautiful little girl, the quintessential cherub, with strawberry-blonde curls, huge blue eyes, and soft, round, rosy cheeks. She was wearing a pink-and-white checked dress, pink socks, and white Mary Jane shoes.

She had blood matted in her curls and blood on her arm from a small cut. She was not crying, just looking at me as if to ask what she had done wrong to cause all the hurt and pain. I lifted her over a turnstile and set her on the floor and started to turn back to the other children.

Her eyes filled with tears, and she held her arms up to me with a soft cry, "Please," to pick her up. I wanted so much to pick her up and hold her close and kiss away the blood and the fright, but I could only pat her quickly and turn back to lift the rest of the children over the turnstiles. I will always feel that I failed her.

I climbed over the turnstiles and started going toward the day-care center. A man went with me, holding my elbow. The devastation was so great that, for a little while, I could not tell where we were.

At one point, I stepped on a shifting pile of debris and would have lost my balance and fallen into a pile of glass, metal, and other debris had not the man with me tightened his hold on my elbow and helped me regain my balance. He had to grip so tightly that his thumb left a small bruise on the inside of my elbow. This with two other bruises and a scratch were the only physical injuries I sustained.

We kept moving until I suddenly saw the day-care toddlers' room. I later learned that all fifty-two children in the day-care center were out of the building and accounted for within seven minutes.

The bomb exploded at 9:02 A.M. The children were scheduled to go out to the playground at 9:30. The playground is located at the very end of the block, the closest place to the Murrah building. Had they been there, they would probably all have been killed or seriously injured.

I remember the feeling of being in a soft, gray fog. I will never see fog again without remembering April 19. Amazingly, I never had any trouble breathing in all the time I was in the building. Others had to have inhalation therapy because of the dust they inhaled but even though I have severe allergies, I never had any symptoms or problems whatsoever.

As I came out into the bright sunshine, the first thing I was aware of were the huge, billowing, black clouds of smoke. It was only then I heard someone say it was the Alfred P. Murrah Building that had been bombed. I turned to look at it and the enormity of the destruction began to set in.

I picked up a little black girl, three or four years old, who was sobbing in fear. The chaos around me was indescribable. I can't remember many details, which probably is a blessing. I think the human spirit can absorb only a finite amount of carnage and horror without going numb or crazy or both. Those details that I do remember are as sharp today as they were that day: crying, terrified, bleeding little children; broken glass; and blood everywhere on everything.

Soon after this, the mother of the little girl found me with her child. I learned later that none of the children in our day-care center were killed or seriously injured physically. I say "physically" because the mental damage is so extensive that it is impossible to measure.

I realize now what someone told me about the grieving process, that it is like hitting your thumb with a hammer. First, it's numb, and then the numbness wears off and the almost unbearable pain starts, continues for awhile, eventually diminishes to a dull ache that is always with you, but sometimes is felt every now and then as a stabbing pain.

About two weeks after the bombing, I was visiting with the employee who had led me out of the day-care center that day, and I asked if he could remember who the man was who had kept me from falling into that pile of glass and debris.

The young man looked at me with a very puzzled expression and said, "Manon, there was no one with you." I told him there had to have been someone with me because he kept me from slipping. I even showed him the bruise on the inside of my arm, but his response was that I had been alone when I came into the day-care center.

Needless to say, I was rather stunned by his reply because I know a short, stocky man walked with me, held my arm, and kept me from serious injury.

The Horror Lingers

Beverly Rankin

---

*A*pril 19, 1995, started just like every other work day. It was 8:50 in the morning and the Social Security employees were working on their pending workloads before the office opened to the public at 9:00.

I had been at work for almost an hour and had just completed a critical payment authorization for a claimant who called in a few minutes earlier. I took the form to my supervisor, Steve Williams, for his signature. Steve had to sign the form before I could transmit the information that would issue a replacement check to the claimant. He was busy and asked me to leave it on his desk. He would review it and bring it back to me before his management meeting at 9:15. Steve's cubicle faced the windows overlooking the sidewalk bordering NW Fifth, just a few feet from where a Ryder truck filled with explosives would park. Little did I know this would be the last time I would talk to Steve or to any of the fifteen other co-workers and the numerous friends and acquaintances I had made over the years I worked at the Alfred P. Murrah Building.

I went back to my desk in the service-representative area located

276

in the one-story part of the building on the northeast corner. About five minutes before 9:00, Sharon Littlejohn, who was working the front windows that open to the lobby, called to say I needed to take an interview in the front. I picked up my pad and pen in preparation for the interview when the phone rang on a fellow employee's line. She was off that day, and since it wasn't yet 9:00, I answered it.

Beverly Rankin

The lady on the phone explained her situation, and we were involved in finding a solution when the bomb went off. Suddenly there was a horribly loud noise and everything went pitch-black. Things were falling from the ceiling and the hutch part of my desk fell over on me.

The air was thick with smoke and grit. When the noise of everything falling finally stopped, there was a deafening silence—I realized I was holding a telephone receiver to my ear but it was not connected to anything. I threw it away from me as if it had been the cause of all the chaos.

After some time—I have no idea how long—my co-workers closest to me started calling out each other's names to see if everyone was okay. I had to crawl over something to get to the others, but there was no panic as we gathered together. We heard another co-worker, Rex Irwin, yell out that we could get out through the break room to Robinson Avenue on the east side of the building. It was still pitch-black as we felt our way over unknown objects and debris toward the thin line of daylight at the back door to the street. Some of our co-workers were bleeding and we helped them get to ambulances that had responded to the call.

Once outside, I saw cars burning in the parking lot across the street from the front of the building, but I still didn't comprehend that we had been bombed. A gas main or something else had exploded. Bombing was not something that happened to ordinary people in Oklahoma City!

I will never forget that horrible day or all that was lost in one brief moment. There are still blank spaces in my memory and no idea of time frames, but the horror lingers. I lose control when it thunders and the lights blink. I miss my friends and co-workers who were lost in the bombing and I still cannot understand how this could have happened. Most of all, I wonder why. My innocence has been stolen. I would give anything to change what happened, to take away the hurt so many have suffered. No one deserves this.

(There is one footnote to the story. Some months after we reopened the office in a new location, the phone rang on an employee's line as I worked at my new desk. The employee was off that day and I took the call. The lady on the phone began explaining her dilemma and recognition flowed over me as she talked that this was the same situation I was working on when the bomb went off! The lady on the phone was in shock. She said her mother was talking with someone at the Social Security office when the bomb exploded and she just knew that person had died. Happily, I informed her that I did not die, and we again took up working on the solution to her problem.)

The Rose

Jana' Redd

WOODROW "WOODY" CLIFFORD BRADY
FEBRUARY 9, 1954–APRIL 19, 1995

On Tuesday, February 9, 1954, God graced the Redd family garden of life with a male rosebud named Woodrow "Woody" Clifford Brady. The beauty of this rose exemplified family dedication, loyalty, kindness, and an ardent affection for life. His free spirit, love for family, and respect for mankind were truly a gift from God.

Woody greeted each day exultantly with a smile and lived as if it were his last. Living a full and fruitful life was a priority. Wednesday April 19, 1995, 9:02 A.M., a senseless injustice was committed.

In 1971, a Future Farmers of America student from Meeker High School, Woody became the first African-American youth to win a state championship in the Farmers Union Youth division of the annual Oklahoma Farmers Union speech contest held in November of that year. He was awarded an expense-paid trip to the nation's capital where he was presented an award, toured the U.S. House of Representatives, and visited other sites during the Oklahoma Farmers Union's eastern

**Woodrow Clifford
"Woody" Brady**

tour of the country in the summer of 1972. He was also extended an invitation by George W. Stone, president of the Oklahoma Farmers Union, to deliver his award-winning speech at the Oklahoma Farmers Union Convention in 1972.

One of his dreams as a youngster was to obtain his diploma from the high school where his mother was the first African American to graduate. In May 1972, graduating at the top of his class, Woody was one of three students to receive Meeker High School's highest student honor, fulfilling one of his many lifelong dreams.

A graduate from Seminole Junior College (where he was awarded a "walk-on" basketball scholarship), and an attendee of Oklahoma City Christian College, majoring in biology/zoology and minoring in art, education was an important tool he often utilized. He felt compelled to project his old-fashioned disciplined ideas, and countless hours were spent encouraging, supporting, and advising children to pursue the basic roots of life: an education, happiness, and knowledge. Brought into this world with love, hope, and honor, Woody felt every human being deserved the best life had to offer. He was an inspiring young man who loved people, especially children. His belief that children of all walks of life needed support and leadership and his unquestionable love for them led to the idea and reality of personalized children's books. He often stated, "A child may read a book if he can identify with a character; put the child's name in the book, his/her picture, something about their family or surroundings, and it should hold their interest." The kindness of his heart would give a book to a child who could not afford to purchase one as long as the child promised to read the story. One of Woody's strongest beliefs was, if you can conceive your dream, you can achieve your dream, nothing is impossible.

Football, tennis, baseball, basketball games, and boxing matches would raise the roof at the Redd household. There was never a quiet moment; everyone had to voice their opinion and hurrah their team to victory. An avid golfer (sunshine, rain, sleet, or snow), this was a sport he enjoyed playing with his brother, Johann, a special cousin, and his best friend. There were many hours spent encouraging his mother to learn to play golf, but she chose to house his many trophies instead.

Woody loved cooking, drawing, playing chess, boating, reading, traveling, telling his mother jokes, and watching his sister, Sarita (who began ballet at the age of three), perform. Whenever his sister performed, he would be there to applaud her graceful gift, truly given to her by God. He called his grandmother, Janie, daily for a different recipe to prepare or for another cookbook.

Pride in the relationship he had with his mother and siblings compelled him to convince young people of the importance of family and family values. "Brady," as his grandmother called him, would spend hours on end with his mother, sharing his dreams and asking advice. Jeanne was her son's confidante, friend, supporter, encourager, and leader.

Holidays were a special time for Woody; even Sundays were considered holidays as far as he and his brother were concerned. Woody and Johann would spend hours playing chess and delighted in changing their mother's menu. Whatever the occasion, they were sure she would meet their request and, of course, she would prepare the menu they put together. Some of Woody's favorite dishes were salmon, steak, shrimp, and quail, and as far as he was concerned, no one could prepare those dishes to his taste except his mother.

Wednesday, April 19, 1995, due to the troubled society in which we live, brought violence to the door of the Redd family garden of life. Though we never thought it could happen to us, it did. Losing Woody's physical presence has left a great void in our lives and though we bid his physical being farewell, we will never spiritually say goodbye. We know God is Woody's rock and that relationship is built on a solid foundation.

For every life touched by Woody's presence for forty-one precious years, we hope their prayer will be as ours, "Love one another, for life is short, and pray for peace."

His spirit will continue to live and be a presence in the lives of his loved ones. We thank God for an incredible creation, our treasured memories, and the joy Woody brought to our lives, for he was truly a chosen one.

A tree was planted and a monument placed in front of Meeker High School in memory of Woody, by the class of 1972, 1995–96 Student Council, and the FFA.

Fighting to Stay Above Water

Angela Richerson

*M*y nightmare began on April 19, 1995, at 9:02 A.M. The morning had started out to be a fairly decent one. I was running on time but my little truck was hot so I dropped by my mom's to bum some antifreeze before heading to Tinker Air Force Base. The last thing I told her was that I loved her.

I was in my office when a friend came and told me that the YMCA downtown had been bombed. It took a few minutes for us to find out for sure that it wasn't the YMCA, but the Murrah building instead. I lost a part of my heart at that moment. I kept trying my mother's office and got no answer. I then made arrangements to meet with both my sisters.

I have never liked to be alone, but on that day I felt like the loneliest person around. We were running through downtown with police officers and rescue workers, helping with children who were being carried down the street, but I could not find my mother. I was lost in my own hometown.

We had gotten right by the Murrah building, and we looked for Momma as hard as we could, but we couldn't see anything except

Norma "Jean" Johnson

that the bomb had blown up right at my mother's office window. All the floors were right on top of where she was; there was nothing left of her office. Somehow though, I knew in my heart that Momma wasn't in the "pit."

We had yet to contact our father and we didn't know how. We just wanted to be able to take our mother home to be with him. We went many places searching for her until we finally ended up at Presbyterian Hospital. There were a couple of women there who fit Momma's description but they were not her. Our brother, Carl, then came and took us to St. Anthony's Hospital and then from there back to the site, but still no word about our mother.

I had some very good friends who helped me with my children during this time. Delisha was eight and Mathew was four. I tried to keep them from finding out but Mathew knew what the building looked like and had seen some of it on TV. When I took Delisha to school, she cried and I had to pry her hands off of me to get her into her classroom. I later found out she had been teased by the other children about her Nana being in the bombing and not being found. No wonder she cried.

Every day we would wait at St. Luke's Church with many other families for news. One by one, people would leave and not be back. Nine days passed and we were not to hear about Momma there. I was in my own little world. The song by Alabama, "Angels Among Us," kept running through my mind. I felt them all around me but I didn't feel as though one of them was Momma. I never gave up and I never quit singing that song; it gave me comfort.

On April 29, 1995, we got a call from Momma's boss. They had found Momma very late the night before. I thought that I couldn't cry anymore but I was wrong. It seemed like my tears would never quit. I couldn't make sense of what was going on and had two close friends come stay with me and the children.

Daddy was unable to help with funeral arrangements so we kids did so. We were able to get a plot for Momma close to Jacob, my three-year-old nephew who had died March 27, 1989. Momma took care of him when he was alive, so it was only right that she be close to him in her next life.

I went to the funeral home and picked up Momma's belongings. We were blessed with her rings, earrings, and watch. Her watch was still running and when I noticed this, I cried like a baby. I then took out a ring that Momma wore which was my grandmother's and placed it on my finger. I was told it was a miracle that the stones survived the blast. I don't take it off now. It means so very much to me. I have Momma just a little closer to me because of it, but I wish I could feel her arms around me.

Momma was laid to rest on May 5, 1995. On that morning, my father had a heart attack. The hospital said it wasn't anything but stress, so they sent him home after a couple of hours. On October 24, 1995, Daddy had a triple bypass after many weeks in the hospital and almost losing him to many more attacks.

I was on the verge of my whole world collapsing around me and it seemed no one cared. There were financial problems and problems with work since I was not able to be there for weeks after the bombing and then with Daddy. I was able to get counseling but when asking for help for my kids, I was told children bounce back quickly. They lied. Delisha was held back in school and she was becoming more violent with Mathew. Something had to be done. I finally was able to get counseling for the children but was threatened with the loss of my job if I didn't quit taking them and myself to counseling. I work for the government. I wouldn't be going through this if my mother had not been murdered.

The first anniversary was approaching and I was feeling more desperate. I had thought out how to take the lives of me and my children. I would not leave them behind to suffer more. They didn't deserve that, but I guess God wasn't going to let go of me and I put myself into St. Anthony's Mental Ward. I was locked in for Mother's Day and missed my children very much, but I couldn't talk to them much because they were having a hard enough time. I went from there to a day program for four weeks and learned a lot from my time there. One person in particular helped me so much during this time; he knows who he is and I want to thank him for all he did for me. I would like to think I helped him a little, too.

I am a person who keeps much locked inside, and Delisha has learned this from me because she is doing the same. She has a lot of anger. She gets so angry at times that she is hurtful to her brother and then Mathew acts that way with her and his pets. I am now dealing with a six-year-old son wanting to die. Delisha locks herself up in her room; she sleeps so much and seems to withdraw more.

I finally got mad at Momma for leaving me the way she did and it took me till March 8, 1997, to be able to get mad about any of this. I got mad at God for taking her the way that He did, but I pray Momma didn't suffer. I never lost my faith in God but I had a hard time praying and I still struggle with all the feelings that keep going through my heart and mind.

It doesn't matter what or how I do anything, my heart always feels heavy. My chest feels like a heavy weight has been placed on it, and the shortness of breath makes it hard to breathe. I also have anxiety attacks and can have them for no reason. I've been on so many different medications. I have a hard time sleeping despite sleeping pills, which then make it hard to wake up. I have trouble seeing things clearly, my head spins, I lose my balance, and I get disoriented.

Even though three years have passed, the pain of losing Momma and how she left us is still very strong. I don't know if the pain will ever quit.

I found a support group for the kids last year at the Kids' Place, where they have someone their own age to talk with and can see other children who are going through the same thing for one reason or another; knowing there isn't anything wrong with the way they are feeling and that it is okay to feel sad, mad, happy, or angry. It's okay and they are not alone. And there are those who helped us make it through bad times and when I couldn't make ends meet. I am so thankful to them and to my good friends. I am also thankful to everyone who found it in their hearts to help my family, even if it was just a kind word or a hug. We will never forget you.

I am really tired of my heart aching so badly and I wish someone would tell me how to stop it. This whole thing has almost ruined my life and the lives of my children. We are fighting to stay above water in so many ways and I don't know when I can stop treading water. I still have a hard time with the fact that my mother is dead and that she won't be coming home. I can finally miss her and remember the good times we had together, but the hurt still remains.

I will always miss Momma and so will my children, but like I try to tell them, as long as we keep Nana in our hearts, as long as we remember her and keep her memories alive, Nana will always be with us. I just wish I could feel her in some small way. I will always love my mother and I thank my mother for doing the best she could with us kids. I would give almost anything to have had more time with her and for her to be with both of my kids. We will see her again though. My faith in God assures me of that.

The Girl in the Yellow Dress

Christi Sanders

At 7:30 A.M. Sonja came bounding through my front door as she did each weekday morning, bringing her kids for me to baby-sit while she worked. She had on a yellow dress, one she rarely wore because she wasn't that fond of it.

She sat the girls down, along with their diaper bag, then headed down the hallway in a beeline for my closet, saying she wanted to find something of mine to wear. She said the yellow dress made her look like a "fat cow." Searching frantically but not being able to find anything, she said she had to leave, that she didn't have time to keep looking. She kissed her girls, said bye, and off she went, yellow dress and all.

Sonja was my idol. She always let me, her kid sister, tag along and she always helped with typical "sister" things. She would give me a boost when I couldn't reach something, and she held my hand on the way to school. She took care of all the bullies for me and stood beside me in a strange crowd. She also kept me humble. She would be the first to point out that my butt looked bigger in my new jeans, and she would let me walk through a crowd with a sock stuck to my back, then tell me when we got home.

She helped me through all the toughest teachers and she saved term papers for me. She helped me through graduation, and clued me in on all the important things, like, if you felt like you were going to puke, lay down in the bathroom and put your cheek on the cool tile floor. She warned me which guys were creeps and which guys were keepers. She was my maid of honor, and three months later, I was hers. We married brothers; now we shared two families.

Sonja laughed and cried with me; we shared family secrets; we were best friends. We could look at each other and know what the other was thinking. She was such a major part of my life,

Sonja Sanders

it's hard to wake up each morning and start another day without her. I know she knew how much we loved her. We just feel so robbed— she was only twenty-seven when she was killed; her daughters only three and twenty-two months. She had so much love to give them. She was so good with her girls and enjoyed her time with them. I know if she had any time to think in those last few seconds of life, she thought of them. I wish they could know her as we did.

For the life of me, I can't understand why someone who never knew her could have taken her life, along with all those other lives, and treated it like it was so worthless. My sister was far from worthless; she was a good mother, wife, sister, and daughter; and she was doing what the bombers should have been doing that day—working.

After the bombing, we told anyone we thought might have connection to the search about the yellow dress Sonja was wearing, and that at 9:00 she was in a staff meeting on the third floor where she worked in the credit union. We supplied them with her dental records and descriptions of birthmarks, scars, jewelry—anything we could think of to help them find her.

During the sixteen-day wait, my dad decided he had to go to the bomb site; the waiting was too much and he couldn't just stay home and do nothing. Mama was afraid to leave the phone, afraid that, by some miracle, Sonja might find a way out and try to call home. Daddy and I headed downtown to the site at 2 A.M., hoping to find her in the rubble—if we could just lay beside her and talk with her and maybe even to hold her hand. To tell her we were there and that we loved her.

When we reached downtown, they wouldn't let us get close to the building. All we could see was the devastated upper floors. It was cold and windy; we could see the debris blowing from the building. Sonja was strong, but how could anyone survive that kind of destruction? I have never seen my dad so out of control emotionally. He cried uncontrollably and pleaded with the National Guard to just let him in and let him move rocks, or at least allow him to point them in the direction of where she would be. The guard at the site said he understood, but that he just couldn't allow him to go any closer. My dad had always faced problems head-on, but this time he had no control.

We tried to keep faith that she was still alive by saying that she was such a fighter, and that they would probably find her and Claudette in a void somewhere, mouthing at each other for more room, complaining about the cramped quarters. Sonja's husband, Mike, joked and said she had such a strong will. "You don't really think it was my idea to have pink carpet and cows in the kitchen, do you?"

On Friday, May 5, after sixteen days of waiting, our worst nightmare became a reality. They found the girl in the yellow dress—our Sonja. My life and our families' lives would never be the same. A part of us died along with her. We didn't have a lot of money growing up so we learned to enjoy those simple things like each other's company and joking and laughing with each other. I wish I could have those days back. One thing we do have that nobody can ever take are our memories. I know I will see my sister again, I just wish I knew how to accept the fact that my life with her here on earth is over. It's so senseless. She should still be here with us enjoying life.

It All Started with a Kiss

Mary Schonberger

*I*t was a cloudy April morning, and Spencer Christian on ABC's *Good Morning America* said we might see some rain here in Oklahoma before the end of the day. Tom was leaving for the base and since I was ready to leave for work early, I opened the garage door for him and gave him a nice long kiss goodbye. As he pulled out of the driveway, I signed to him "I really love you" and shut the door.

After eating my breakfast, I packed a drink for the ride downtown and headed to the office on schedule for a change. The April morning was a little cool and with a forecast for rain I grabbed my umbrella and the outer shell of my ski jacket—it also made a great raincoat. When I arrived at my parking space just a half block west of my office, I realized I had made great time and had twenty minutes before I had to start work. With that in mind, I leisurely made my way up the alley between Fourth and Fifth streets to go smell the lilacs blooming in the yard of the house behind the church. Those lilacs were the only ones that I had seen in Oklahoma since I left New England only a year and a half before: they reminded me of

291

home. It was a nice change from my usual trek up the hill on Fifth Street. Once I finished enjoying the flowers, I continued to the credit union where I was the new accounts officer, and thought to myself, This is going to be a good day.

I worked for the Federal Employees Credit Union of Oklahoma City and had been there since September 1993. The office, located on the third floor of the Alfred P. Murrah Building, was space provided to us at no charge since we provided a service to the federal workers. Since the space was free, the various credit union departments were all in different areas but on the same floor. It was at times awkward to explain to members where the departments were located, but the space fit our needs for the time being.

I worked in the operations department, and it was the same as always on a Wednesday morning. Four of our tellers—Christi, Tresia, Bobbi, and Enterice—were opening mail. Jason, the telephone teller, was answering the early morning calls. Joe, the share draft officer, was playing practical jokes on Frankie, another teller. Sonja, the head teller, was telling Kathy, the Vice President of Operations, about something her two little girls had done the night before. Kathy and Sonja had a meeting in the CEO's office at 8:30, but as usual it would start late. I was trying to get caught up. All of this before the doors opened at 9 A.M.

I made my way across the hall to the loan department to use their copier. Over there, I said good morning to my friends and co-workers and caught up on the latest office news and made plans for lunch. I was not sure yet if I was going with Kim and Ellen as I did almost every day or if I was going to meet Tom again today which was always a special treat. The last I saw of them, Kim was making copies, Ellen had just gotten off the phone, and Terri was in Pam's office since Pam was out on sick leave.

The office doors opened for business at 9 A.M. according to our clock on the wall that always ran a few minutes fast. I was opening a new account that I received in the morning's mail when Duane Miller came in asking me to locate a check copy he ordered. Jason handled the check copies, but when it involved Mr. Miller, either Sonja or I took care of it. As I had not talked to Jason since I had returned from my honeymoon two weeks earlier, I thought I would check his log to see when Duane placed the order. Jason's desk connected to mine, both facing the north wall of the building. With no record of the order on his desk, I walked over to Bobbie and she also did not know anything about it. I then decided to look at Jason's log one more time, but I never made it back to his desk.

As I reached the corner where Jason's desk met mine, the nightmare began. It was as if I was suddenly being buried alive. There was a big whoosh as debris and ceiling insulation came down on top of me. My first thoughts were Oh no, the ceiling is coming down and, I can imagine what Duane Miller is thinking. I didn't even scream, there was no time. Before I could think anymore, I was sitting on the floor, it was quiet, and I was completely trapped. What for some must have felt like a lifetime went quickly for me, defined by only what I could hear.

The next sound I heard was Bobbie's voice yelling. Thank God, I thought. Someone else is all right. Screaming meant to me that she was alive and that gave hope for me. Over her screams I could hear Jason. Good, another person. He was trying to calm Bobbie down and to get over to her. I had no idea what it was like outside my dark cocoon, but their voices led me to believe that maybe it was safer inside than out. Once Jason settled her down, I could ask him where I was; that was my cue to start calling for help. There was no way anyone would have heard my soft voice over Bobbie. With that, I started to call for Jason and once he heard me I was able to poke a hole through the debris with the pen that I had held onto the whole time (don't ask me how). Jason saw the pen but could not get over to me. Then out of what appeared to be nowhere, I heard Joe, and Jason began to tell him that I was buried. Joe sat only a few feet away from Jason so I could not understand how they became separated and why he could not see where I was located. Sitting there in my cocoon, I started to become scared. I could not tell what was going on outside and the only three voices I could hear were either hysterical or getting there. Joe eventually got close enough to hear me, and my voice led him to my location. He found me by stepping on the debris that covered me. Joe then began to dig me free.

As he pulled the various materials off me, I was able to help though everything I saw was hazy. My long hair had been covering my face and for that I was thankful as it acted like a filter, preventing dust from entering my lungs. I realized I had been sitting on the floor with my knees bent and there was a high-backed chair with its legs on either side of my chest and its back over my knees. Jason was holding up a filing cabinet that was hanging over me. Joe then said, "Oh my God, oh my God" very quietly. When I asked, "What?" he told me there was a large item that he needed help moving. Jason's hands were tied so he couldn't help, but I told Joe if he could just lift it a little then I could get my leg free. With that he told me that the item was one of the desks from army recruiting... their office was on the fourth floor. After a brief pause, I asked Joe to try again. With that he lifted the desk and I was able to get free. At that time I felt no pain. My foot was sore and I had no shoes, but I thought I was fine. I was alive and at that point I guess that is all that truly mattered.

As I stood up with Joe's help, everything went black. For a few moments I could not see and realized I was going to need help to get out of the building. As I stood in the darkness, I could hear loud, popping noises and Joe saying that he thought it was gunfire. Slowly, within minutes, my eyesight came back. As it returned, I could see fire and it looked like it was in the parking lot across the street. That meant that at least three walls were now gone. The operations office was located in the center of the building, the loan and Visa departments were to the north of us, and I could not see anything that resembled their offices. Jason and Bobbie were asking if we should stay or try to get out of the building. When I turned around I saw that what had been our teller lobby and teller area was now a big, gaping hole. I could not see my desk or anyone else. Mr. Miller was gone. Everyone and everything was gone. I realized we had no choice, we had to get out. I informed Jason that I was getting out with or without them, preferably with them.

My first step was unsuccessful. My right ankle was badly injured and could not sustain any of my weight. Since I had Joe to lean on, I did not attempt another step. Using Joe to brace myself, we slowly started to climb over the rubble with Jason and Bobbie following. We got just past what I thought may have been Joe's desk when I heard a voice that sounded like Patti, our Visa clerk. Before we could respond to her cries, a man who I think was a U.S. marshal appeared in front of us. He picked me up in his arms and carried me over the next pile of debris. As we looked up, there was another person who took me from the marshal. I told the marshal who the voice crying for help belonged to and where her office used to be. I never turned around again as the other man carried me toward the stairwell.

As we approached the stairs, the outer door was lying on the hall floor, blown off its hinges. The man, who I learned was a member of our credit union, had been driving by just as the blast occurred. When we arrived at the stairs, I sent him back to help the others and informed him that there was a day-care center on the second floor, which he had not known. I then proceeded to use the railing to lower myself down the steps. There were large amounts of glass on every step. As I was almost to the bottom, another person came in the second-floor entrance and carried me out to the south side of the building onto the plaza. He also had no knowledge of the day care. He left me on a bench as we saw my three co-workers emerge from the stairwell's exit. Bobbie was so hysterical that she was almost hyperventilating. Jason and Joe went to pick me up when I told Jason to let Bobbie help instead. I do not know why I was the calm one, but I was. I felt if Bobbie helped carry me she might calm down a little, and it worked. While Joe and Bobbie carried me to the makeshift first-aid station on the corner of Fourth and Harvey, I tried to make jokes. I remember saying something about how I worked in Boston for three years and nothing ever happened. I have to move to Oklahoma for all the excitement. I thought they were going to drop me for that comment. Then Jason asked me for Tom's phone number. I could not think about calling him. Somehow I knew that he would know I was okay and I would call him when I could.

Bobbie and I were seated on the curb just east of the corner, searching for familiar faces. Next to me were two women who had come up from Dallas for a one-day training session. We all sat there on the curb for what seemed to be an eternity. The bleeding injured were tended to by paramedics and volunteers, the seriously injured were being taken care of immediately and transferred to a hospital as soon as an ambulance was available, and the "walking wounded" were being bused to hospitals out of the downtown area. I just sat there and waited my turn.

Everyone was terrific, from the paramedics (who apologized for the lack of icepacks) to the volunteers. One of those volunteers was Joe's wife, Laniece. She was helping to bandage people when she saw me. She had already found Joe and knew that he was fine. She took Tom's phone number from me and said she would call when she could. I understood, what she was doing was more important than calling Tom and I knew that he would want me taken care of first. After Laniece left I saw various credit union members wandering around. Some had only minor injuries and others were more seriously hurt. The worst part though was seeing the rescue workers carry out the children from the day-care center. All of the employees in the federal building took the same risk when we accepted our jobs, but those children had no choice. They were the innocent victims.

It was an hour later when I finally received an icepack for my ankle. I had been sitting on the curb surveying the damage done to the federal courthouse in front of me and the church to the west of the federal building. By this time Laniece was able to contact Tom, so he knew that I was alive and I was to call him when I got to the hospital. One of the volunteers said that he was not sure if a gas explosion or a bomb had caused all the damage. At that point, I don't know if any of us cared about what it was, but just how many of us would survive. Then, before I knew it, I was being transported to a backboard and carried to an ambulance. A volunteer named David stayed with me until I was in the vehicle. It was not until the ride that I realized I had more injuries that I thought. But the worst of it all, I would never be able to thank those people for all they had done.

Since the events of that morning, I learned that I had suffered a concussion, shattered my right heel into over one hundred pieces, crushed my right ankle, fractured my right tibia and fibula, broke my tailbone in half, and ruptured a disc in my lower back among all the bruises to my ribs, shoulders, and legs. Still, all that was nothing compared to not being able to thank all those on the street who helped and all the workers at Children's Hospital and the Tinker AFB Hospital where I was later transferred. Nothing will ever hurt as much as losing so many of my colleagues, my co-workers, and most of all, my friends. People who have lost loved ones by accidents or in a war tell me that they know what I am going through. However, everyone knows that car crashes occur everyday and that when people go off to war, not everyone returns. But how do you prepare for a bombing? How can anyone ever understand what we are going through?

Five Minutes
to Eternity

Anna Sterling

---

*P*rying myself out of bed and out from under cozy covers was especially difficult. It was already light outside. The alarm had gone off as usual at 6 A.M., but I had fallen back to sleep. I began to make my bed still feeling the effects of a midnight snack I had eaten over the sink after raiding the refrigerator.

I opened the balcony drapes to see the weather condition and turned on *Good Morning America* on the way to the kitchen. Sunlight was softly filtering through a haze. No time to go out on my balcony or to sit down with a cup of coffee. Turning the TV up loudly enough to hear in the next room, I hurriedly got ready.

Walking back through the living room, I could always catch a glimpse of the city's skyline. "I love a hazy morning—a great morning for a walk. I can use the fresh air." Mentally, I mapped out my route. Walking down the alley between the *Journal Record* building and the parking lot north of the Murrah building, I would catch the full benefit of the sun.

No cold, dark shadows on that side—only one lonely tree unexpectedly protruded its branches out of the asphalt. Taking that direction, I would be able to bask in the translucent iridescence of the morning, even if it would only be for the five minutes required for the walk to work.

I'm not an apartment dweller at heart and never thought I would wind up living in one, much less a high-rise in the downtown area without a wonderful yard with flowers and shrubs. But when my job relocated to the *Journal Record* building downtown and I sold my home in Oklahoma City, the convenience of living at the Regency Towers apartments, one block from work, appealed to me.

Anna Sterling

The view from my balcony was spectacular, particularly at night and on holidays. I could clearly spot certain buildings—the Oklahoma County Courthouse directly south and the Alfred P. Murrah Building and the Water Resources Board building in the blocks directly east. From my balcony, the fireworks displays at both New Year's and the Fourth of July were a dizzying extravaganza.

At 8:35 A.M., dressed and still puttering, a thought came to mind about the interesting discussion I'd had the night before at a prayer meeting. A friend had posed this question: "If all of a sudden we experienced an emergency and had to hurriedly leave our homes knowing we may never be able to return, and we could take with us only what we could carry, what would we choose to take?"

My answer was that, since I had sole possession of them, I would take the family's pictures. Everything else could be replaced but the pictures.

At 8:55 A.M. I turned the TV off, closed and locked the door behind me, boarded the elevator alone, and automatically pushed the "Lobby" button fully intending to stop in at the deli for a donut and then to walk to work. In this age of fitness consciousness, it is a little ridiculous to drive one block from one parking garage to another. Besides, I'd been made fun of one time too many lately. I was definitely walking!

My walk would have taken me one-half block east on Fifth Street toward the Murrah building and past the Water Resources Board building, down the alley just fifty yards north of the Murrah building. I had walked that way dozens of times before.

Suddenly, for some unexplained reason, I found myself reaching up and pushing the "2" button to the parking garage where my car was parked. Why did I do that? "Well, it is windy and cool and the weatherman did say it may rain later today." When the elevator doors opened on the second level, I hesitatingly got off, not fully understanding my indecision in this simple matter.

At 9:00 A.M. I got into my car. As I headed east on Fifth Street to Harvey toward the Murrah building, sunlight beamed through the haze into my eyes. It would be the only sunlight I would experience for weeks. I crossed the normal-looking Sixth Street, entered the north entrance of the *Journal Record* parking garage on the fifth floor, and backed into an end space.

At 9:02 A.M. I had just reached across to the passenger seat to get my purse when I felt a thundering jolt knock me forward into the steering wheel. It felt as though something had either fallen on my car, or something had picked the car up and rammed it against the wall behind me. From inside the car, everything looked intact. I opened the car door and peered outside.

There was an eerie stillness. The sky seemed almost green, filled with dust whirlwinds, dirt, flying bits of paper, debris, and smoke. The roof of my car was washboard, but nothing appeared to have fallen on it.

I could see people on the sidewalks below beginning to run haphazardly, and I was hearing car horns and alarms going off. "An explosion, there's been an explosion!" I heard faint screams from the opposite side of the garage, and running to the other side, I saw the huge skeleton of the *Journal Record* building looming before me with black smoke billowing from behind it. I stared in disbelief and horror—"A gas explosion at the office!" I began to tremble.

It appeared I was alone in the garage. I saw the impossibility of using the elevators, and, reaching the door of the stairway, started my descent cautiously on each glass-covered step. Following a trail of blood, I finally reached the street.

The area was coming back to life, but not the safe, secure, comfortable life I'd grown to expect here in Oklahoma City. The few people I began to see looked like I felt—dazed, bewildered, and shocked. The air was thick with unbreathable substances. People began streaming out of that skeleton of a building I had inhabited for the past couple of years, some coughing, some screaming, some crying, and some bloody with paper towels or articles of clothing wrapped around their wounds. All were covered with building debris.

It felt as if I was in a protective bubble, that I could see everything that was going on, but I wasn't really a part of it. My legs and body were numb, but my mind was amazingly clear and calm. I was bent on getting into the building and going to work, or at least checking in on my friends.

My search was over, when, one by one, I began seeing the familiar faces of the people I love. Once my small group of coworkers was safely gathered on a street corner, I learned it was the Murrah building that had suffered the fatal blow.

I would eventually learn that eleven of my thirty-one coworkers required emergency treatment, but all were alive. I would learn that many members of our office were heroes on that tragic day, a day that demanded more compassion, more courage, more determination, and eventually more faith and inner strength than any of them ever dreamed possible.

I would also learn that first night that there was an unknown number of dead buried under the pancaked floors of the Murrah building, and that hundreds of family members were waiting with some faint hope for the word that missing loved ones could still be found alive.

One week later, I would learn the personal horror of the bomb's aftermath when I was allowed a five-minute access to my apartment to retrieve necessary items. My apartment looked as though a wrecking ball had battered it, with glass sprayed everywhere. The balcony that once confidently pursued the cityscape that included the massive Murrah building now overlooked its pathetic ruins.

I am now permanently relocated in a residence of my own. But how can I ever forget that five-minute time frame in which I could have been catapulted into eternity? How could I know that getting myself back into a more normal pulse of living would span more than two years? How could I know of the anxiety attacks that would overtake me in the middle of the night? How could I know I would emerge from that pit a different person, with different priorities, perspectives, and perceptions?

Different. I am not the same person I was on April 18, 1995. The impact of the bomb set my feet on an entirely different pathway.

I am forever changed.

The Horror Prevents the Healing

Dixie and Kerry Van Ess

*M*y husband of forty-five years was born October 23, 1927, in Muskogee, Oklahoma. John attended college at Oklahoma State University, in Stillwater. In 1945, he played basketball under Henry Iba, when OSU won the National Basketball Championship which was played at Madison Square Garden.

We had four children, two girls and two boys: our oldest daughter, Kevin; Karl, a son; Kerry, a daughter; and the youngest, our son Dan. Kerry said, "Dad loved jokes and he loved to laugh. I will always miss his laughter. He liked to take care of his yard, take Mom for rides in the country. Dad loved family gatherings; he would drive anywhere for a home-cooked meal."

On April 19, 1995 my husband was on the seventh floor of the Murrah building. He worked for HUD and had just finished meeting with a gentleman from an abstract company when the bomb went off. When the bomb exploded, my husband was hurled down seven floors into the "pit." During our seven-day wait we received several reports that he had been found—all false reports.

Nearly every bone in his body was broken and there was gravel

John Karl Van Ess III

embedded in the side of his face. We were discouraged by the funeral director from seeing him. Kerry said, "I would say to anyone who has lost a loved one suddenly not to let them be buried without seeing them, a mistake I will always regret. I believe not seeing him kept me in denial about his death. I always expected him to come home.

"We got a card from the family of the man who worked for the abstract company, and who was the last one to see my Dad alive. They said that 'John had been very helpful and was in a good mood.' I will always appreciate that they took the time to write and let us know. An act of kindness I will never forget."

I live with the visions of my husband's death every day. It is like the bombing was yesterday.

I want people to understand the difference in loosing a loved one due to illness or accident and losing a loved one due to an act of terrorism. The absolute horror of this death prevents any healing. I cannot accept his death because it did not have to happen!

There Is Hope
If We Don't Stop
the Love

Janet Walker

O n Wednesday, April 19, 1995, my world was torn apart. My husband, David Jack Walker, was killed in the bombing of the Alfred P. Murrah Federal Building. At 9:02 A.M., I heard the loudest boom I have ever heard. It reminded me of the old sonic booms I had heard as a child, only many times louder. My third floor office is located approximately five miles north of downtown. The windows face southwest. The boom was so loud my windows shook and I literally ran out of my office. My boss, Sherwood Washington, called me on the phone to ask if I was all right because it sounded like the noise came from my corner of the building. I went back in my office and looked out my window. I could see black smoke billowing upward in the sky. I am not good with distances, so I asked a co-worker, "Is there any way it could be downtown?" I did not want to hear the reply! I grabbed the phone and called the HUD office. I still can't remember if the line was dead or busy. All I remember is that it didn't ring and David's secretary, Fran Williams's friendly voice did not say, "Just a minute, Janet, I'll find him for you."

I have a radio in my office and along with many co-workers, we

David Jack Walker

tuned in to hear what had happened. First we heard it was the federal courthouse. My heart was beating so fast as I felt both saddened and relieved. Knowing my mother would be watching TV, I again picked up the phone. "Mother, what's going on? David's office is downtown. What building is it?" In shock herself, she calmly said, "Honey, it's not David's building, it's the federal building." I remember saying, "Oh, Mother, that *is* David's building."

The next thing I remember is my friends and co-workers hugging me, touching me, and trying to console me. Then our son-in-law, Herby, called from Tulsa. I told him the explosion was from David's building and I could not get hold of him. Herby said he was picking up Jacqueline, David's middle daughter, and would be in Oklahoma City as soon as possible. Again, the phone rang. It was David's oldest daughter, LeaAnn, calling from California. I remember thinking, how did she hear so fast? and I wished so desperately I could tell her everything was all right.

After a while, I asked to be alone in my office. I turned out my lights, picked up my Bible, and got down on my knees. "Oh Lord, my God, please don't take my David. Our lives are just beginning, I love him so much. Oh God, he can retire in three months, the new business is ready to go, and in three months we will celebrate our fifth wedding anniversary. We're going to the movies tonight, and fishing this weekend—oh please, God, please."

Then I was told all the federal and state buildings were being evacuated. "No," I remember saying, "he will call me here. This is where he knows I am, please don't make me leave." Kathy, a co-worker, drove me home in my car and Norma, another co-worker, followed. My son, David, was soon by my side and then the youngest daughter, Jennifer, was home. I can't remember when my mom came. It seems she was always there, silently taking care of everyone. Herby and Jacqueline went directly downtown and would call from the cell phone while running from the bomb site to the hospital, asking questions and showing David's picture to anyone they could find. "This is my father. Please, have you seen him?" Everyone was so kind, but no one had seen him. Toward dark they came home.

That night I spoke to David's best friend, Calvin Moser, who also worked on the eighth floor of the federal building. He said he and David had just got back from coffee. He reminded me that I had just talked with David. I was so numb from the bombing, I had forgotten I had talked to David around 8:45 A.M. I had bought him a spotlight for his boat and he was so proud of the light and his bargain-hunting wife, he wanted to know if I could pick one up for Calvin. I told him I had purchased the last one, so Calvin was out of luck. I reminded him we had a date to go to the movies but that I would talk to him before the end of the day. That was our last conversation. Thank God, Calvin went back to his office. Though he worked within seeing distance of my husband, he escaped the building with only minor cuts and scrapes. He did not escape from the trauma, nightmares, and loss of many friends, including my David.

The next eight days were so foggy. We watched TV, listening for any word. We went to the First Christian Church and met with many other struggling families. I remember it got so cold and rainy, and I hoped David wasn't cold, but I knew he had to be hungry. I still had hope! I think it was day two or maybe three when it was reported, a woman on the eighth floor was waving her arm. Our hopes grew stronger. We knew it was Fran, and that David was somewhere by her. When we heard it was only loose debris, we stopped watching TV. However, I would get up early in the morning before the kids and see if the count had changed. We went to our church and we prayed together. My neighbors brought our evening meals. Church families, office employees, and friends brought food and supplies, called, and visited. The Red Cross and Salvation Army offered their assistance. Everyone was so kind and everyone shed tears with and for us. We started receiving cards and letters from everywhere.

And the wait went on...

On day eight, April 26, Jennifer and I attended Dana and Chris Cooper's funeral at our church. Sadly, five church-family members were killed in the bombing. On our way home from the funeral, Herby called us on the cell phone. We were about three miles from the house so he said to come straight home because I had received a call. The call was from the First Christian Church and although we were told the call would come from HUD, I knew in my heart they had found David. When I reached home and called the First Christian Church, they asked me to come to the church. The three girls, both sons-in-law, my mother and father, and I met at the church and were led to a room where the medical examiner, two clergy, two medical staff, and a representative from HUD were waiting. We were told David's body had been identified. I wanted to know if he had suffered? That information was not available and could only be obtained from the funeral director. I later found out, and thank God, he had not suffered—he died instantly. That was my greatest relief. I also wanted to know where his body was found. The medical examiner said it could be weeks before that information was released. It was months, however, before I found out that his body was found in the approximate area that his desk was setting—only eight floors down.

We wanted everyone to know the husband, father, and grandfather we knew. He was big, he was funny, and he made us laugh. He was a Christian and he loved his family. He was more than a man who wore a suit and tie five days a week for almost thirty-five years. Like an angel, my friend and co-worker Gary Heerwald knocked on my door. "What can I do?" he asked. The next thing I knew, we were planning a life-history collage. The girls and I spent hours looking through hundreds of pictures, picking out our favorites. The collage measured four-by-five feet and was placed in the foyer of our church on Sunday, April 30, the day the funeral service was held. People laughed, cried, and remembered.

I find myself reflecting back, with good memories, to the day I met David. It was on February 23, 1989, at a workshop in downtown Oklahoma City. He was the HUD Environmental Officer and I work for the State of Oklahoma. Our jobs were entwined and we worked together almost on a daily basis. We were married at First Baptist Church of Nicoma Park on July 14, 1990. I'm not going to say my marriage was perfect, but it was the greatest thing that ever happened to me. This man showed me a love I never knew existed. He not only was my husband, but my best friend. I remember my co-worker Kathy asking me on Monday, two days before the bombing, "How are you and David?" and I replied, "It's so good right now, I feel like we're on our honeymoon again."

David led me to my Lord, and for that I will forever be grateful. At a time like this, we all ask, "Why did God let this happen?" Many people have asked me if I lost my faith. To that I proudly say no! In fact, it is stronger than ever.

The love and kindness this tragedy had brought is known world-wide, and I pray that it will continue for all our sakes, and perhaps, someday we can say some good has come from this horrible loss.

Although my heart is hurting now, I know I will soon be with David, for this life is so short compared to eternity.

I Just Called
to Say Hello

Judy Walker

*I*nterstate 40 stretched endlessly before me. It was June 1995 and
I was coming home from my first family reunion without Bob.
Memories of our short nine years of marriage flooded through me.

We both worked for the Social Security Administration and had
chosen to transfer from the program center in Birmingham, Alabama,
to the new teleservice center in Albuquerque, New Mexico, six years
before. After three years, we accepted positions in a field office in Oklahoma City, a move we needed for future advancements.

In February 1995, a ten-week training session for a promotion had
sent me to Dallas, Texas—a session cut short by the news of a bomb
ripping through the Alfred P. Murrah Building in Oklahoma City. My
Bob was in that building.

When Bob and I first met, he was putting together a tape of love
songs titled "Twenty Years of Loving You," gleaned from albums and
45s borrowed from friends, some of whom were unattached women
with their own agenda. I offered him the use of my record collection
and asked him to use my favorite, Stevie Wonder's "I Just Called to Say
I Love You."

By the time Bob finished the tape, we had been dating for several weeks. One Saturday, he called and asked if I would like to take a ride with him, he had something special to show me, and "dress casually." Wearing jeans and a pullover shirt, I was ready when he pulled up outside. We drove to a place that sold semitrailer cabs. Bob got out of the car and went into the office. He spoke with the salesman, gesturing toward the rows of semis. He came out with a wide grin.

"Have you ever wondered what a semi looked like inside?" he asked as he held the door for me.

**Judy and
Robert N. Walker Jr.**

"I never really thought about it," I said warily. "I just always try to stay out of their way on the road."

He had told the salesman he was a truck driver and asked if he could show his girlfriend the inside of a fancy semi. The salesman said, "Sure, look around all you want."

We crawled in and out of a half-dozen cabs: some had sleeping areas almost as big as a double bed; small, built-in televisions; refrigerator units; microwaves; cleverly hidden storage spaces; and many of the comforts of home. Bob loved to plan unconventional dates.

We got in the car again and as we headed for the highway, he took out a cassette and slid it into the tape deck. My own voice, taken from a message I had once left on his answering machine, came out of the speaker: "I just called..." The tape then faded into the music of Stevie Wonder. "I made this one especially for you," he said.

Close to the Oklahoma state line, I happened to see the sign "Oklahoma Trading Post—50 Miles Ahead—Exit 287" and it occurred to me that

Bob and I always meant to stop on our return trips from Alabama but we never did: we had already gassed up an exit or two before, we were tired, we just wanted to get home. "This time," I decided, "I'm going to stop."

As I drove, my mind wandered; how could I ever make it without Bob—my big, strong husband whose comforting arms held me when I cried, whose sense of humor melted my anger, and whose sense of adventure had enriched both our lives. Tears stained my cheeks, but I kept driving. Suddenly, there was Exit 286. Damn! I had passed the trading post. Well, maybe next time.

Just as suddenly as I made the decision to drive on, I decided I would go back! I swerved the car at the last instant and drove up the ramp. Reaching the main road, I realized I was on the Turner Turnpike—no exit for who knew how many miles. I looked for a flat place in the median and drove across, mindless of whether a state trooper might be watching, and headed back toward the trading post.

As expected, the trading post was like many Bob and I had stopped at on our travels: a mixture of Southwestern goods and souvenirs. As I wandered through the store, I came upon a wrought-iron-and-wooden-bed setup showcasing Indian blankets, prickly cactus plants, and strings of red and green peppers.

Beside the bed was a small table holding Aztec vases, delicate desert flowers, and a howling coyote with a bright scarf around its neck. Unobtrusively nestled among them sat a small, old-timey wooden telephone with a carved mouthpiece and a rotary dial, its receiver resting on the black prong and connected with a thin black cord. My first thought was, How unusual. Everything else is so Southwestern, the telephone looks out of place. Picking it up, I lifted the receiver.

A musical tinkling began from the base of the phone. Tears filled my eyes and coursed down my cheeks. A wave of warmth swept over me as I stood sobbing, clutching the phone, oblivious of other customers walking warily around me. The tune I was listening to was "I Just Called to Say I Love You."

Making my way toward the front to pay for my newfound treasure, there was no doubt now that I could make it. I was not alone; my Bob just called to say he loved me.

Those I Knew

Raymond Washburn

$\mathcal{M}$y name is Raymond Washburn and I operated the snack bar on the fourth floor of the Murrah building. I would like to name a few people I knew very well in the building who were killed on April 19, 1995. I cannot name them all in this brief account, but I will try to take certain people from certain areas and tell you what they bought and what conversations we had. Like I said, I can't put them all into one story, but each and every person who died was very special.

I knew Ethel Griffin from Social Security. Ethel came in and we talked. We talked about smoking. I remember Ethel used to kid me about smoking because she had quit. Ethel came in and bought taco potatoes on Wednesday. I will never forget, if that potato wasn't right, she'd send it back and I don't blame her. Ethel was a fine person.

Richard Allen and I used to kid around about going out after hours and having a good time. Richard came in and bought coffee during the day. He was a nice person. Richard was always there if you ever needed assistance of any kind.

Sandy Avery came in mornings and afternoons. Sandra bought a

Raymond and Mary Lou Washburn

large Pepsi and if I didn't have Pepsi, she'd go downstairs to my vending machine and buy a can of Pepsi there. I knew Sandra and to me, she was rather a quiet person, but very nice.

Raymond Johnson I didn't really know that well, but I knew of him. He was a quiet person. He came in and bought coffee and just had an all-around nice personality.

I could name more from Social Security, but I'm sure survivors from Social Security miss those people and they will always be missed. I still keep in touch with survivors from Social Security. To me, we were like a big family. We worked together, they came to the snack bar, and some of them were people that you could really get to know. I felt like they treated me fairly and I tried to treat them fairly.

I knew the children from the day-care center. I treated those children with Cokes or ice cream every so often. Here are the ones who we really have to look out for, because these are the ones who never had a life to begin with. They were very nice children and I just can't believe that someone would want to destroy their lives.

The Federal Employees Credit Union...I remember Robbin Huff. Robbin came in on her lunchbreak and sat off in the non-smoking section. She sometimes bought a special we had but most of the time she bought popcorn. She liked to sit over there, eat her popcorn, and read the newspaper.

Claudette Meek was a very cheerful person. She was outgoing. We had a deal going on about making a loan since she was a loan officer and I would tease her about making a loan whenever she came up. Her reaction was, "Come down whenever you have time, and we'll discuss it." I did make a few loans with Claudette. Like I said, Claudette was a very nice person.

Sonja Sanders came up to the snack bar quite a bit. Sometimes she would run errands for the girls, she'd get ice and pop or whatever items they needed, and take them back to the office. On occasion, she'd call the snack bar and ask if we could bring down an order for them, and we would.

Karen Shepherd... I remember when she became a loan officer. Karen came by one day and I overheard her talking to Terry and she made the statement that she was glad she was a loan officer. Karen was a very likable person and I enjoyed doing business with her. Karen would come in sometimes and buy a cinnamon roll.

Frankie Merrell was a nice person. I enjoyed Frankie because she came in every morning before it was time for her to go to work. Like Sonja, she was the person who would go get things for the rest of the credit union staff. She'd come up and get popcorn or ice and a lot of times she didn't have enough money to pay the bill. I'd tell her not to worry about it, that I'd get it later since I had to go down to the credit union anyway. That's how we worked, I trusted those people. I don't believe you could find any other people who were as honest as they, because they were super people.

I remember survivors from the VA on the fifth floor. Dr. Paul Heath, George, Diane, Dennis, and John were all customers. They bought mostly coffee or lunch specials or popcorn. I sold a lot of popcorn and I think my customers really enjoyed it. I sold cherry limeades and ice cream in the summer, and they went really well. Those are days we will never forget.

From the sixth floor, I remember the marines. They came down, had lunch, enjoying sitting around and talking. I don't remember the marines all that well, but what I do know of them is that they were very interesting and very complimentary of things that you did for them. I think they really appreciated the snack bar.

Let's go back to the fourth floor. Across the hall from the snack bar was Army Recruiting. I knew Karen Carr from Army. Karen was a very nice person. Karen and her boss would come in mornings and their special was a pimento cheese sandwich, which they split. I guess that was for their breakfast. Karen also liked tea and hot choco-late. One thing I also remember about her is that she liked the heels of the bread toasted; most people don't like that, but that was Karen's favorite. Those people who were killed there will always be missed.

I used to make tea and coffee for meetings or parties of the Fed-eral Highway Administration on the fourth floor.

The seventh and eighth floors were Housing and Urban Devel-opment (HUD) and I remember HUD having big parties. HUD had a women's group and I will never forget when they made me an hon-orary member of the women's group. I lost in the bombing a plaque they presented me but it was replaced with a plaque when I retired and that is something I will always cherish. The person who sticks out in my mind from HUD is Diana Day. Diana was a very comical person. She seemed like a cheerful person. I remember when Diana got her new van. She brought it to work the next day and she turned a Coke over in it, so she came in and wanted some towels to help clean it up.

Colleen Guiles from HUD was a very nice person. She came in on Wednesdays and wanted a taco potato. She always wanted a taco potato before we had them done so we knew we'd better get one done before she came in. I enjoyed Colleen, she was very interesting and had a lot going for her. I am sorry this happened to her. I knew her son Matt who was also very nice. It's a shame that somebody like that had to lose their mom—he lost a very nice mother.

On the ninth floor was the Secret Service and Bureau of Alcohol, Tobacco and Firearms (BATF). I remember Linda Mc-Kinney coming in the snack bar. She always ran around with Valerie. Linda was a very cheerful person; she was outgoing and spoke highly of other people. I never heard her say a bad thing about anybody. She used to come in and tell me jokes and I'd tell her jokes and we'd kid around. Keep in mind, these were clean jokes because Linda was not the type of person to tell anything else. At this time I wish I could think of one of her jokes, but I cannot.

I knew all the people from the BATF. I remember Don Leonard. I could go on and name all of them but I cannot remember them all at this time. When I hear their names, I remember them and know who they are, but I could speak highly of all these people, and all of them will be missed.

I would like to add a few things to this article in remembrance of the 168 people who were killed. I would like to state that as you know, on December 23, 1997, there was a verdict reached in the trial of Terry Nichols, codefendant in the bombing. I was not pleased with the verdict. I felt like he should be charged with all the counts. You know, you'll never bring these 168 people back, but I felt like the man was wrong in doing what he did regardless of what he knew or didn't know; he was involved. In my mind he knew that Timothy McVeigh was going to blow up that building; he wasn't going to be there, but Terry Nichols helped build the bomb. I feel like there are numerous people involved in this but that's something we will never know. We have to live with the jury's decision for now but Terry Nichols will stand trial again in Oklahoma. Right up front, I am for the death penalty.

These men took many, many lives, especially the children who had barely begun a life. How low can you go to be someone who takes somebody's children who never had a life to begin with and comes along and destroys it?

In Memory of Wanda

Mildred Watkins

---

y husband, Jim, and I were in Leavenworth, Kansas, helping my sister, Florence, get settled into her new home when we first heard of the bombing in Oklahoma City.

Junetta, our daughter, was in Rogers, Arkansas. She called us and asked the name of the building where our other daughter, Wanda, worked. She was crying and said she was sure Wanda was in the building that was bombed. I assured her that I thought Wanda was all right.

Until Junetta called, we had not turned on the television, so we did not know what was happening. Even after we turned on the television, I did not want to admit that Wanda could have been in that building—that sort of thing always happens to other people.

I tried calling Wanda's home but could not get through. By then, I was feeling pretty anxious. I called the Salvation Army and the Red Cross from Leavenworth and then, again, that evening when we arrived home in Rogers, but they couldn't help me. Again, I called Wanda's home, hoping to hear her answer, but heard my own voice on her answering machine instead. I had recorded the announcement for her when she bought the machine. I did get through to

Wanda's landlady, who checked on her dog, Twigg, for us.

Jim, Junetta, my grandson Bob, my sister Peggy, and I arrived at Wanda's home in Midwest City about noon the next day. Even Twigg seemed to know there was something wrong and would not eat, drink, or go outside for us. She had always been happy to see us in the past, but now she wouldn't even budge from under the bed.

I called numbers that appeared on television but could not get through to any of them. The frustration and the feeling of helplessness were overwhelming.

I had terrible visions of

Wanda Lee Watkins

Wanda lying in a twisted manner, covered with concrete, debris weighing her down and in excruciating pain. I actually felt relieved when we were informed she was dead. I knew she wasn't suffering.

Even when we knew she wasn't coming home, I felt as if I was invading her privacy, as I searched through her papers looking for documents and photos we needed. I felt as if she should be doing that herself.

Jim has Parkinson's and to drive in heavy traffic makes him pretty nervous, as well as being unfamiliar with Oklahoma City, so it meant a lot to us when the Department of Army Recruiting Battalion took us to places we needed to go. They were so good to us.

Wanda was planning to retire in about five years and move to Rogers, so she could be close to us. She loved to square dance and line dance. We had talked of taking lessons together. She used to jokingly say, "When I win the lottery, I'm going to buy that house next door to you and put a gate in that back fence so Twigg can go back and forth. Then I'm going to buy a riding lawnmower so Dad can keep my grass cut." She worried about Dad working in that hot sun though, so I knew she would probably be the one cutting the grass.

Her home really reflected her personality. She loved flowers and had silk flowers on the walls, in vases, bowls, and sitting on the furniture. She had potted plants in every room. She laughed a lot and liked to joke and tease. She did not like jokes that hurt people's feelings though. She was a very sensitive and compassionate person, but she also had a stubborn streak, especially if she thought she was right.

Her hands were rarely idle when she was sitting, as she crocheted so much when she was here. I didn't pay much attention to what she was making. She usually went to the store with me, but, a couple of times before her last Christmas with us, she didn't want to go with me. After Christmas Day, I knew why. She was crocheting a tablecloth for me and wanted to measure the cloth to the table.

I am not an extremely religious person, but I do believe in God and life hereafter. In October 1995, I had a mild stroke. I was in a hospital room alone, half asleep, half awake, when I felt a hand over mine. I seemed to be high up on a broken floor with a jagged edge. When I felt the hand, I jerked, and it seemed I saw a woman in a short gown float over the edge of the floor. I know I was dreaming, but it still gave me an eerie feeling.

We have received numerous gifts: tapes, books, poems, songs, teddy bears, angels, and one little boy sent a jewelry box full of chocolate kisses. That was so sweet. I tried to send thank-you cards, but I know I have missed some. I tried to write a card of thanks to the newspaper in Oklahoma City to thank all of the rescue workers who risked their lives and to all of those who did so much to help the survivors and the families, but I just couldn't find the words. I do appreciate every one of them.

I play in a country western band, and although Wanda was not very fond of country music, she would go with me to nursing homes when I played. Sometimes she would go with me and visit the residents. I have recovered sufficiently from my stroke that I have been able to continue with that part of my life.

I am the eldest of eleven children. I helped raise my younger siblings. I loved everyone of them. I have lost two brothers and a sister but none of their deaths have been as hard for me to accept as the death of our daughter. There is hardly a day that goes by that we do not shed tears for our loss.

Wanda's nephew, Bob, refuses to talk about his aunt. She was his second mother: when he was small, he and his mother lived with Wanda. She really spoiled him, always buying him a new toy when they went to the store together. It's a shame she never had any children of her own. She would have made a wonderful mother.

Wanda was a daddy's girl, and Jim mentions her a lot. I suspect he cries a lot, too.

I am grateful for the family I have left. We call or write more often now. Although our family has always been close, this tragedy seems to have brought us closer.

I believe this terrible event has made me more sensitive to the things that have occurred since then. I was never insensitive to the feelings of others, but I think I can better understand the agony of those people who awaited the recovery of the bodies of their loved ones in the TWA Flight 800 disaster. I thought of the grotesque visions I had of Wanda lying in all that rubble. I thought of the relief I felt when I was told she never knew what hit her. It doesn't ease our pain, but I am grateful that she did not suffer.

I hope our government will continue digging until they find all those responsible for this tragedy. It scares me to think of the organizations that plot against our government. So many of them think they are above the law and should live by their own rules, right or wrong.

As for my family and myself, we are trying our best to get on with our lives, though our lives will never be the same.

I Lost
My Best Friend

Bud Welch

---

*M*y daughter, Julie Marie Welch, was twenty-three years old. She worked for the Social Security Administration as a Spanish translator and claims representative. Around 8 A.M. on April 19, 1995, Julie and three other women began straightening files in the stockroom of the Social Security office located on the first floor of the Murrah building. About 9 A.M., Julie took her final steps to the front of the Social Security office to meet Emilio Rangel Tapia, a father of five, and the Reverend Gilberto Martinez, the pastor of El Tabernaculo de Fe Church. Tapia, who spoke no English, had an appointment to obtain his Social Security card, and Martinez came to help. Julie's three co-workers started to return to their offices when a supervisor suggested that they stay in the stockroom until they finished throwing out dated forms. Julie had left the file area approximately ninety seconds before the bomb went off. Her co-workers in the stockroom survived.

I want people to remember Julie for her kindness and her willingness to help other people, especially the poor. She worried about that all the time. She started volunteer work in high school when she became a member of the National Honor Society, which required a certain number of hours of community service. Julie chose to go to the Hispanic Center in Capitol Hill and volunteer there. She was helping people who couldn't read or write in either Spanish or English, trying to work out utility-payment plans for them. After her official community service hours were completed, she continued volunteering. It meant a lot to her.

Julie Marie Welch

Years later, Julie's journey to the Dominican Republic as a translator for the Society of Saint Vincent de Paul in Milwaukee was a very moving experience for her. During the three weeks she was there, she lived in the countryside in the barrios with one family. She was shocked that the whole family shared one towel. It was suggested to the visitors that they take an extra set of linens and leave it behind with their host family. Julie went the extra step and left the linens and towels she was using as well. When Julie returned home she told me that they didn't have any electricity or running water. I asked her, "What did you have to do, use an outside toilet?" And she said, "No, Dad, they didn't have those. You used a pan." She struggled with why they had nothing and she had so much.

In Milwaukee she worked for Habitat for Humanity, helping to build houses on Saturdays. I remember one week she called me on a Saturday night and said, "Dad, I'm getting so tired of chopping weeds and picking up tires and automobile parts out of backyards. I wish they'd let me do something else." I encouraged her to do this for a few weeks before asking for a new task. She was so enthusiastic. She said, "I want to paint and build some cabinets." But, hell, she didn't know anything about building cabinets! She felt really good when she finally got to paint and even hang some wallpaper. Julie got so much satisfaction out of seeing the big smiles and the happy tears of the families when they were able to move into their own homes.

Julie was very devoted to God, thanks to her mom, I think. By the same token, Julie was not one to wear her faith on her sleeve. Her faith was inside her.

Every Wednesday at 11:30 A.M. Julie Marie and I would meet for lunch at a Greek restaurant across the street from the Murrah building. We had a lot of wonderful times, but I always thought we would have more wonderful times in the future. Now my future will be without my best friend. Julie had met a wonderful air force lieutenant named Eric Hilz. There were so many things to look forward to, but now I will never know the joy of walking her down the aisle on her wedding day, I will never hold her children, and I will never again hear her sweet voice saying, "I love you, Daddy."

Sometimes when I go down to the fence, I go to the Survivor Tree. I lean against the trunk, close my eyes, listen to the leaves, and think about the way it used to be. Julie would not want us to be sad. She loved God and now she is with Him in a better place. We must remember the joys of life because that is what she would want of us.

You can kill the body, but you can't kill the soul.

The Story of the Death of Robert G. Westberry

Tillie Westberry

*T*he morning of April 19, 1995, started as any other morning. I got up at 5:30 A.M., walked on the treadmill for one and a half miles, then during my cooldown I had my Bible reading and prayer. Bob also did this when he got up. We both had our showers and were at the table for breakfast at about 6:40 A.M. Our conversation was the usual small stuff along with that tomorrow, April 20, was the anniversary of our eldest daughter's death seven years earlier. That morning I wasn't ready to leave for work at the same time Bob was, but as usual I went to the door with him to kiss him goodbye and wish him a good day. That morning I patted him on the tush and said, "I really love you." I watched as he drove away in his red Grand Jeep Cherokee. When I finished fixing my lunch, I also left for work at Aetna Health Plans, where I worked as a nurse consultant.

Work for me that morning was the same as any other morning. Phones were busy. People either needed surgery or they needed a referral from their primary-care physician to a specialist. Shortly after 9 A.M. we heard this massive explosion at which time our building shook really hard. Janet, the nurse who sat next to me, thought we were having an earthquake. I stated that it sounded more like an explosion of some kind. There was a lot of hustle about the office to try to find out what had happened. Someone said there was a huge fire in downtown Oklahoma City. I tried to call Bob's office but I only got a recording saying that the circuits were busy. By this time they had the

Robert G. Westberry
(right, with his son, Glen)

TV on in the conference room and Janet said, "Tillie, you need to go look, it is really bad," but for some reason I stayed at my desk and continued to take calls. At some point someone said it was the courthouse that was damaged. I tried to call Bob's office again and this time it just rang and rang. I thought, Well, if there was a bomb threat at the courthouse, then the federal building would have been evacuated and no one would be there to answer the phone. At about 9:40 Paul, who had a desk in the nurses' area, walked in and said it wasn't the courthouse but the federal building. I rolled back my chair and said, "Paul, are you sure?" He said he was sure. At that time I had a client on the phone and she asked if I was okay and I told her, "No, there was a big explosion at the federal building where my husband worked." I transferred the call to Karen, a nurse who was there with her arms around me, and then went to the conference room to see if I could find out anything else. At first, I couldn't recognize the building.

When they showed the aerial shot of the terrace behind the building, then I knew it was the federal building. In my mind, all I remember about that first picture was that the front wall was gone. I did not see the gaping hole exactly where Bob's office was so I did not understand when I was told that the area where Defense Investigative Services (DIS) offices were located was totally gone. Greg, one of the Aetna managers, asked if I knew anyone who worked there and I told him that my husband worked on the third floor in the front.

I left the conference room and started back to my desk, thinking, What do I do now? I walked back and forth in the hall several times and then realized I needed to call our children because they would be seeing this on the news. When I returned to my desk my voice-mail light was on and it was my pastor, Ken Nesselroade, who had seen the news and said that if I wanted to I could come to the church office to wait for word. He said he would be happy to come get me if I didn't feel like driving. I told him I would come as soon as I notified the children of what had happened.

The telephone company building just north of the bomb site was very heavily damaged and it was difficult to make any calls. After what seemed like forever, with multiple tries, I was able to reach Glen, our son in Orlando, Florida. I tried to explain to him what happened and that I had no idea of his father's condition, but not to do anything until I called him. I figured it would be cut and dried and I would have some word by that afternoon. I also told him if they had a TV to turn it on, that the building looked like a war zone. I gave him the phone number of my pastor's office and continued making calls to Robin in Keystone Heights, Florida, and I asked her to call Sue since I was having such a terrible time getting an outside line.

I left the office with Debbie, who drove me to my pastor's office. I was totally in shock and unaware what the next several days would bring, nor did I realize that on that day my life was forever changed. Pastor Ken had the TV on in his office, and it was there that I realized the extent of the damage. When I first saw that huge hole that was blown out of the building, I felt this awesome peace that Bob was safely with our Lord. The verse Romans 8:28 was constantly on my mind in the days that followed: "And we know that in all things God works for the good of those who love Him, who have been called according to His purpose."

When I saw the extent of the damage, I also wondered if there would be anything left of his body. Having been a nurse for over thirty years and working many years in ICU or the ER, I knew what to expect. I asked the Lord to please give me his wedding band. Not only did I get his wedding band, which was identical to mine, but I also got his wallet, coin holder, and a small pocketknife that had been a gift from Ann.

I spent the rest of the morning at the church office, with several men stopping by to offer their help. About noon the pastor's wife, Elaine, arrived. We ate a bite of lunch and then went to my house to watch the coverage and to wait. I had called the DIS regional office in Dallas to let them know where I was and to give them the names of the people that I knew would be in the office that day.

After 3:30 P.M., they announced that there was a list of the injured and the dead at a church in Oklahoma City, so Elaine and I left to go over there. When we arrived there was no list. The church was set up for taking information and for people to wait. I filled out the first of many forms asking where Bob's office was located in the building, what he was wearing, did he have any identifying marks on his body, and where I could be reached. They asked me to get his dental records, which I picked up the following morning. I had the option of staying there with all the other people, but I just couldn't handle being in big crowds so I opted to go home and wait. After we left the church, we went to St. Anthony's Hospital where they had a list of all the injured who had been rescued so far and which hospital they were in, but Bob's name was not on any of those lists. I filled out more paperwork and was able to talk on the phone to the medical examiner's office which again asked all the same information and also asked me to get the dental records.

We returned to the house physically and emotionally exhausted. By that time my stomach was hurting so badly that it felt like it was in one big spasm, so we stopped at the drugstore to get some antacids. When we arrived home, Pastor Ken called and told me that my son, Glen, would be flying in that night.

There are many gaps in my memory but the one real thing I felt through the entire time was the awesome presence of the Lord and the prayers of people from around the world. At the time, I had brothers in New Zealand and Brazil, and I had nephews in Japan and Brazil, all missionaries. My younger brother is vice president of Jungle Aviation and Radio Service in North Carolina and through e-mail, people from all over the world sent their prayers, not just for me and my family, but for all the families.

The next day Glen and I picked up Bob's dental records and took them to the church where we had been the day before. They said to take them to the medical examiner's office, but we had no idea where this office was so we went back home. During the day my daughters arrived with their families and the following day Glen's wife and son also arrived.

The DIS supervisors—Jim Rogner, Harold Rankin, and Rich Barry—were in Oklahoma City to do what they could to assist. They, along with Bob's assistant, Floyd Carter, were wonderful. They came to our home several times and worked endless hours. They picked up the dental records, and Bob's Bible to get fingerprints.

Late on Saturday afternoon all the DIS men arrived to let us know that Bob's body had been identified. I later found out after I got the medical examiner's paperwork that he was found in front of the building in the rubble just below his office window.

We had a memorial service at our church, Springdale Christian Missionary Alliance, on Tuesday, April 25, 1995. Rich Barry accompanied Bob's coffin to Orlando where we had services at Longwood Presbyterian Church and burial was at the Highland Memorial Gardens, close to our daughter Ann.

Through all of this I have nothing but praise to my Lord for His strength and direction. I also have endless praise for all the wonderful things and for all the love people have shown me and my family, especially the DIS family and the Sprint family in Orlando. My heart goes out to all the rescue workers for what they suffered and saw during the rescue effort, and also to the medical examiner and his staff who worked endless hours under the worst possible conditions identifying and putting all the parts back together.

Afterword

Penny Owen

$\mathcal{A}$ s a reporter for the *Daily Oklahoman*, I have been covering this tragedy since the first hour. I reported on the rescuers who took breaks in the shade and cried, on the body count as these loved ones were removed from the debris, on the tree plantings and memorial services and the hope that comes with time. I spent nearly a year in Denver covering the trials of Timothy McVeigh and Terry Nichols. Through it all, I've come to know many of the people you've just read about.

But I don't know them all. And after more than three years, that amazes me, because it shows how far this single act of hatred stretches. You don't know them all either. There's P. J. Allen, the toddler whose lungs were burned beyond repair when the bomb rumbled through the America's Kids Day-Care Center. He will wheeze his way through life, never normal or complete. Martin Cash lost his eye—and three years later, his home to a fire. He says he's a survivor twice over, thanks to good neighbors and a stroke of fate. Cash has that same Oklahoma attitude which helped this state outshine its darkest hour.

And the good news did come: little Brandon Denny made it out of the hospital alive, despite the brick lodged in his brain. Aren Almon Kok got married and bore Bella, her second daughter. Bella will learn all about her sister, Baylee, the limp child cradled in fire-fighter Chris Fields's arms. Aren has also opened a delicatessen adjacent to the bomb site. Her customers are bombing survivors, downtown workers, and tourists who pass by the Murrah fence to remember.

Our sound-bite lifestyles encourage progress, if you will. There are plane crashes to mourn over, classmates shooting classmates. There are blizzards and gang rapes and floods. It is time, some say, to get over the bombing. Tragedies happen. Indeed, the loudest cries come from Oklahomans themselves. We've had enough, they say. Get it off the front page. Isn't it time we move on?

We haven't even talked about the police officers and firefighters who are only now unearthing their trauma. Project Heartland, a counseling consortium for bombing victims and survivors, is still getting new cases, many of whom are rescuers who kept a stiff upper lip—until the nightmares became unbearable, until the drugs became their friends and their marriages fell apart. They moved on, but were forced to return to the building over and over, night after night.

Closure is a dirty word in Oklahoma. Time and again I've heard there is no such thing; better to suggest a new normal. It's like having your arm chopped off, one widow told me. You can learn to function again, but never as well. For many of those we know and don't know, it will never be over completely.

Yet above it all comes this wonderful strength from citizens like you from across the country, who sent flashlights, teddy bears, poems, and search dogs. We used your many volunteers, including emergency personnel, federal employees, and even funeral providers, and smiled at your hand-colored cards and stitchery. The phone never stopped ringing. So many here are comforted in knowing how much people care. A quiet confidence has also attached itself to this tragedy. At least we pulled together, people here say. We made the best out of the worst.

Perhaps most encouraging is a Scripps-Howard News Service poll conducted in June 1998, which found that antigovernment sentiment has "cooled significantly" since 1995. Analysts believe this lessening of tensions is partly due to the emotional aftermath of the bombing. To me, that means people haven't forgotten what hatred does to a society. Those who shared their stories, and those who read them, will keep the history alive. And that is the trick to preventing another sad story like Oklahoma City.

In Memoriam

The following is a list of those who were victims of the April 19, 1995 bombing of the Alfred P. Murrah Federal Building in Oklahoma City, Oklahoma, according to the government indictment of suspects and reports in the *Daily Oklahoman*. Their ages and places of employment (if applicable) are included.

Lucio Aleman Jr., 33, Federal Highway
    Administration (FHA)
Teresa Alexander, 33
Richard Allen, 46, Social Security
    Administration (SSA)
Ted Allen, 48, Housing and Urban
    Development (HUD)
Baylee Almon, 1
Diane Althouse, 45, HUD
Rebecca Anderson, 37, nurse
Pamela Argo, 36
Sandy Avery, 34, SSA
Peter Avillanoza, 56, HUD
Calvin Battle, 62
Peola Y. Battle, 56
Danielle Nicole Bell, 15 months
Oleta Biddy, 54, SSA
Shelly Turner Bland, 25, Drug
    Enforcement Administration (DEA)
Andrea Blanton, 33, HUD
Glen Bloomer, 61, U.S. Department of
    Agriculture (USDA)
Lola Bolden, 40, Army recruiting
James Boles, 51, USDA
Mark Bolte, 27, FHA
Cassandra Booker, 25
Carol Bowers, 53, SSA
Peachlyn Bradley, 3
Woody Brady, 41
Cynthia Brown, 26, Secret Service (SS)
Paul Broxterman, 43, HUD
Gabreon Bruce, 4 months
Kimberly Burgess, 29, Federal Employees
    Credit Union (FECU)
David Burkett, 47, HUD
Donald Burns, 63, HUD
Karen Gist Carr, 32, Army

Michael Joe Carrillo, 44, FHA
Rona Linn Chafey, 35, DEA
Zackary Chavez, 3
Robert Chipman, 51, Oklahoma Water
    Resources Board
Kimberly Clark, 39, HUD
Peggy Clark, 39, HUD
Anthony Cooper II, 2
Antonio Cooper Jr., 6 months
Dana Cooper, 24, America's Kids Day-
    Care
Harley Cottingham, 46, Defense
    Department (DD)
Kim Cousins, 33, HUD
Aaron Coverdale, 5
Elijah Coverdale, 2
Jaci Rae Coyne, 14 months
Kathy Cregan, 60, SSA
Richard Cummins, 55, USDA
Steven Curry, 44, General Services
    Administration (GSA)
Benjamin Davis, Sgt., 29, Marine recruit-
    ing
Diana Day, 38, HUD
Peter DeMaster, 44, DD
Castine Deveroux, 49
Sheila Driver, 28
Tylor Eaves, 8 months
Ashley M. Eckles, 4
Susan Jane Ferrell, 37, HUD
Chip Fields, 48, DEA
Katherine A. Finley, 44, FECU
Judy Fisher, 45, HUD
Linda Florence, 43, HUD
Donald Fritzler, 64
Mary Anne Fritzler, 57
Tevin Garrett, 18 months